Social Work and
Human Development

Social Work and Human Development

Third Edition

KARIN CRAWFORD AND JANET WALKER

Series Editors: Jonathan Parker and Greta Bradley

LearningMatters

First published in 2003 by Learning Matters Ltd.
Reprinted in 2003
Reprinted in 2004
Reprinted in 2005 (twice)
Reprinted in 2006
Second edition 2007
Third edition 2010

© Karin Crawford and Janet Walker

British Library Cataloguing in Publication Data
A CIP record for this book is available from the British Library.

ISBN 978 1 84445 380 1

This book is also available in the following formats:

Adobe ebook ISBN: 978 1 84445 745 8
EPUB ebook ISBN: 978 1 84445 744 1
Kindle ISBN: 978 0 85725 013 1

Cover and text design by Code 5 Design Associates Ltd
Project management by Deer Park Productions, Tavistock, Devon
Typeset by Pantek Arts Ltd, Maidstone, Kent
Printed and bound in Great Britain by Bell & Bain Ltd, Glasgow

Learning Matters Ltd
33 Southernhay East
Exeter EX1 1NX
Tel: 01392 215560
info@learningmatters.co.uk
www.learningmatters.co.uk

Contents

Life course development and social work practice •
Understanding your own life experiences • The impact of values
on understanding human development • Ways of explaining human
life course development • Interprofessional practice

What is theory? • Taking a life course perspective
on human development • Theories of human life course
development • Comparing and contrasting the theoretical
approaches • The biographical approach

Social work practice and child development •
The developing child • Child development overview •
The social and emotional development of infants and
children – developing attachments • Safeguarding children:
Children in need and children in need of protection

Series Editors' Preface

The Western world including the UK and England face numerous challenges over forthcoming years. These include dealing with the impact of an increasingly ageing population, with its attendant social care needs and working with the financial implications that such a changing demography brings. At the other end of the lifespan the need for high quality child care, welfare and safeguarding services have been highlighted as society develops and responds to a changing complexion.

Migration has developed as a global phenomenon and we now live and work with the implications of international issues in our everyday and local lives. Often these issues influence how we construct our social services and determine what services we need to offer. It is likely that as a social worker you will work with a diverse range of people throughout your career, many of whom have experienced significant, even traumatic, events that require a professional and caring response. As well as working with individuals, however, you may be required to respond to the needs of a particular community disadvantaged by world events or excluded within local communities because of assumptions made about them.

The importance of social work education came to the fore again following the inquiry into the death of baby Peter and the subsequent report from the Social Work Task Force set up in its aftermath. However, it is timely to reconsider elements of social work education – indeed, we should view this as a continual striving for excellence! – as this allows us to focus clearly on what knowledge is useful to engage with in learning to be a social worker.

The books in this series respond to the agendas driven by changes brought about by professional body, Government and disciplinary review. They aim to build on and offer introductory texts based on up-to-date knowledge and to help communicate this in an accessible way preparing the ground for future study, as you develop your social work career. The books are written by people passionate about social work and social services and aim to instil that passion in others. The current text introduces you to aspects of human development that are central to social workers' understanding of people at various stages in their life course. The theories and knowledge introduced in this book are important for all social workers in all fields of practice; they set the scene for exploring more specialised areas of practice.

Professor Jonathan Parker
Greta Bradley

Foreword

This new edition of *Social Work and Human Development* is being published at a critical time in the history of professional social work education and training. In the wake of the tragic death of Baby Peter, the then ministers for the Department of Children, Schools and Families and the Department of Health announced (in December 2008) the setting up of a Social Work Taskforce. The final report was published in December 2009, with 15 recommendations, entitled *Building a Safe, Confident Future*.

In accepting the report on behalf of the Labour government, Ed Balls (Children's Secretary) stated: *The public rightly want to know that social workers are properly trained and well supported. This is the best opportunity we have got to build a professional, well trained and respected workforce and everyone including social workers should work together on this*. What does being *properly trained* mean?

One of the recommendations of the report (Recommendation 2) requires an overhaul of the content and delivery of social work degree courses and will result in further steps towards a national curriculum for qualifying social work programmes. So what would need to be in a national curriculum in order for the public to be reassured that social workers are 'properly trained'? When the social work degree requirements were published (in May 2002), five specific areas of learning were identified, one of which was *human growth, development, mental health and disability*. Fortunately, the government has reaffirmed its commitment to the qualifying social work degree as being generic in nature, and so students continue to need to understand how people tick across their life course.

It is inconceivable that any curriculum for social work could do anything other than explore the ways of making sense of human experience, as each person makes their individual way as a 'traveller from the cradle to the grave' (Shelley, *Prometheus Unbound* IV, 549). Social work is almost always about engaging with human beings in unusual and extreme circumstances. When facing unexpected difficulties and personal crises, the well-being of vulnerable people – whether children, young people or adults – needs to be assessed and a *judgement* made as to whether their situation merits and demands a particular type of intervention, sometime of legal nature.

This is what makes social work such a difficult professional activity. One of the hallmarks of 'professionals', according to Codd (1997), is that they *make judgements in non-routine situations*. Social workers can only benchmark the well-being or vulnerability of an individual older person, for example, if they have an understanding of the biological, historical, sociological, psychological and cultural meaning of being an 'older person' in any given society. When Tolstoy asserted (in *Anna Karenina*, I, Ch1) that *all happy families resemble one another, each unhappy family is unhappy in its own way*, he was inviting us to consider what those common preconditions of 'happiness' might be, so we could better understand what was lacking in the family that was not providing 'good enough' care for its children and family members.

In short, we can only begin to consider undertaking social work roles and tasks with an underpinning understanding of human experience through the life course. This new and updated version of Karin Crawford and Janet Walker's text *Social Work and Human Development* will enable the social work student to comprehend and grasp the fundamentals of life-course theory that is necessary to inform effective practice across all social work service domains.

Nigel Horner
School of Health and Social Work
University of Lincoln

Introduction to third edition

This book is about human development across the life course through an examination and application of theoretical concepts and ideas; policy initiatives; legislation and research that informs professional practice. It takes a life course perspective, supporting you to understand the whole of life from birth to death as a progressive and developmental path with opportunities for growth and change across all facets. Critically it invites you to apply ideas about human development to practice situations through the use of case studies and invites you to reflect on the implications for professional practice and for your personal and professional values.

This third edition of *Social Work and Human Development* is written primarily for students studying for their degree in social work who are beginning to develop their knowledge, skills and understanding of the requirements for professional practice. Whilst it is primarily aimed at students in their first year or level of study, it will be useful for subsequent years depending on how your programme is designed, what you are studying and especially as you move into learning in practice. Additionally the early chapters of this book also relate to the *Common Core of Skills and Knowledge of the Children's Workforce* (CWDC/DfCSF, 2010), specifically the area of expertise titled *Child and young person development*. This book should appeal to people considering a career in social work or social care, but not yet studying for a degree in social work. It will also assist students undertaking a range of social, health and education-related courses in further education. Additionally nurses, occupational therapists and other allied professionals will be able to gain insight into human development across the life course and the role and requirements for social work, particularly to support the interprofessional context of practice. Experienced and qualified social workers, especially those contributing to practice learning, or undertaking their own professional development within the General Social Care Council post-qualifying framework, will be able to use this book for consultation, revision, teaching and to gain understanding of the expectation of the qualifying degree in social work.

In developing this edition we have sought to maintain its value and usefulness, including the overall philosophy and structure of the book. There is a particular emphasis on integrating the context of contemporary practice with theoretical concepts of life course development. Each chapter has been revised to include current policy agendas and legislative frameworks. Further reading sections at the end of each chapter have been developed and updated to included annotated references to recent texts and internet resources. Diagrams, activities, case studies and research information have been reviewed and added to.

Requirements for social work education

Social work education ensures that students develop knowledge, skills and values for professional practice and qualified social workers are educated to at least honour degree level. Social work operates in complex, demanding and uncertain human environments, reflected in the international definition of social work:

> *The social work profession promotes social change, problem solving in human relationships and the empowerment and liberation of people to enhance well-being. Utilising theories of human behaviour and social systems, social work intervenes at the point where people interact with their environments. Principals of human rights and social justice are fundamental to social work.*
>
> (International Association of Schools of Social Work (IASSW) and
> International Federation of Social Workers (IFSW), 2001)

This definition seeks to encapsulate that social work is concerned with individuals and with wider society. Social workers intervene with people at the point at which individuals interact with the environment (Hollis, 1970; Stevenson, 2004). Social workers will intervene in a wide variety of human situations; they are more likely to undertake their practice with people who are vulnerable and at risk, who are struggling in some way to participate fully in society. Consequently as a social worker you may feel you walk a 'tightrope' between marginalised individuals and the wider political and social environments which may have contributed to their marginalisation.

Social workers need to be highly skilled and knowledgeable to work effectively. Social workers have to use a range of theoretical approaches with different people in different contexts, assessing needs, planning and intervening within their social context, constructively challenging individual, institutional and structural discrimination. They should work in partnership with people who use services and carers, seeking to empower and emancipate individuals, and work with other professionals. It is critical that you as a student social worker develop a rigorous grounding in, and understanding of theories and models for social work. Such knowledge helps social workers to assess what to do, when to do it and how to do it, while recognising that social work is a complex activity with no absolute 'rights' or 'wrongs' of practice for each situation.

This book aims to meet the learning needs outlined in the Department of Health (2002c) requirements for social work education and the prescribed curriculum for competence and knowledge and understanding of human growth and development, incorporating the development of knowledge and skills relevant to social work, to interprofessional working and in the development of values.

It will also meet subject skills in the Quality Assurance Agency (2008) academic benchmarks for social work. The Subject Benchmark Statement for social work as an applied academic subject at honours level sets out expectations concerning the subject knowledge, understanding and skills of an honours graduate in social work; the teaching, learning and assessment methods employed in their education and the standards expected of them at the point of graduation. This includes understanding the nature of social work and developing knowledge and understanding of: social work services, service users and carers; the service delivery context; values and ethics; social work theory and the nature of social work practice. In addition social work graduates should acquire and integrate in problem-solving; communication; working with others; personal and professional development and ICT and numerical skills.

The book will also meet the National Occupational Standards (NOS) for Social Work (GSCC, 2002a) provide the criteria for the assessment of competence in practice. They outline the range of knowledge, skills and values that the student must demonstrate, evaluate critically and apply to their practice. Within the Standards the importance of working with individuals, families, carers, groups and communities to achieve change and development and to improve life opportunities is clearly stated.

National Occupational Standards for Social Work

Key Role 1: Prepare for and work with individuals, families, carers, groups and communities to assess their needs and circumstances.

- *Prepare for social work contact and involvement.*

- *Work with individuals, families, carers, groups and communities to help them make informed decisions.*

- *Assess needs and options to recommend a course of action.*

Key Role 2: Plan, carry out, review and evaluate social work practice, with individuals, families, carers, groups and communities and other professionals.

- *Respond to crisis situations.*

- *Interact with individuals, families, carers, groups and communities to achieve change and development to improve life opportunities.*

- *Prepare, produce, implement and evaluate plans with individuals, families, carers, groups and communities and professional colleagues.*

- *Support the development of networks to meet assessed needs and planned outcomes.*

- *Work with groups to promote individual growth, development and independence.*

- *Address behaviour which presents a risk to individuals families, carers, groups and communities.*

Key Role 3: Support individuals to represent their needs, views and circumstances.

- *Advocate with and on behalf of individuals families, carers, groups and communities.*

- *Prepare for and participate in decision making forums.*

Key Role 4: Manage risk to individuals, families, carers, groups and communities, self and colleagues.

- *Assess and manage risk to individuals, families, carers, groups and communities.*

- *Assess, minimise and manage risk to self and colleagues.*

National Occupational Standards for Social Work (continued)
Key Role 5: Manage and be accountable, with supervision and support, for your own social work practice with your organisation.

- *Manage and be accountable for your own work.*

- *Contribute to the management of resources and services.*

(GSCC, 2002)

In addition there are six value and ethical requirements (each with a number of criteria), summarising the expectation of social workers from the perspective of service users, carers and organisations, following a number of consultations with them.

The 'Value and Ethics: Statement of Expectations' have six key headings, each with a number of expectations.

1. Communications skills and information sharing.

2. Good social work practice.

3. Advocacy.

4. Working with other professionals.

5. Knowledge.

6. Values.

(GSCC, 2002)

In essence this book will focus on developing your knowledge and understanding of human development throughout the life course and its importance and relevance to social work practice. An action-orientated approach helps to facilitate evaluation, review and reflection of your learning and practice. Case studies, which focus on different aspects of the human life course, will be used throughout to enhance this process and to illustrate key learning points. Additionally theory and research summaries are provided to underpin the developing knowledge with theories, models and evidence.

Book structure

Understanding the way in which individuals develop before birth, as babies, children and adolescents through to young, middle and older adulthood towards death is fundamental to social work practice. Having an understanding of such knowledge supports the worker in assessing and planning to meet individual needs. It allows them to be sensitive and appropriate in their communication with people and in the services they offer and provide. It is important that social workers have an understanding of human development to work effectively with other disciplines and to demonstrate a professional literacy commensurate with their status. This book will demonstrate how theories of human life course development inform social work practice in key areas.

Throughout the book, you will examine how an understanding of the theories of human life course development is necessary to establish effective partnerships with people who use social work services, with other professionals and when using the law to protect and enhance service-users' rights. The importance of taking a biographical approach, listening to the narrative stories of individuals and their constructions of their own lives, is highlighted. Links will be made to the skills needed at various stages of development, including communication and working with other professionals. Additionally other key elements of the prescribed curriculum, such as the knowledge of child development and legal intervention to protect, will be incorporated. Throughout the book, you will be encouraged to examine your own views and perspectives and to interrogate the origins of these.

The book takes a case-study approach throughout, with case studies being used to illustrate and draw out key points, to aid and reinforce learning. You will also be provided with summaries of relevant contemporary research, suggestions for further reading and current government guidance and policy documents, all of which give evidence for and support best practice. The emphasis in this book concerns you achieving the requirements of the curriculum and developing knowledge that will assist you in meeting the Occupational Standards for social work.

The book has seven main chapters covering human development through the life course. In the first chapter you will be introduced to the reasons why knowledge and understanding of human development throughout the life course are important to social work practice. The chapter starts by outlining the importance of recognising the impact that personal values and your own life events can have upon practice. You will also consider the concept of life-events and transitions. The chapter makes the links between practice and inquiries into social and health care that have come into the public domain. By introducing you to a range of theoretical approaches to human development and the significance of knowledge from other disciplines, this chapter creates the links to the specific practice-focused chapters that follow.

Chapter 2 develops the introduction to theoretical models for understanding development across the life course. This chapter will outline the theoretical approaches commonly used by social workers and other professionals when working with people in a variety of settings, across the whole life course. The connections, similarities and differences between the theories are examined and you will compare and contrast models and apply them to practice situations. The chapter will suggest that no single theory alone can explain the complexity of human life course development. Having introduced a range of perspectives and developmental theories in this chapter, the remaining chapters of the book will focus on specific phases in the human life course. These practice-focused chapters will build on this introduction to theories, examining particular approaches and their usefulness to social work practice with individuals at certain age points along the developmental spectrum of their lives.

Chapters 3 and 4 focus on human development and social work practice with children. Both of these chapters are set within the context of the national strategic development programme *Every Child Matters: Change for Children* (DfES, 2004) and the legislative conduit for this programme, the *Children Act 2004*. Additionally, the chapters make the links between understanding children's development and the practice standards within *The common core of skills and knowledge for everyone working with children, young people and their families* (DfES, 2005a) and specific practice developments, such as *The Common Assessment Framework* (DfES, 2006a).

In Chapter 3 you will explore life course development knowledge in social work practice with infants, young children and their families. This chapter will set out knowledge in respect of early child development. You will examine pre-natal, peri-natal and neo-natal periods of life development and will consider the relative importance of hereditary factors and environmental factors in determining the individual's development. This chapter will specifically develop your understanding and ability to critique theories that explain human development taking a cognitive approach and theories taking a biological or physical perspective.

Chapter 4 looks at using life course development knowledge in social work practice with older children and their families. The chapter will specifically develop your understanding and ability to critique theories that explain human development taking a systemic approach. The Department of Health *Children-in-Need Assessment Framework* will be used to explore this approach.

In Chapter 5 you will look at life course development knowledge in social work practice in respect of young people in their teenage or adolescent years. The chapter will explore issues related to the transition to adulthood and the particular significance that this may have for young people with disabilities. You will develop your understanding and ability to critique theories that explain human development taking a behavioural and social learning approach. The discussion of adolescence and development through teenage years is contextualised within contemporary strategic policy approaches outlined in *Youth Matters* (DfES, 2005b).

In Chapter 6 life course development knowledge in social work practice with people in early and middle adulthood is examined. You will focus on developing your understanding of human life course development and the significance of transitions in adult life. Drawing on situations related to adults experiencing physical disability, adults with learning difficulties and adults who have caring responsibilities, the chapter will consider how transitions present opportunities for growth and development or conversely potential crisis points. This chapter will specifically develop your understanding and ability to critique theories that explain life course development in stages or phases. This chapter and the final chapter, Chapter 7, have been developed to enable you to frame your learning in the context of current social work practice with adults and older people. Most significantly, you will read about *Our Health, Our Care, Our Say* (DoH, 2006a) and, specifically in Chapter 7, *Next steps in implementing the National Service Framework for Older People* (DoH, 2006b) and how knowledge of human life course development supports your practice within this policy context.

The final chapter examines ways in which an understanding of the theories of human development is necessary for effective social work practice with older people and their families. The chapter considers older age in terms of opportunities for growth and development, it addresses issues related to ageing, older age and how it is constructed in our society. An exploration of the significance of transitions in later life will enable you to consider effective ageing and end-of-life issues. This chapter will further develop your understanding and ability to critique theories that explain life course development in stages or phases.

Concluding remarks and signposts are offered at the end of the book. At this stage you will be invited to review the learning outcomes set at the outset. You will be encouraged to review your progress by charting and monitoring your learning, taking developmental needs and reflections forward to other books within the series.

Learning features

This book is interactive. You are encouraged to work through the book as an active participant, taking responsibility for your learning, in order to increase your knowledge, understanding and ability to apply this learning to practice. You will be expected to reflect creatively on how your immediate learning needs can be met in the area of understanding human development and how your professional learning can be developed in your future career.

Case studies throughout the book will help you to examine theories and models for social work practice. We have devised activities that require you to reflect on experiences, situations and events and help you to review and summarise learning undertaken. In this way your knowledge will become deeply embedded as part of your development. When you come to practice learning in an agency the work and reflection undertaken here will help you to improve and hone your skills and knowledge.

This book will introduce knowledge and learning activities for you as a student social worker to demonstrate how theories of human life course development inform social work practice in key areas.

Professional development and reflective practice

This third edition of *Social Work and Human Development* places great emphasis on developing skills of reflection and analysis about, in, and on, practice. Reflective practice is a critical skill for social work practice to constantly examine and improve your practice skills in the ever-changing complexity of practice situations.

> ## Some definitions:
> We reflect in order to learn or we learn as a result of reflecting.
>
> *(Moon, 2004 p.186)*
>
> The goal of reflective learning is a transformation of perspective (Mezirow, 1991), a significant shift in perspective that allows professionals not only to critically review their practice, but also helps them to work in a more responsive, creative, and ultimately more effective manner.
>
> *(Redmond, 2004 p.1)*
>
> Reflective practice involves the ability to be aware of the 'theory' or assumptions involved in professional practice, in order to close the gap between what is espoused and what is enacted, in an effort to improve both.
>
> *(Schön, 1991)*

This book will assist you in developing a questioning approach that looks in a critical way at your thoughts, experiences and practice, as well as key theories and models that explain human development and the life course. As a result of these deliberations, the book seeks to heighten your skills in taking a critical approach and reflecting on your work within the context of contemporary professional practice. This third edition is supported by a companion *Reflective Reader* (Crawford, 2006), where the concepts and skills of reflection and professional development in relation to human development are furthered. Reflection is central to good social work practice, but only if action and further development result from these reflections.

Reflection about, in and on your practice is not only important during your education to become a social worker; it is considered to be key to continued professional development and is an underpinning principle to the *Framework for post qualifying education in social work* (GSCC, 2007). As a professional that acknowledges life-long learning as a way of keeping up to date, ensuring that knowledge and research inform practice and in honing skills, values and ethics for practice, it is essential that you begin this ongoing process at the start of your learning. The importance of professional development is clearly shown by its inclusion in the *National Occupational Standards for Social Work* (GSCC/Topss 2002b) and the *Codes of Practice for Social Care Workers* (GSCC, 2002c).

As you undertake reading and work on the chapters in this book, you are invited to reflect on your learning and the implications for your practice. You could address the following questions as you complete each chapter:

REFLECTION POINT

- *What do I know, or can I do now, that I did not know or could not do before I did this section of studying?*

- *Is there anything I do not understand or want to explore further?*

- *What else do I need to know to extend my professional development and learning in this area?*

Chapter 1
Understanding human development through the life course

A C H I E V I N G   A   S O C I A L   W O R K   D E G R E E

This chapter will help you to begin to meet the following National Occupational Standards:
Key Role 1: Prepare for and work with individuals, families, carers, groups and communities to assess their needs and circumstances.
- Prepare for social work contact and involvement.
Key Role 5: Manage and be accountable, with supervision and support, for your own social work practice within the organisation.
- Manage and be accountable for your own work.
Key Role 6: Demonstrate professional competence in social work practice.
- Research, analyse, evaluate and use current knowledge of best social work practice.
- Work within agreed standards of social work practice and ensure own professional development

It will also introduce you to the following academic standards as set out in the social work subject benchmark statement:
3.1.4 Social work theory.
3.1.5 The nature of social work practice.

Introduction

In this first chapter, we shall be setting out some of the key terms and perspectives that the book will develop in respect of life course development and social work practice. We will outline the importance of human growth and development, in particular how it relates to social work practice. We shall be considering your own life course, how it has developed and how an understanding of this can help you in your social work practice. This chapter will cover why it is important to recognise your personal values, and be aware of the impact that these may have on your practice. The critical importance of reflective practice will form an element of this discussion. This chapter will also look at some of the broad debates on human development, as an introduction to the next chapter which will look in more detail at different theoretical perspectives on how human beings become the people they are. The chapter will show how the contribution of other professionals can enhance developmental knowledge, improving the social work response and thereby improving practice.

In order to demonstrate the importance of knowledge and skills in human development for social work, this chapter will make the links between practice and public inquiries into health and social care practice in relation to specific cases.

Social work practice involves interactions between people, which are influenced by each person's life course and their experience and perceptions about their own life. Social workers need to understand people, and how they develop and place people's life situations in the context of the expectations of normal life course development. This will enable the worker to appreciate that a person's experience, their growth, development and life experiences have a direct impact on who they are and how they see their world.

The social work profession is based on the supposition that people can be helped and supported to change and grow as a result of their experiences. Therefore, in order for you to be sensitive and appropriate in your communications with people and in the services you offer and provide, you need to appreciate and understand their life course and what makes them who they are. Understanding how people grow and develop is central to the role and tasks of a professional social worker.

Social work is an activity that requires an ability to thrive and embrace dilemmas, conflicts, uncertainly and not knowing; practice is central to shaping the identity of social work:

> *Social work derives from the society of which it is part. The preoccupation of social work with people and their social circumstances creates its main occupational risk – a lack of specificity an inherent ambiguity.*

> (Butrym, 1976)

In acknowledging the constantly changing context of social work organisations and social work practice, Cree and Davis (2002, p.12) stress that:

> *. . . the necessary qualities of social workers do not change; their ability to listen to people, to advocate on behalf of others and see them in the context of their whole lives. These are qualities that stand out in social work . . .*

Life course development and social work practice

Development goes on throughout life. Because human beings are complex, the study of life course development is inter-disciplinary, drawing on a many disciplines. This includes biology, genetics, history, psychology, sociology, anthropology, philosophy, medicine and education.

As you learn about human development through this book and your further reading, you will come across a number of terms that may appear to describe similar concepts. In this section you will be introduced to some of the key words that are commonly related to this topic. We shall explain our interpretation of those words and how they are used in this book.

Throughout the book we take a life course perspective. This will be expanded upon in the next chapter when you consider theoretical approaches to the study of human development. Taking a life course perspective means to adopt an approach that considers the whole of a person's life as offering opportunities for growth, development and change. You will notice that we use the words *life course*, however, in other texts you will find the words *life span* and *life cycle* used in similar contexts. Léonie Sugarman (1986) writes from a psychological perspective and adopts the term *life-span development* as she discusses *life-span developmental psychology*. Paul Baltes (1987), also a developmental psychologist, describes the concept of a *life-span perspective*. You will read more about his ideas in Chapter 2. In contrast Erik Erikson (1982), another theorist whose approach is explored in the following chapters, writes about the *life cycle* from a psychosocial approach. The term 'psychosocial' describes an approach that considers both the individual psychology and the social context of people's lives on their individual development. The psychosocial perspective enables social workers to consider the influences of the relationship between the internal world of the service-user and the social environment in which they live (Howe, 1987). Erikson describes the concept of *life cycle* as implying *some kind of self-completion* (Erikson, 1982 p.9). The use of the word *cycle* brings the notion of time and progression to life development, but it can be criticised for implying a circular process whereby in the later years of life there is a return to the dependency of childhood. Thus from psychosocial and sociological perspectives, the term *life course* has become favoured and is the term that we shall adopt for the remainder of this book.

In order to develop your understanding of social work and human development the chapters of this book will introduce you to a range of theories, research and ideas. However, the under-pinning philosophy of a life course perspective is emphasised and its application to social work practice is developed through an understanding of the narrative approach. The narrative approach, or biographical approach as it is sometimes called, focuses on the individual's experiences through their first-hand account of their life. Within this book you will develop your knowledge and ideas by studying human life course development in the context of individuality and difference. You will learn about development in respect of people of different ages, gender, levels of ability, race, ethnic and cultural background. However, where it has not been possible to cover each of these topics in detail, the significance of the narrative approach coupled with a whole of life course perspective is that stereotypical assumptions are challenged and diversity is valued. The narrative approach is explained further in Chapter 2.

Summary of definitions and key concepts

Life course	The progression and path an individual takes from conception to death.
Life course perspective	A viewpoint that considers the whole of a life (from conception to death) as offering opportunities for growth, development and change.
Life-span	An alternative term used to describe the life course, often used in developmental psychology.
Life cycle	An alternative term used to describe the life course, this is now considered to be an out-of-date term.
Development	A complex, continuous, progressive series of changes that occur as a result of maturation and experience.

Narrative or biographical approach	A way of working with individuals that focuses on the importance of their own first-hand account of their life, their experiences and the meanings they attach to them.

The ideas explained above will be considered in more detail as you progress through this book. In the next section you will consider your life course, and what this has meant to you from your personal perspective, much as you would take a narrative approach with a service user.

Understanding your own life experiences

To understand the impact of human growth and development on social work practice we will begin by asking you to look at your own life course development. Examining your own life, and the experiences that have influenced it, is an important stage in learning the significance of life course development. By understanding and making sense of your own life experience, you will be able to appreciate the importance of the key events in shaping you as a person. First, we shall start by exploring your own life course development.

ACTIVITY **1.1**

Think about your own life, your childhood and the time you were growing up. By following the activities below, you will represent your life in a diagram.

- *Draw a line to represent the 'ups' and 'downs' of your life so far.*
- *Now place the life events against the peaks and troughs of your line.*
- *Consider the line you have drawn, identify for each of these points the main influencing factors, in other words what made the change happen, were you able to make choices?*

When you have completed this, consider your thoughts and feelings at these times, for example 'happy', 'sad', 'excited', 'uncertain'.

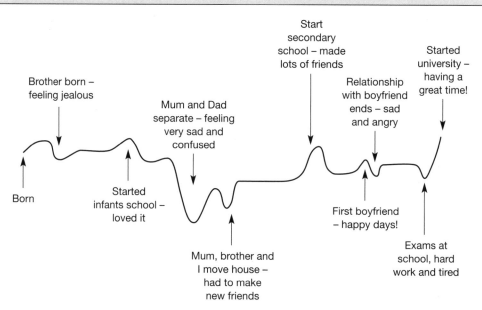

Figure 1.1 Example of a life course line

COMMENT

Every person completing this activity will have drawn a different diagram. However, if you have the opportunity to compare the life course line that you have drawn with another person, perhaps another student, you are likely to find a number of common themes. Figure 1.1 is an example that we have completed.

You will find the concept of life road maps developed in Chapter 2 of *Social work practice: assessment, planning, intervention and review* (second edition) (Parker and Bradley, 2007).

You may recognise many similarities that may be linked to events that have occurred at certain ages, for example we are all dependent upon others for the first few years of our lives; there may be other similar milestones in our lives, such as starting school, moving to secondary school or biological development, such as puberty and so on. There will also be differences that may be linked to your history, age, class, gender, culture, disability and/or ethnicity, such as living in the same town all your life or moving around; the influence of family life events, such as marriage, children or divorce, the impact of your race and culture on your upbringing and so on. Thinking about your own life, and making sense of the experiences you have had, will be invaluable in having some insight into the impact of your life course on your development and growth as a person.

You may feel that you have had a fairly uneventful life, or conversely that a lot has happened in your life. However we have all experienced changes and obstacles. What you have been doing in this activity is identifying the personal and social impact of life events. These can also be called periods of transition, which are phases or stages within a person's life course when people move through life events.

All people will experience transitions in their lives. An example of this might be the impact of making a choice to study at university.

ACTIVITY **1.2**

Think about the impact of making the decision to study at university. What influenced your decision? What impact has this had on your life and life style? What impact do you hope that gaining a qualification will have for your future life course?

COMMENT

Some of the issues you may have raised may be related to your family, friends, finance, where you live and so on. What will be apparent is that this decision can be described as a major life decision as it has been influenced by your past life experience, has an impact on your immediate experience and will significantly influence and impact on your future life experiences.

Understanding the impact of transitions within a person's life course is important for social work practice in order to help us understand other people's lives. Although people may experience the same life event, their response to the transition and the decisions they make will be different. People will have different perceptions of what is happening to them as they move through a transition in their lives, their response and the learning they gain from it will be different. For example, you may have enjoyed school, tolerated it or hated it. This may be due to academic ability, the influence of peers or the attitude and response of a particular teacher. People's response to these transitions may be different; for example, a response to 'hating' a particular teacher may have been that you took no part in the learning or it may have been to work hard to 'show them' what you can do. Thinking of life development in stages or points of crisis, which we all attempt to move through successfully, can assist us in understanding the challenges faced by people at different points in their lives.

You may be aware of people who have complex life issues but appear to cope with them. There are other people who appear to be unable to cope with any issues within their lives. As social workers we need to recognise the opportunities to work with people through transition as an opportunity to grow. We need to try to enable people to use these events to trigger change and move on and develop. People can have crises and still have happy and fulfilling lives. Additionally there is the opportunity to support people through, for example, providing services; linking them with other people in similar positions for sharing and support; working with communities to promote change.

The case study below is an example of a major life transition.

CASE STUDY

Following a violent outburst from her children's father, resulting in her receiving broken ribs and a broken arm, Christine has moved into her mother's home with her children, Ashley (2 years) and Chloe (3 months). Ashley is 'clingy' and demanding. Christine finds it difficult to 'bond' with Chloe; she is fretful and difficult to feed. She is lonely and depressed, missing her friends and home. Recently the children's father has been texting her, demanding to see the children and threatening legal action.

ACTIVITY 1.3

Think about ('reflect on') the case above:

- *Write down your thoughts and emotions that you feel in considering this case.*

- *How might those involved in this case be feeling?*

- *What issues seem to be the significant issues? As a social worker for this case what might you be trying to achieve? What are the consequences of this for Christine/her children/the children's father/Christine's mother/yourself?*

- *What do you need to do in order to make things better/improve the situation/resolve the situation/feel better/get on better?*

- *What broader issues need to be considered if any action is to be successful? What might be the consequences of this action?*

An important aspect of your practice as a social work student and as a social worker is that of 'reflective practice' (Schön, 1983). The notion of reflection is evident in many different disciplines, for example, education or health professionals. Reflective practice is fundamentally thinking about ('reflecting on') your approach before, during and after any intervention. It seems to include such complex activities as: 'learning from experiences', 'thinking about', 'turning back on self', 'deconstructing'. Schön (1983) describes technical rationality ('rules') and professional artistry ('reflection in action'). For Schön very often the `theory' or rules espoused by practitioners are quite different from the `theory' or assumptions embedded in the actual practices of professionals. Reflective practice therefore involves the ability to be aware of the `theory' or assumptions involved in professional practice, in order to close the gap between what is espoused and what is enacted, in an effort to improve both. Fook (2002) suggests reflective practice involves learning from experience, by examining fundamental assumptions, reintegrating experiences (and reformulating meaning and principles for living) resulting in new guidelines for action.

CASE STUDY *continued*

Following a visit by the Health Visitor to support Christine and monitor the children, Christine allowed her to contact the local Family Centre. The social worker visited and provided support and advice. They have planned together ways in which Christine and her children can move forward with their life: this has included opportunities to talk about her feelings and concerns; seeking legal advice in relation to the children's welfare; identifying a playgroup for Ashley and help with seeking her own accommodation. In addition the social worker has supported Christine in attending a support group at the Children's Centre providing an opportunity to share her experiences with people in a similar position, to learn ways to cope and to develop strategies for the future.

As social workers we also need to recognise the impact of our own role and decisions as they impact on people's lives and major life transitions. Potentially, professional intervention itself can have an impact on a person's life development. For example, where someone who experiences mental ill health is made the subject of a compulsory admission to hospital under the mental health legislation. Whilst this may be in the best interest of their safety and the safety of others, the potential impact on that individual's life and life course could be enormous. Equally a lack of social work intervention or poor practice, when working with young people moving from foster or residential care to independence, can impede their progress through this important transition period. Therefore the potential for social work interventions to interrupt and damage people's life course is considerable.

Another important part of social work practice is 'reflective practice' (Schön, 1983). Reflective practice is concerned with thinking about (reflecting on) the best approach before, during and after any intervention. Thus, as a social worker you recapture the experience, think about your practice in the situation and evaluate it. This requires you to be aware of the knowledge, experience and skills that inform your actions and decisions and how you apply them to your practice. Personal and professional values will underpin every aspect of this practice.

The impact of values on understanding human development

As we have seen so far our own life experiences help us to understand a great deal about the experience, shape and course of our lives. This experience has helped to shape the person that we have become and our responses and choices. Our beliefs and values are deep rooted and impact on the way we live our lives. It is critical that we recognise and acknowledge the impact of these on our professional practice as it could shape our attitude and response to others.

Being aware of the impact of people's life experiences on their values, beliefs and their own identity can also help us to make sense of other people's lives and life course, for example through understanding and sharing experiences with others such as the experience of going to school, being a teenager, studying at university and so on. However we should not make assumptions that our experience is the same as everyone else's. Everyone's experience is unique and his or her interpretation of it will be different. Whilst our own experiences are important, this is not sufficient in itself as a criterion, on which to base our understanding of others. We cannot assume that we know everything on the basis on our own experiences. At a personal level, it may be hard to understand how an adult can sexually abuse a child or how one person can be violent towards another. It is important that we recognise how our own life experiences impact on our understanding of other people's situations and shape our personal values, beliefs and assumptions of others.

To give you an example of how a particular value and belief, which has developed through a person's life course experiences, may impact upon their thoughts and practices as a social worker or student, we shall briefly consider religion. Gilligan and Furness (2006) report on research undertaken with social work students and practitioners to explore the role of religion and spirituality in social work practice. The following research summary gives short extracts taken from their research findings.

The significance of taking account of and valuing difference in people's life courses, cultures, own beliefs and experiences was highlighted through the report into the death of Victoria Climbié.

RESEARCH SUMMARY

... As humans, we internalize many of our early beliefs. Our actions and behaviour tend to be shaped by our experiences and to some extent by the dominant religious legacies that have become enmeshed with and translated into the cultural traditions, rituals and customs of communities.

Gilligan and Furness (2006, p.625)

A (further) comparison of responses from students to specific interventions suggests a fairly consistent pattern between particular groups; 64 per cent of the Muslim students considered 'The use of religious or spiritual language or concepts' as potentially appropriate, in contrast to only 25 per cent of Christian students and 36 per cent of those holding no current beliefs. Also, a higher number of Muslim students considered 'Recommending participation in a religious or spiritual program' and 'Participation in a client's rituals as an intervention' as potentially appropriate. This difference seems likely to result from the fact that religious beliefs and customs are central to the lives of Muslims and that they are, as a result, more likely to recognize the potential importance of religion and spirituality in the lives of others. However, while most of the Christian students saw the intervention 'Helping clients develop ritual as an intervention (e.g. visiting graves of relatives, house blessings, etc)' as potentially appropriate, most Muslim students did not, possibly because of the essentially euro-centric nature of the examples offered.

(ibid, pp.631–2)

CASE STUDY

Victoria Climbié died on 25 February 2000, aged 8 years and 3 months. Her aunt and partner were subsequently convicted of her murder and are serving sentences of life imprisonment. A number of professionals had contact with Victoria, her aunt and partner, including Social Services. On 20 April 2001, Lord Laming was appointed by two secretaries of state to conduct three statutory inquiries. Together they would become known as the Victoria Climbié Inquiry (Laming, 2003). This report has raised significant practice issues and has been the conduit for widespread reform of services for children and families: Every Child Matters: Change for Children (DfES, 2004). Evidence from the Victoria Climbié Inquiry indicated that a lack of understanding of cultural difference, by a range of different professionals, contributed to the death of this child (Laming, 2003, cited in Gilligan and Furness, 2006 p.634).

CASE STUDY

In December 1992 Christopher Clunis attacked and killed Jonathon Zito, who was a stranger to him. Clunis had been diagnosed as having paranoid schizophrenia in 1986 when living in Jamaica. Where a murder has taken place and one of the parties is receiving a mental health service, an independent inquiry is held. The inquiry report on the care and treatment of Christopher Clunis was published in February 1994.

Continued

CASE STUDY *continued*

Within the report the Inquiry team stated that

> the added factor of his blackness may have contributed to the different manner in which some professionals treated him and it may have caused them to defer against his best interests, to his own expressed wishes.
>
> *(Ritchie et al., 1994 p.4)*

Amongst the many recommendations made in the Inquiry report, the panel stated that

> young black males should not be type-cast as suffering from schizophrenia unless the clinical indications warrant it and clinicans and others who care for black mentally ill people should not be too ready to ascribe odd behaviour to the abuse of drugs.
>
> *(Ritchie et al., 1994 p.129)*

The previous case study is another example that demonstrates how assumptions, stereotypical views and an absence of a multicultural perspective on the life course (Paludi, 2002) have contributed to poor practice.

In summarising the findings of their research into the role of religion and spirituality in social work practice Gilligan and Furness state that

> *... there is a clear need for all social work practitioners and educators to give greater priority to exploring the potential significance of religious and spiritual beliefs in their training, in their professional practice and in the lives and perspectives of service users and colleagues. Social workers need to be able to respond appropriately to the needs of all service users, including those for whom religious and spiritual beliefs are crucial. 'Culturally competent' practice depends, amongst other things, on an understanding and appreciation of the impact of faith and belief.*
>
> (2006, p.617)

The research and the examples shown in this chapter provide powerful lessons for us to reflect upon. Within our practice we need to ensure that we balance our personal beliefs and values about how we should live our lives, such as those based on religion and culture, with those of the service users and carers we work with.

Ways of explaining human life course development

In this chapter, so far, you have considered how your own life experiences may have influenced your growth and development; you have also explored the significance of personal beliefs and values in understanding the individual and the critical importance of developing skills in reflective practice.

CASE STUDY

Casey is 14 years of age, living on a large inner city housing estate which has a reputation for anti-social behaviour among teenage 'gangs'. Casey has not attended school for some months. John, her father, has recently been sent to prison to serve a seven-year prison sentence for drug dealing. Jackie, her mother uses drugs and alcohol and is known to 'deal' in soft drugs. Casey's paternal grandfather has also spent a period of his life in prison, including a current ten-year sentence for arson. Her maternal grandmother is a long-term user of alcohol.

ACTIVITY **1.4**

Think about the range of responses that Casey's situation raises from you and answer the following questions:

- *How do you feel about Casey? Casey's situation?*

- *What might Casey feel about her life?*

- *What might Casey's family feel about her?*

- *How might the public/society feel about Casey/young people in 'gangs'?*

COMMENT

While you will have had to make judgements based on limited information, it almost certainly will have raised a range of different views and dilemmas for you. Your response to this activity will not only be concerned by considering your professional response and values but also will be influenced by your personal values and beliefs. For example, some people may feel that Casey's behaviour is a 'cry for help'; others may feel that there are aspects of 'normal' behaviour for young adolescents, especially those with Casey's background; others may feel this is unacceptable behaviour that needs to be dealt with by public agencies such as the police. As a professional social worker you need to think about how you can balance the support, care and rights of young people against your responsibility and accountabilities to the community and wider society.

Within this case study there seems to be some indication in Casey's background that certain of her characteristics are part of her biological make-up. We also need to consider how individuals are influenced by their upbringing and surroundings.

CASE STUDY continued

As a child Jackie attended a special school because of emotional and behavioural difficulties, spending a number of periods in care as a child, due to neglect by her parents. John's background was stable, growing up in a more affluent area and being more academically able. At 14 years he began to spend increasing time with a disaffected group of young teenagers, becoming involved with drug use. At the age of 15 Jackie gave birth to Casey.

Continued

Following this Jackie and John began to live together living in a series of bed and breakfasts and a hostel for homeless people. In order to survive and have money for their increased drug use, John would steal and Jackie would work occasionally as a prostitute. Casey was placed in the care of a series of relatives. Her parents finally obtained a council house when Casey was three years old. By the age of five Casey had two brothers and a sister. Although her parents are still together, they have a volatile relationship. The family continue to have an erratic lifestyle, largely due to her parents drug and alcohol use. Since John was sent to prison, Jackie has been earning money to fund her drug and alcohol use through prostitution in her own home; one of these men recently made an 'advance' to Casey; this has frightened her. Casey has being attending school on a regular basis and is considered an 'able' student; lately her attendance has been giving cause for concern. Casey is a member of a local 'gang', a group of young people who are involved in shoplifting from local shops, using alcohol and experimenting with 'soft' drug use. They hang out at a local park, verbally abusing and bullying the children who come to play there.

ACTIVITY **1.5**

Now you know more about Casey's situation, list 5 possible explanations for her behaviours.

COMMENT

You may have come up with a number of ideas. Your thoughts are likely to arise from two main perspectives. Perhaps you thought that Casey's behaviour had some natural, inborn predisposition for bad behaviour that was part of her individual make-up. Or perhaps you thought that Casey's childhood, her background and upbringing have led to some of these behaviours.

These two explanations are examples of opposing theories that attempt to account for individual behaviours and qualities. This is known as the 'nature or nurture' debate.

The 'nature' viewpoint argues that our genes predetermine who we are and our characteristics are inherited. We have inborn biological characteristics that are hereditary from our birth-parents at the point of conception. There is certainly significant evidence to suggest that certain of our characteristics are inherited such as intelligence and personality. The danger in purely assuming this perspective is that it assumes that change is not possible – we are the way we are and that there is little that we can do about it. This argument can stereotype characteristics and people, this potentially supporting prejudice and oppressive behaviour, as we have shown in relation to the care of Christopher Clunis earlier in this chapter.

The 'nurture' viewpoint argues that fundamentally our environment, experiences and the way we are brought up influence our development – the complex forces of the physical and social world that influence our biological make-up and psychological experiences before and after birth. Evidence can be found of this in patterns of family behaviour, for example whether family members are 'introvert' or 'extrovert', the way they demonstrate affection to one another and others. However does this argument stereotype individuals and families into certain 'types'? For example in some 'extrovert 'families, there may be a member of the family who may be extremely introverted.

ACTIVITY *1.6*

You may wish to reflect on your own background and family and consider what aspects of your/your families' personality reflect 'nature' or 'nurture'. How might you account for 'differences' between family members? Can you identify ways in which your up-bringing influences your values and beliefs?

CASE STUDY *continued*

Jill is Casey's aunt, her father's sister. She is married to a software development consultant and they live in a pleasant home in the suburbs of the city. Jill and her husband have offered to care for Casey. They have an active lifestyle and, although they have no children, appear committed to Casey and supporting a change in her behaviour, believing that their lives and lifestyle can present a positive model for her.

COMMENT

This case example raises a number of fundamental questions: are people's behaviour and actions predetermined? How do we 'inherit' our behaviour? What effect does the environment we grow up in have on our behaviour and actions? Some people would argue that genes and the family we come from determine the way that we make choices and therefore the causes of our behaviour are predetermined, such as the way we live our lives. Others would argue that it is 'free will' – that we change by our own efforts.

The issues that this case raises show that it is too simplistic to argue from one point of view. It is most likely that the complex interaction between a range of factors contributes to who we are, for example:

- the genes that we inherit;
- physical appearance and characteristics, for example the way we look;
- our behaviour, which may attract a favourable or unfavourable response;
- the way we are brought up: for example by a range of carers;
- environmental factors: for example, the area we live in, the food that we eat;
- cultural background and appearance;
- cultural stereotypes: for example those associated with age, the social class we are judged to come from;
- cultural values: each culture has certain values associated with different ages;

- role changes: attitudes towards different ages are greatly influenced by the roles that are played; for example for those who have retired, social attitudes are less sympathetic;

- personal experiences;

- the choices we make;

- the opportunities that come our way; and

- the impact of other people on and in our lives.

As you have been thinking about Casey, her behaviours and her family, you have been examining different aspects of her situation and this shows how difficult it can be to understand people's life courses, the influences upon them and the complex events that they may have been through.

The exploration of these 'nature' and 'nurture' theories in this chapter has introduced you to one of the fundamental broad debates on human development. Within Chapter 2 of this book we shall be looking in more detail at the key theoretical models used to help us understand development across the life course and consider how theory is applied to social work practice. One of the benefits of looking at different theoretical ideas is that it gives us a wider perspective taking us beyond our own particular life experiences.

Interprofessional practice

We have seen, therefore, that social workers need to be open to a range of interpretations, critical approaches, theories and debates in relation to life course development in order to understand their use in practice. Social work practice from a human life course development context is no different. The logical consequence of taking this approach and developing an understanding of theories from a range of disciplines is that social work practitioners will take a holistic approach to their practice. This means taking account of every aspect of the individual's life, in other words, building up an understanding of the whole person. A truly holistic understanding of an individual's circumstances can only be achieved by working in partnership with other professional disciplines, with service-users and their carers. Interprofessional practice will enable us to bring together a range of knowledge and understanding about all the different aspects of a service-user's life and thereby ensure a holistic approach to practice.

CASE STUDY

In August 1995 Anthony Smith killed his mother Gwendoline Smith and his half-brother who was 12 years old. In June 1995 Anthony Smith had been diagnosed as having schizophrenia. The Inquiry report was published in October 1996 and one of the recommendations included:

> It appears essential that a psychiatric patient with a severe psychiatric illness whose recent history is not known should be assessed by a social worker after admission to hospital and prior to the decision to discharge. Where there appear to be difficulties, an assessment of family or employment circumstances should be made.

Continued

Given the psychosocial nature of the impact of schizophrenia, and other severe psychiatric illnesses on the patient, relatives and carers, it is important to ensure that a multidisciplinary and multiagency approach is always adopted.

(Recommendation 1, Wood et al., 1996)

The Smith report commented that the

failure to recognise fully the social aspects of Anthony Smith's problems ... (were) one of the most important and unfortunate aspects of his care.

(Wood et al., 1996 p.19)

The examples in the case study opposite demonstrate the importance of taking all perspectives into account.

The importance of this approach has also been highlighted by the Victoria Climbié Inquiry that was referred to previously.

It is deeply disturbing that during the days and months following her initial contact with Ealing Housing Department's Homeless Persons Unit, Victoria was known to no less than two further housing authorities, four social services departments, two child protection teams of the Metropolitan Police Service (MPS), a specialist centre managed by the NSPCC, and she was admitted to two different hospitals because of suspected deliberate harm. The dreadful reality was that these services knew little or nothing more about Victoria at the end of the process than they did when she was first referred to Ealing Social Services by the Homeless Persons Unit in April 1999.

(Laming, *Victoria Climbié Inquiry* Summary Report [2003] p.3)

We have provided this example to demonstrate one aspect of the significance of interprofessional working. It can be seen that there are many different professional perspectives and areas of knowledge that need to be brought together and co-ordinated. Within social work, therefore, if we are to ensure good practice, we need to work across disciplines, taking account of all aspects of the individual's life course in developing an holistic approach to social work practice.

- *What do I know, or can I do now, that I did not know or could not do before I did this section of studying?*

- *Is there anything I do not understand or want to explore further?*

- *What else do I need to know to extend my professional development and learning in this area?*

CHAPTER SUMMARY

Life course development is about each one of us and our life experiences from birth to death. It is important that social workers understand about human growth and development and the impact that this has on individuals, their experiences and their own interpretations of their lives.

This chapter began by introducing you to some of the terms that are used in the study of human life course development. We also explained the importance of taking a life course perspective and supporting this with the application of a narrative approach to practice. These concepts are core features of this book and are revisited in the later chapters.

Social workers need to understand their own life course development and the significance that this has had on the values and beliefs that they have developed themselves. This will enable individual professionals to be aware of the importance of taking a non-judgemental approach to practice. Social work practice must take account of individual, social and cultural differences, otherwise it risks being oppressive and discriminatory. Therefore, social workers must also use their background knowledge and skills to enable service-users to express their own interpretation of their life course and its impact on the situations in which they find themselves.

As well as an awareness of the course your own life has taken, social work practitioners need to have a wide range of knowledge from a span of theoretical disciplines to ensure that all aspects of an individual's make-up are considered and appreciated when working with them. In this chapter, we have shown how a number of formal inquiries into health and care practices, following specific incidents of concern, have identified how knowledge and understanding of human development and growth can improve social work practice. By using appropriate skills, involving service-users and working in partnership across professional disciplines, poor practice and resultant mistakes can be reduced and the overall understanding of individual service-users' needs will be greatly enhanced.

Within the next chapter of this book we shall explore theoretical perspectives in more depth, outlining the models commonly used by social workers and other professionals when working with people in a variety of settings. We shall develop the concepts outlined in this chapter and begin to compare and contrast these models and apply them to familiar social work practice situations. This will form a link to the subsequent chapters which will deal with more specific areas of social work practice, with Chapters 3 and 4 focusing on social work practice with children, young people and their families and Chapter 5 exploring social work practice with adolescents. Chapter 6 will develop your knowledge of life course development in early and middle adulthood and the final chapter will concentrate on practice with older people and their families.

FURTHER READING

Cabinet Office/Social Exclusion Task Force (2009) *Understanding the risks of social exclusion across the life course.* London: Cabinet Office. Available from: **http://www.cabinetoffice.gov.uk**

This project provides quantitative data on the complex relationships between different risk markers of social exclusion and how they vary among the British population. The background, aims and methodology, and key messages and implications for policy in the four projects on children and families, youth and young adulthood, working age adults without dependent children and older age are outlined.

Connolly, M and Ward, T (2008) Navigating human rights across the life course. *Child and Family Social Work*, 13(3), pp.348–56, August.

This paper takes a broad look at human rights issues that occur across the life course, and uses examples of life course transitions to illuminate issues related to moral rights and human rights. The examples include family formation, raising children, adolescent maturation in the context of youth offending and grandparents parenting their grandchildren.

Horner, N (2009) *What is social work?* 3rd edition. Exeter: Learning Matters.

This social work text explores the foundations of social care in the UK, how it evolved and why. It answers key questions on mental health, working with older people, working with families and children, with expanded chapters on international social work, the new directions for social care and the implications of interprofessional working.

Paludi, MA (2002) *Human development in multicultural contexts: A book of readings.* New Jersey: Prentice Hall.

This text focuses on the issues of life span development from a multicultural perspective. It explores the impact of cultural influences on development within each of the life stages and dimensions of development.

Parrott, L (2010) *Values and ethics in social work practice.* 2nd edition. Exeter: Learning Matters.

This text identifies current issues in social work and then applies an ethical dimension. These issues are then investigated further within an anti-discriminatory framework and against the background of the code of practice for social care workers and employers. Traditional value perspectives are clearly explained and current developments in virtue theory and the ethics of care for social work are also introduced.

Chapter 2

An introduction to theoretical models for understanding human life course development

Introduction

In this chapter we will explore theoretical approaches to understanding human life course development, particularly approaches commonly used by social workers and other professionals when working with people in a variety of settings, across their life course. You will develop an understanding of the importance of theory that is based on researched concepts and critical explanations of human development.

The chapter will therefore start by explaining the importance of theory and research to social work practice, it will then provide you with an explanation of the perspective that we have taken throughout this book, as our overall approach to human development. The chapter will then examine how a range of disciplines contribute to the knowledge base of social work, by looking at the similarities and differences between approaches and applying them to a case study. The chapter will draw on the importance of listening to and understanding the individual service-user's story and the meanings that they attach to the lives they have lived. This is known as a biographical or narrative approach. Over the course of this chapter we aim to provide you with a background to the theories, models and tools that you can use in effective practice.

What is theory?

Students and some professional workers often believe that theory is complex and unnecessary and that they need to take a more 'pragmatic' approach and learn or study information or facts alone. In reality though, facts alone cannot simply be understood – they need to be interpreted and explained. This interpretation will be influenced by theoretical approaches. Theories at their simplest can be described as 'an attempt to explain' (Thompson, 2000 p.20). They provide a framework to support understanding and so help us to make sense of social problems. Students and social workers need to understand the underpinning theoretical approaches in order to analyse and evaluate the information that is presented to them as 'fact'. For example in Chapter 1 you looked at how theories of biological determinism ('nature') and theories of environmental determinism ('nurture') were the basis for different explanations of behaviour and development in the case study of Casey and her family. We shall reconsider the situation of Casey and her family in this chapter, as we investigate how the different theoretical perspective influences the social work practice intervention chosen.

Theories, and the research that accompanies them, can contribute towards our understanding of people and situations. Life course development theories help to explain and analyse the life course and may enable us to predict outcomes. In this way, theories and researched evidence are important tools to help and guide practice. However, different theoretical approaches can be seen to lead to different approaches to social work practices. Therefore, as a professional social worker you need to be prepared to assess and critically evaluate theories – for example, be aware of their origins, underlying assumptions, their strengths and limitations. The relationships and oppositions between theories provide a context in which their value can be assessed against ane another, and against the modern social context in which they must be used (Payne, 2005 p.39).

It is also important for professional workers to appreciate that theories themselves reflect the history, culture, assumptions and values of those who have developed them. In Chapter 1 we looked at how imposing your own values and beliefs on other people could infringe their rights as individuals to develop their own interpretations and understanding of their life. Similarly when examining well accepted theoretical concepts, social workers need to ensure they question and explore the values and concerns that lie beneath them.

Taking a life course perspective on human development

Before you learn about specific theoretical ideas that explain how human beings develop, it is important that you understand the perspective that we are taking throughout this book. In Chapter 1, you read about the definitions of key terms and the concept of life course used in this text. The notion of life course has informed the approach that we introduce you to throughout the chapters of this book.

Each of the chapters that follow will concentrate on age-related periods of life. The book has been put together in this way to assist you to develop your understanding of specific issues through the life course. However, we have taken a life course perspective throughout, which means that we have maintained that human beings develop and grow across the whole of their lives, from conception to death. You may think that babies, children and young people go through the most noticeable growth and development and that there is little change in adulthood, with possible decline or degeneration in older age. We dispute that view and within the chapters of this book emphasise that growth and development, change and opportunity are features of human development throughout the whole of life. Paul Baltes (1987) developed seven theoretical propositions of life-span developmental psychology. These propositions are the characteristics or assumptions that underpin the life course perspective that we adopt in this book.

You will find it helpful to refer back to this page as you study the rest of this chapter, which will explore how different disciplines have developed theoretical perspectives on life course development.

RESEARCH SUMMARY

Paul Baltes (1987) Theoretical propositions of life-span developmental psychology

- *Human development is **multidimensional** – it is made up of biological, cognitive and social dimensions.*

- *Human development is **studied by a number of disciplines** – as above, researchers and theorists from across the disciplines have investigated human development.*

- *Human development is **multidirectional** – it will be characterised by both growth and decrease or loss, but not with any single predetermined pathway that can be deemed as normal. The dimensions, noted above, will vary in terms of growth and decline, throughout the life course.*

- *Human development is **plastic** – it is varied and may take many different paths dependent upon the person's life conditions.*

- *Human development is **embedded in history** – it will be influenced by the person's life history and the sociocultural and socio-economic conditions that they have lived through.*

- *Human development is **contextual** – it is dependent upon how the individual responds to the things that are going on around and within them, the context in which they live their lives. Thus development is influenced by the interaction between the person, their experiences, their history, their environment and their biological make-up.*

Theories of human life course development

There are a number of different perspectives that can be taken to form an understanding of how we develop into who we are. As you work through this book about life course development you will be looking at various ideas and theories broadly taken from the disciplines of sociology, biology and psychology. Each of these disciplines has a different emphasis in its underpinning assumptions of what influences life course development.

Theories arising out of the sociological disciplines emphasise social and environmental factors. Sociologists attempt to explain situations in terms of the views and interpretations taken by society as a whole. Social relationships and the individual's situation within the society in which they live and how that is understood or explained by members of society are the main focus of this approach. Karl Marx (1818–1883) took a sociological perspective, emphasising the importance of social and economic structures in influencing our development.

Theories derived from the discipline of biology focus on the physical well-being of the individual. Thus physical development, genetic influences, human growth stages and instinct can be seen as key elements of any biologically based theory. Charles Darwin (1809–1882) was one of the earliest theorists who argued that human behaviour is genetically determined.

Theories formed taking a psychological perspective concentrate on what goes on in people's minds, their emotional development, the development of personality and related behaviours. Theories from this school of thought often describe human life course development in terms of stages or phases that individuals progress through. Sigmund Freud (1856–1939) explains human behaviours and psychological problems by exploring stages of early childhood experiences.

The diagram below represents the different perspectives that will be explored further in this chapter and throughout this book.

Figure 2.1 Theories of human life course development

As can be seen, each of these disciplines takes a different approach to explain what influences life course development. These explanations in turn would suggest different approaches to social work practices. In the following sections of this chapter you will consider each of these disciplines in more detail and develop an understanding of how these perspectives impact upon social work practice. The case study introduced in Chapter 1 will be used as the example in each instance. A summary of the case study is given overleaf.

Casey is 14 years of age, living on a large inner city housing estate which has a reputation for anti-social behaviour among teenage 'gangs'. Casey has not attended school for some months. John, her father, has recently been sent to prison to serve a seven-year prison sentence for drug dealing. Jackie, her mother uses drugs and alcohol and is known to 'deal' in soft drugs. Casey's paternal grandfather has also spent a period of his life in prison, including a current ten-year sentence for arson. Her maternal grandmother is a long-term user of alcohol. At the age of 15 Jackie gave birth to Casey. Following this Jackie and John began to live together living in a series of bed and breakfasts and a hostel for homeless people. In order to survive and have money for their increased drug use, John would steal and Jackie would work occasionally as a prostitute. Casey was placed in the care of a series of relatives. Her parents finally obtained a council house when Casey was three years old. Although her parents are still together, they have a volatile relationship. The family continue to have an erratic lifestyle, largely due to her parents drug and alcohol use. Since John was sent to prison, Jackie has been earning money to fund her drug and alcohol use through prostitution in her own home; one of these men recently made an 'advance' to Casey; this has frightened her. Casey has being attending school on a regular basis and is considered an 'able' student; lately her attendance has been giving cause for concern. Casey is a member of a local 'gang', a group of young people who are involved in shop lifting from local shops, using alcohol and experimenting with 'soft' drug use. They hang out at a local park, verbally abusing and bullying the children who come to play there. Jill, Casey's aunt, is married to a software development consultant, Ian, and they live in a home on the suburbs. They have an active lifestyle and, although they have no children, appear committed to Casey and supporting a change in her behaviour.

Sociological approaches

The discipline of sociology and theoretical perspectives that can be categorised within this discipline explain human development by examining the interactions between people and the society in which they live. Sociological theories may start from this wide perspective, but then explain development and influences upon it by looking at different levels of that society. The work of Bronfenbrenner (1979) has been particularly influential to social work practice. He proposed a theory of human development that explores the different levels of society that may influence the individual's life course.

Bronfenbrenner's theory of ecological development

Bronfenbrenner (1979) described the influences of environmental factors on children. He uses the terms microsystem, exosystem and macrosystem. He suggests that there is a reciprocal process of interaction, in that the child is both influenced by and influences its environment at each of the levels.

Continued

The **microsystem** refers to those factors that are located within the immediate environment of the child, such as people and events in the home. These factors have the greatest impact on the child, because the child experiences them directly and concretely.

The term **exosystem** is used to describe those factors that lie beyond the immediate environment of the child, such as the neighbourhood in which the child lives.

The **macrosystem** includes larger societal factors, such as overall economic conditions and cultural values.

Bronfenbrenner's theory also describes two further levels of analysis, the **mesosystem** and the **chronosystem**. The mesosystem describes the way in which factors in two or more microsystems interact. The chronosystem is used to account for the influence of time on development. Each of these levels interacts with one another to make up the integrated and complex lives of people.

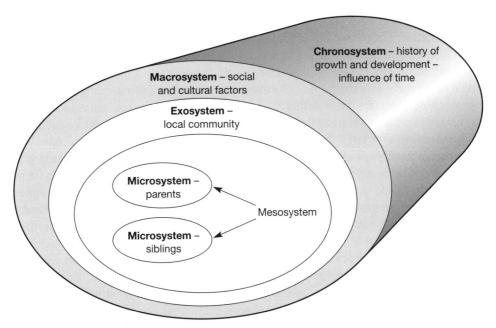

Figure 2.2 Diagram of Bronfenbrenner's theory of ecological development

Look back at the case study of Casey. What would be the influences in Casey's life at the different levels described by Bronfenbrenner?

- At the microsystem level?
- At the exosystem level?
- At the macrosystem level?
- How might Casey chronosystem affect her development?

Using Bronfenbrenner's model of development to explain Casey's life course would enable us to break down the many influential factors that we have found. When looking at Casey's microsystem we would need to consider the influences of her parents, siblings and immediate family. While exploring her exosystem would lead us to look at the local community in which she lives, the council estate, her school and peer groups. At another level, the macrosystem in which Casey lives would include social factors such as the economic and political climate in the country that may impact on Casey and her family.

We could go further and examine some of the mesosystem evident in Casey's situation, such as where her parents and grandparents may interact. Looking at Casey's behaviour through the chronosystem would enable us to account for changes and development as she has grown older and, for example, perhaps the influences of moving between different relatives when she was younger.

From this example, you can see how a sociological approach would concentrate on how wider factors and expectations of our society influence how Casey's behaviour are construed and how they have developed. It would do this by considering the influence of Casey's social class, her immediate environment and relationships on the behaviour that has been expected of her.

This explanation, understanding and assessment of Casey's behaviour and her life course will influence the form and method of social work practice considered appropriate. Thus, this brief analysis would suggest that Casey needs 'listening to', support and guidance to enable her to make safe choices and to explain and support in understanding her own life-course history. There are issues within the family that need to be explored, especially with her mother, in order to ensure that Casey is 'safe' within the environment. Work would need to be undertaken with Jackie, her mother, to ensure she has sufficient insight to understand the impact of her lifestyle choice on Casey and has the motivation and ability to ensure that Casey's emotional and social needs are meet and that she can be protected from harm. There are issues to do with her school attendance and support that would need to be given to help her to return to school and to achieve her academic potential. It may be that Casey's aunt and uncle, Jill and Ian, can provide support and guidance to her. This approach suggests that the social and environmental influences are significant contributing factors in Casey's development. Social work interventions linked to community development work and improving education and employment opportunities through partnership working with key organisations are good examples. In Chapter 4 of this book you will further develop your understanding of Bronfenbrenner's theory of ecological systems and the importance of this approach to social work practice. Within Chapter 4 you will be encouraged to consider how this approach to understanding human growth and development can contribute to the assessment of a child's needs, as this model underpins the *Framework for the assessment of children in need and their families* (Department of Health, 2000). You should also look at Parker and Bradley (2010, 3rd edition) *Social work practice: assessment, planning, intervention and review* to help to inform your understanding.

Physiological approaches

The disciplines of physiology or biology explain human development by examining the physical development and genetic make-up of the individual. So within childhood, for example, biological theories explain a child's growth and development, focusing on characteristics inherent in their biological family. In Chapter 3 of this book patterns of children's growth and development are explored further. Biological explanations of later adulthood, on the other hand, concentrate on bodily changes and decreased physical and psychological functioning associated with increased age. In Chapter 7 of this book biological changes in later adulthood are discussed.

ACTIVITY **2.2**

Think about Casey again. Taking a biological perspective, write down the key factors that might influence her life.

COMMENT

The perspective from a biological based discipline would consider Casey's behaviour in relation to her age, looking at her physical development and how this relates to expected courses of growth and physical development. Additionally theories taking this approach would consider Casey's parents and grandparents, looking at how the genes she may have inherited could explain Casey's development.

Psychological approaches

Psychology is about the study of people and how they are influenced by their thoughts, feelings and emotions. There are many specialist areas of psychological study and theory, so within this book we have chosen to explore two specific perspectives: developmental psychology and psychosocial approaches.

Developmental psychology

Theories that have been developed taking a developmental psychology approach consider how people develop across the life course, by exploring their thoughts, ideas, feelings and behaviours. Theories of cognitive development, which are about how we learn, take a developmental psychology approach. In the next chapter you will develop your understanding of cognitive perspectives on children's development. One of the key theorists that you will read about in Chapter 3 is Jean Piaget (1896–1990).

RESEARCH SUMMARY

Jean Piaget's (1936) theory of cognitive development

Piaget believed that the child seeks to understand and adapt to the environment. In doing so the child undertakes certain actions as it moves through progressive stages of development. (These are explored further in Chapters 3 and 4.)

Piaget's stages of cognitive development

Stage	Age	
Sensorimotor	0 – 2 years	Using senses and movement to understand the environment.

Continued

RESEARCH SUMMARY *continued*

Stage	Age	
Preoperational	2 – 6 years	The child begins to be able to use basic logic, but is not able to understand how other people might perceive the environment.
Concrete operations	7 – 12 years	The child can now take account of different perspectives on the environment and is able to undertake more complex logical reasoning.
Formal operations	Aged 12 years +	The child has developed the ability to imagine and speculate. At this stage, the child can conceive new ideas underpinned by reasoning, without the need for prior experience.

Another approach to understanding the human life course from a developmental psychology perspective is presented through theories that focus on our behaviours and how behaviours and the consequences of our actions influence our learning. In Chapter 5, you will look in more depth at behavioural and social learning theories and how they influence social work practice with adolescents.

RESEARCH SUMMARY

Behaviourism – B.F. Skinner (1904–1990)

Skinner explained development as the acquisition of behaviours, which are learned through responses to experiences. Skinner did not see the individual, their thoughts or conscious mind as influencing their behaviours, but rather behaviour being a response controlled by the rewards and punishments in the individual's environment.

Social learning theory – Albert Bandura (1977)

Social learning theorist Albert Bandura also emphasised the importance of behaviour and the environment, but also saw cognition, or thought, as being a significant factor in the person's development. Therefore social learning theories consider the influence of values, beliefs, reasoning, self-determination, emotions and thought on the learning process.

Psychoanalytic perspectives

According to this perspective people move through a series of stages in which they confront conflicts between biological drives and social expectations. The ways in which these conflicts are resolved determine that individual's ability to learn, to get on with others and deal with personal conflicts and anxieties.

Freud's theory

Freud (1856 – 1939) believed there were three parts to a personality:

Id This is the largest part of the mind and is the source of basic biological needs and desires. It is largely 'unconscious'.

Ego This is the conscious, rational part of the personality, emerging in early infancy so that the id's impulses can be discharged on appropriate objects at the right time and place.

Superego Between the ages of three and six years the superego (or pre-conscience) develops from interactions with parents who mediate the child's conformity with society's values.

According to Freud the relations established between the id, ego and superego during the pre-school years determine the individual's basic personality.

In addition Freud believed that during childhood sexual impulses developed and changed:

Table 2.1

Period of development	Psycho-sexual stage	Explanation
Birth – 1 year	Oral	The dominant 'ego' directs the baby's behaviour to sucking activities towards the breast or bottle.
1– 3 years	Anal	The focus of pleasure is holding or releasing urine or faeces. Holding it in and letting it go are greatly enjoyed.
3–6 years	Phallic	This relates to Freud's Oedipus conflict for boys and Electra complex for girls and relate to the sexual desire for the other sex partner. To avoid conflict they adopt the same-sex parents characteristic and values. The relations between the id, ego and superego established at this time determine the individual's basic personality.
6–11 years	Latency	As sexual instinct dies down, the superego develops further, the child learns new social values form adults outside the family and from same-sex peers, for example, through play.
Adolescence	Genital	Puberty causes the sexual impulses of the phallic stage to reappear: if development has been successful in the earlier stages then it leads to mature sexuality and the continuation of the reproductive urges.

From these theories Freud and his daughter Anna, developed a number of ideas and propositions based on these foundations, including: anxiety; denial; repression; displacement; projection; identification with aggressor; regression.

'Treatment' for Freud was through such areas as: a relaxed atmosphere in which the 'client' is free to express themselves ('the Freudian couch'!): free association, in which the client may talk about anything at all. However, in therapy, there is the therapist, who is trained to recognise certain clues to problems and their solutions that the client would overlook; and dream analysis.

Whilst there are some significant critiques of Freud's theories and its limitations, Freud's theories highlighted the importance of family relationships for children's development and was the first theory to stress the role of early experience.

Psychosocial theories

Some of the theories we shall consider in later chapters in the book arise from a combination of perspectives from psychology and sociology disciplines and are seen as psychosocial theories. David Howe describes psychosocial as being

> created by the interplay between the individual's psychological condition and the social environment.

> (Howe, 1998 p.173)

Later in this book you will develop your knowledge of psychosocial theories by looking at theories that explain the human life course as a series of stages. One of the important models that will be examined in Chapters 6 and 7 is that of Erik Erikson. Erik Erikson's (1995) 'eight stages of man' is a model of development, which states that individuals move through each of eight life stages.

RESEARCH SUMMARY

Erik Erikson's model of life stage development

Erikson (1995) saw people developing their identity as they move through stages or 'crisis' points in their lives. Erikson saw individuals moving through the stages by virtue of increasing age, however the successful progression through each stage, by the negotiation of the particular 'crisis' to a positive outcome, ensures healthy development.

Erikson's eight stages of develoment are:

- **Birth to one year** *Trust versus mistrust, in which the child learns to trust others based upon the consistency of their caregiver(s). If trust develops successfully, the child gains confidence and security in the world around him and is able to feel secure even when threatened. Unsuccessful completion of this stage can result in an inability to trust, and therefore a sense of fear about the inconsistent world. It may result in anxiety, heightened insecurities, and an over feeling of mistrust in the world around them.*

- **One to three years** *Autonomy vs. shame and doubt, in which children begin to assert their independence. If children in this stage are encouraged and supported in their increased independence, they become more confident and secure in their own ability to survive in the world. If children are criticised, overly controlled, or not given the opportunity to assert themselves, they begin to feel inadequate in their ability to survive, and may then become overly dependent upon others, lack self-esteem, and feel a sense of shame or doubt in their own abilities.*

- **Three to six years** *Initiative vs. guilt, in which children assert themselves more frequently. They begin to plan activities, make up games, and initiate activities with others. If given this opportunity, children develop a sense of initiative, and feel secure in their ability to lead others and make decisions. If the child experiences either criticism or over-control, children develop a sense of guilt they may develop a lack of self-initiative.*

Continued

- *Six years to 11* Industry vs. inferiority, in which children begin to develop a sense of pride in their accomplishments. They initiate projects, see them through to completion, and feel good about what they have achieved. If children are encouraged and reinforced for their initiative, they begin to feel industrious and feel confident in their ability to achieve goals. If this initiative is not encouraged, then the child begins to feel inferior, doubting his own abilities and therefore may not reach his potential.

- *Adolescence* Identity vs. role confusion, in which children are becoming more independent, and begin to look at the future in terms of career, relationships, families and so on. During this period, they explore possibilities and begin to form their own identity based upon the outcome of their explorations. This sense of who they are can be hindered, which results in a sense of confusion about themselves and their role in the world.

- *Young adulthood (20–30s)* Intimacy vs. isolation, in which the person begins to share themselves more intimately with others, exploring relationships leading toward longer-term commitments with someone other than a family member. Successful completion can lead to comfortable relationships and a sense of commitment, safety, and care within a relationship. Avoiding intimacy, fearing commitment and relationships can lead to isolation, loneliness, and sometimes depression.

- *Middle adulthood (40–60s)* Generativity vs. stagnation. Careers are established, relationships are 'confirmed' and families are established. A feeling of contributing to society is achieved. By failing to achieve these objectives, the person may feel stagnant and unproductive.

- *Late adulthood* – ego integrity vs. despair There is a tendency to slow down productivity, and explore life as a retired person. Life and its accomplishments are explored and a person develops integrity if they are leading a successful life. If life is seen as unproductive, the person may feel guilt about their past, or feel that they did not accomplish their life goals. They may become dissatisfied with life and develop despair, often leading to depression and hopelessness.

As you can see, explanations of human life course development that take a psychological perspective explore human behaviour from a number of different positions. In order to understand how people develop psychologists investigate thoughts, feelings, emotions and behaviours, looking at how these interact with the person's social environment.

ACTIVITY **2.3**

Think about Casey again. She is 14 years of age and has developed a number of behaviours that are labelled as 'anti-social', such as theft, misusing substances and non attendance of school.

List some of the aspects of Casey's life that would be particularly relevant if using a psychologically based theory.

COMMENT

If we take a general overview of the theories taking a psychological approach, we can see that they would look at Casey's own perspective on the behaviours. This approach would also consider Casey's development in respect of her life stage, with a focus on Casey's learning, analysing her reasoning and motives. Developmental psychology might emphasise the importance of Casey's relationship with her mother during the early stages of her life and how this has led to certain behaviours. A social learning or behaviourist approach would consider the influence of how Casey has been responded to by others, including her parents, the school and her peers, looking at, for example, how she has been rewarded or punished for her actions as she has developed in her childhood.

As stated earlier in the chapter, the theoretical perspective chosen will affect and influence the approach the social worker takes to intervention and practice. Practice interventions that arise from behavioural perspectives usually take the form of cognitive-behavioural therapy which aims to enable the service-user to reconsider the meanings they attach to their behaviours and thereby change the behaviours (Ronen, 2002).

Comparing and contrasting the theoretical approaches

In this chapter you have been presented with a brief overview of the theoretical perspectives that will be developed through the rest of this book. You have looked at some competing theoretical approaches and considered how each might explore the situation presented in the case study of Casey and her family.

You have seen how these theories attempt to explain and develop our understanding of people and how they have developed. You have also considered how the different underpinning theoretical approaches can be seen to lead to different forms of social work intervention. Therefore, when considering even the most acclaimed theoretical concepts, you should not think of them as 'fact'; social workers should question and explore the assumptions, values and ideas that are evident. As you develop your knowledge and experience as a professional social worker, it is important therefore not only to understand the different perspectives being offered, but also to be able to analyse and evaluate the theories and subsequent intervention in respect of its appropriateness in any given situation.

Each of the disciplines that have been described in this chapter reflects a specific focus and certain assumptions. For example, a biological approach concentrates on the physical being and takes, as its focal point, the individual person. In contrast, theories from a socio-logical base explore the issues by starting to examine the society in which individuals grow and develop. These theories explain human development as being largely dependent upon the impact of the environment, social and cultural influences. Theories can also be critiqued for their strengths and weaknesses in how they explain and describe certain aspects of development. For example, Jean Piaget's theory of cognitive development could be considered as one of the most comprehensive and coherent theories in helping us to understand children's mental development. However, Piaget's theory is not as useful if you want to understand how life events and challenges influence growth and development in adulthood. For this area of life course development Erik Erikson's model of life stage development is likely to be more relevant.

At this point, it would be useful to refer back to the work of Paul Baltes (1987) described earlier in this chapter. In defining the features of a life course perspective, Baltes states that human development is *multidimensional*. This is a view that we support, seeing human development across the life course as complex and, in reality, a concept that can be seen to be influenced by the interaction of biological, social, psychological and environ-mental factors. It is, therefore, important to appreciate that in social work practice a range of theories from across the disciplines needs to be considered. It is not possible for any one theory to explain all aspects of human life course development, taking any one approach in isolation would lead to the other aspects of the person's life being ignored. Each of the models and theories introduced within this book has made a valuable contri-bution to our understanding of human development through the life course. Thus, as described in Chapter 1, social workers need to develop an understanding of theories from a range of disciplines in order to take a holistic approach to their practice.

The biographical approach

The most important skill in taking a holistic approach is to understand the individual's life course, as they describe it. Listening to and taking account of the individual's description of their life, the events they consider to be important or influential, and the high and low points of their development, means you are listening to their biographical narrative, or taking a narrative approach.

ACTIVITY **2.4**

You have considered the case study of Casey throughout this chapter. Note down your thoughts on what Casey's own story, her narrative account, might consist of.

The narrative or biographical approach, by definition, will enable you to understand that person's life from the life course perspective we described earlier. In other words, taking account of the whole of their life and the growth (or high) and decline (or low) points as they see them. The appreciation of social and cultural diversity is integral to this approach, as it negates stereotypical assumptions or discriminatory attitudes, enabling the individual to take control of the life that they portray. Chamberlayne et al. (2000) state that

> *working with the 'whole person' calls for knowledge of that person's past as well as their current needs and preferences.*

They also suggest that biographical approaches provide

> *... an opportunity for the development of appropriate and sensitive care practice and interventions and the promotion of more socialised and empowering perceptions of the self in circumstances when stigma, segregation and disempowerment may have been a more common experience.*

> (Chamberlayne et al., 2000 p.10)

More specifically in relation to social work practice, Cree and Davis (2007 p.8) reinforce *the central idea that personal stories are a legitimate way of exploring and understanding the world*. Furthermore that such narrative approaches that build upon the stones of individuals have *the capacity to recgnise people's strengths and engage people in active, meaning-making dialogues* (Fraser, cited in Cree and Davis, 2007 p.8).

In their book on *Social work practice: assessment, planning, intervention and review* (second edition), Parker and Bradley (2007) describe a number of aids and activities that social workers use when they are gathering and analysing information as they make assessments with service-users.

CHAPTER SUMMARY

This chapter has introduced you to theoretical approaches to understanding human life course development. As required by the social work academic standard subject benchmark statement, you will have developed your knowledge of:

research-based concepts and critical explanations from Social work theory and other disciplines that contribute to the knowledge base of Social work, including their distinctive epistemological status and application to practice.

You have looked at the significance of theory and research and how they can support your knowledge, understanding and skills as a social worker.

We introduced the concept of taking a life course perspective, which sees human development as a life-long process and is an underpinning value throughout this book. You have then looked at three broad disciplines or schools of thought, from which some key theoretical perspectives on life course development have arisen. Using the case study that was initially introduced in Chapter 1, Casey and her family, you have had the opportunity to think about how these theories explain a life situation and how this explanation might impact upon social work practices.

Having looked separately at some approaches and key theories from sociological, biological, developmental psychological and psychosocial perspectives, you considered how these might be compared, contrasted and analysed in order to develop effective social work practice, based upon robust theoretical and research-based knowledge.

In the final section of this chapter, you have learnt about taking a biographical or narrative approach. We have stated that understanding the person's life experiences and the 'meaning' that they give to those experiences is fundamental to developing holistic social work practice.

FURTHER READING

Baltes, PB (1987) Theoretical propositions of life-span developmental psychology: On the dynamics between growth and decline. *Developmental Psychology*, 23, 611–626.

In this journal article Paul Baltes describes the characteristics of taking a life course perspective.

Berryman, J, Smythe, P, Taylor, A, Lamont, A and Joiner, R (2002) *Developmental psychology and you*. Oxford: BPD Blackwell.

This second edition of Berryman et al.'s book is a comprehensive, introductory text to developmental psychology across the life course. The theories of cognitive development are particularly clearly explained.

Cree, V and Davis, M (2007) *Social work: Voices from the inside*. London: Routledge.

This book provides a vivid example of how the narrative, biographical approach enables social work practitioners to see people within the context of their whole lives.

Ingelby, E (2010) *Applied psychology for social work*. 2nd edition. Exeter: Learning Matters.

This book shows that, for social workers, it is important for psychology to be studied in the contexts of social care, as it offers potential explanations of complex aspects of human behaviour and development.

Slater, A and Bremner, G (eds) (2003) *An introduction to developmental psychology*. Oxford: Blackwell.

An introduction to developmental psychology, written at an understandable level by an international team of respected researchers.

Chapter 3

Using life course development knowledge in social work practice with infants, young children and their families

A C H I E V I N G   A   S O C I A L   W O R K   D E G R E E

This chapter will help you to begin to meet the following National Occupational Standards:

Key Role 1: Prepare for and work with individuals, families, carers, groups and communities to assess their needs and circumstances.

- Work with individuals, families, carers, groups and communities to help them make informed decisions.
- Assess needs and options to recommend a course of action.

Key Role 2: Plan, carry out, review and evaluate social work practice, with individuals, families, carers, groups and communities and other professionals.

- Interact with individuals, families, carers, groups and communities to achieve change and development and to improve life opportunities.
- Address behaviour which presents a risk to individuals, families, carers, groups and communities.

It will also introduce you to the following academic standards as set out in the social work subject benchmark statement:

3.1.1 Social work services and service users.
3.1.4 Social work theory.
3.2.2 Problem solving skills.
3.2.2.3 Analysis and synthesis.

Introduction

The following three chapters focus on infant, child and adolescent development. Whilst the chapters will consider specific age related issues, these three chapters in particular are inter-related in developing the themes and issues in relation to child growth and development.

This chapter will set out knowledge in respect of early child development. It begins by outlining themes in relation to social work and child development. The section sets out the importance of an understanding of infant, child and adolescent development for social workers. It will then explore the contexts of development – the 'social construction' of childhood – considering the relative importance of history, hereditary, environmental and cultural factors in determining the individual's development. This chapter will specifically develop your understanding and ability to critique theories that explain human development taking a cognitive approach and theories taking a biological and physical perspective. In particular it will explore social and emotional development, developing themes in relation to the critical issues of attachment, vulnerability and resilience. It will introduce issues in relation to child protection and related issues of legal intervention.

Social work practice and child development

Why an understanding of infant, child and adolescent development is important for social workers

This book is set within the context of contemporary social work practice and related policy and legislation.

> *Peter Connelly (1 March 2006 – 3 August 2007) was a 17-month old boy who died in London after suffering more than 50 injuries over an eight-month period, during which he was repeatedly seen by social and other services. Peter's mother, Tracey Connelly, her boyfriend, Steven Barker, and Jason Owen were all convicted of causing or allowing the death of a child, the mother having pleaded guilty to the charge. The child protection services of Haringey Council and other agencies were widely criticised. Following the conviction, three inquiries and a nationwide review of social service care were launched.*

We have already highlighted the case of Victoria Climbié (Chapter 1, p.9) and the consequences following her death. Following the tragic case of 'Baby Peter' Lord Laming was invited to undertake an update on the progress of implementation arrangements for safeguarding children (Laming, 2009). He made further recommendations, including the need for in-depth understanding of child development. In 2009 the Department for Children, Families and Schools and the Department of Health launched a joint Social Work Taskforce, with the remit to undertake a comprehensive review of frontline social work practice, which included recommendations for reforms to social work education. The 15 recommendations of the Task Force are comprehensive and far reaching, and will affect all stakeholders concerned with the profession including children's services and adult services (Social Work Task Force, 2009).

More specifically for social work practice with children, their families and carers, the policy document *Every Child Matters* (ECM) (DfES, 2003), the national strategic development programme *Every Child Matters: Change for Children* (DfES, 2004) and the *Children Act 2004* ('the legislative spine' on which reforms will be built (DfES, 2004 p.5)) have widespread implications and are relevant to your reading of this chapter and Chapters 4 and 5.

The Children's Plan: Building brighter futures *(DfCSF, 2007a)*: The Children's Plan *aims to strengthen support for all families during the formative early years of their children's lives, achieving 'world class' schools, involve parents in their children's learning, and help to make sure that young people have things to do outside of school.*

The Children's Plan: Two years on *(DfCSF, 2009b)*: In this document the government *takes the opportunity to chart the progress that has been made so far and share their next steps.*

Every Parent Matters *(DfES, 2007)*: Explains ways in which practitioners can assist *parents in helping their children learn, enjoy and achieve. It sets out what we are doing to promote the development of services for parents and encouraging them to get involved in shaping services for themselves and their children.*

Reaching Out: Think family *(Social Exclusion Taskforce, 2007)*: Against a backdrop of *increasing prosperity and progress for the majority, a small minority of families are still experiencing poor outcomes. Their complex problems provide significant challenges to public services if we are going to break intergenerational exclusion and close the gaps in achievement. This report shows the impact of families is rarely neutral: they can sometimes be a great source of resilience and protection, but they can also pose grave risks. There is scope to link up the progress being made through public service reform in the children's and adults' sectors to create a coherent system of support for the most vulnerable families.*

Support for All: The families and relationships green paper *(DfES, 2010)*: This Green *Paper sets out a wide range of measures to support all families as they bring up their children and help families cope with times of stress and difficulty. The proposals recognise that while all families need some help, there are families in our society with complex needs and others who require additional – and sometimes non-negotiable – support.*

Additionally, the *Every Child Matters: Change for Children* agenda has supported the development of other initiatives including *The Common Core of Skills and Knowledge* for everyone working with children, young people and their families (DfES, 2005a). One of the six areas of expertise highlighted in the *The Common Core* is *Child and young person development*. Furthermore, and of specific relevance in this chapter, the Department for Education and Skills (DfES) have published frameworks to support practitioners working with young children. The standards framework *Birth to three matters* (DfES, 2002) and the more recent *Early Years Foundation Stage: Setting the standards for learning, development and care for children from birth to five* (EYFS) (DfES, 2007) are available from www.standards.dfes.gov.uk. Both frameworks recognise *the 'holistic' nature of development and learning* (DfES, 2002 p.4) with each child being unique.

Within this, development occurs across a number of dimensions – biologically, socially, emotionally and cognitively. As children develop physically, they also learn about the social and emotional skills that will support them in relationships within the family, with friends, their community, culture and their relationships within the larger society. They show changes in their thought processes. Whilst theorists often appear to compartmentalise these changes, the reality is that development progresses in many different directions at the same time.

Understanding the stages and processes of development can help us to identify the achievement of developmental milestones; an important developmental event in a child's life, such as the age a child takes their first step or says their first word. It also helps us to understand developmental norms – the age at which they achieve skills and understanding compared to other children and 'normal' expectations. Understanding the achievement of milestones and what is 'normal' in relation to development is important for social workers so that we can judge and make sense of the child's progress and experience. However whilst development is concerned with how people change over time these changes are not always predictable. Some children may demonstrate steady, predictable changes whilst others may not.

Development is influenced by a number of different and interrelated processes or systems. Change in one part of the system may have a direct or indirect influence on the development of the child. An example of this is the impact of race and culture on the individual child and the family and community in which they live.

As a social worker you will need to gain an understanding of the 'whole' child, their development and their life course. It is important to take a range of theories and perspectives into account that support us in understanding the child's growth and development and individual experience, the role and impact of their families and the influence of processes and systems on their lives. Through this you should be able to see beyond the description of the child, to give meaning to their lives and experiences. You will also be recognising the individuality of that child.

> It is important to keep in mind that even a tiny baby is a person. Holistic development sees the child in the round, as a whole person – physically, emotionally, intellectually, socially, morally, culturally and spirituality.

> (Meggitt, 2006 p.1)

We need to acknowledge there are children with unique and specific needs that may impact on their individual development and behaviour, certainly on their experiences and how others view and respond to them (DfES, 2007 p.6). An example would be the experience of children with a disability.

The social construction of childhood

We begin by posing some questions: do we have shared understanding of what constitutes 'childhood'? In what way does the experience of childhood change – across history, as the result of different personal understanding from the experience, in relation to the community in which you were raised and as a result of different cultures?

We probably have a clear idea of what we mean by childhood as we have all experienced childhood. Generally it is assumed to be a distinct phase in our lives, which should be 'protected', free from worries and responsibilities, a time in which we play, learn and are nurtured and supported along our path towards adulthood. As a social worker a critical part of your role will be to work with children and families in empowering them to be involved in processes and decisions that affect their lives. Social workers need to develop skills in communicating and working with children and with their families to support this. The right of children to have their voices heard has been enshrined in an international treaty, the *Convention on the Rights of Children 1991*.

The *Convention on the Rights of Children 1991* is a universally agreed set of standards and obligations in relation to the basic human rights that all children have – without discrimination. Children are defined as persons up to the age of 18. It incorporates the full range of human rights – civil and political rights, economic, social and cultural rights.

- The right to survival.

- The right to develop to the fullest.

- The right to protection from harmful influences, abuse and exploitation.

- The right to participate fully in family, cultural and social life.

In addition there are two optional protocols in relation to the involvement of children in armed conflict and the sale of children, child prostitution and child pornography.

The Convention has been signed up to by the United Kingdom.

Within England and Wales the legislative and policy context of social work practice with children, young people, their families and carers is framed by the national strategic vision within *Every Child Matters: Change for Children* (DfES, 2004). This overarching strategy underpins the Children Act, 2004. The *Children Act 2004* does not replace or even amend the basic principles of *Children Act 1989*, but supersedes some of them (Johns, 2007). Whilst the *Children Act 2004* sets out the process for integrating services to children so that every child can achieve the five outcomes laid out in *Every Child Matters*. The *Framework for assessment of children in need and their families* (DoH, 2000) provides a systematic way of gathering, analysing and recording the experience of children within their families and communities. This has been supplemented, through the *Every Child Matters: Change for Children* programme with a Common Assessment Framework (CAF) (DfES, 2006a). The CAF is a standardised, interprofessional approach to conducting an assessment which is integrated and focused around the needs of the child, in particular exploring the child's additional needs and deciding how those needs should be met. Furthermore, to develop support for children who are 'looked after' in local authority care, *Care Matters: Transforming the lives of children and young people in care*, a consultation Green Paper also under the 'umbrella' of the *Every Child Matters* programme, was launched in October 2006 (DfES, 2006b). This Green Paper set out a package of proposals to address the significant gap in experiences and achievements between children in care and their peers.

In many ways this legislative and policy context can be seen to inform the views, perceptions and meanings that are attached to childhood in contemporary society.

However, this view of childhood has not always been so. Ariès (1962), studying the concept of childhood from the Middle Ages to the end of the eighteenth century, found that children were viewed as small-scale adults; childhood as a distinct age grouping did not exist, rather, he suggests, it was a later historical creation. Therefore based on Ariès' views, childhood could be viewed as a 'new' concept.

ACTIVITY *3.1*

Think about your experience of childhood. Think about such things as:

- *Family structure: what sort of family were you brought up in, for example, in a two-parent or single-parent family? How many children were in your family? Were you the only child, the middle child or the youngest child? Can you identify any impact you feel that this may have had on you?*

- *Roles within the family: what role did your mother have in the family? Did she work outside the home? What role did your father have in the family? Did he work? Did you have an extended family? What impact did these relatives have on your family's life? How did these arrangements impact on your experience of childhood?*

- *Social circumstances: where did you live? What kind of neighbourhood was it? Did you have any hobbies and pastimes? At what age did you go to school? What was your first experience that you remember at school?*

- *Economic circumstances: how would you describe the economic circumstances of your family? What impact did this have on the way you lived, for example the toys that you had, the holidays you took, going on outings and excursions?*

- *Culture: what kind of cultural group would you describe yourself as coming from? What impact did this have on the way you were raised? What, if any, impact did this have on the way others viewed you? What impact did religion have on your childhood? Can you identify any specific values and beliefs that your family held as important?*

Compare your experience to that of people older or younger than you, for example your parents and grandparents.

COMMENT

Your experience and those of your children, or your parents and grandparents, will be unique and will have been shaped by specific circumstances and events. Different generations of the family will be influenced by personal circumstances, historical, cultural and societal contexts. You may have found similarities. However it is more likely that your experience of your childhood is different from your parents', almost certainly from that of your grandparents. One of the principal reasons is simply because of the era in which you were raised – your life course will differ from that of your parents and grandparents because of the historical age in which you and they were brought up.

Across history as society has progressed, we can see the emergence of 'childhood' due to the influence of a number of factors. Improving medical and health care has increased the survival rates for babies and for their mothers; additionally there is the opportunity to plan for families through improved birth control methods. With increasing industrialisation, there was campaigning to protect the rights of children. Education within Britain has made a major impact in prolonging childhood with the gradual raising of the school leaving age. Consequently children spend distinct and prolonged periods of their lives in education, in being socialised and prepared for adulthood. This can be seen in the emergence of 'adolescence' as a further distinct period before adulthood is reached.

Generations of families are also influenced by significant political, social and personal events. Some may be experienced as having an intense effect on the family, such as economic depression or war. The impact may be experienced differently because of age: for example war may have no direct impact on the experience of a baby compared to that of a young person of fighting age. However they could have a profound effect on their families and consequently the way in which they have to care for their children; for example being displaced from their home, lack of water and food.

Other impacts on the experiences of different generations of families will be linked to changing social and economic circumstances. An example of this would be the changing role of women in relation to work. For instance, today 65 per cent of women with families are in work (Goldson et al., 2002). Previous generations of women were 'normally' expected to give up their jobs in order to stay at home to bring up the children and take care of the home. This changing role for 'mothers' could be attributed to women campaigning for rights and equality, especially as compared to men. There are also economic reasons. These may be personal to the individual woman such as to increase the available resources, and therefore potential opportunities available, for that family. There is also a 'political' dimension in recognising the powerful 'voice' and experiences of women requiring more people to be available within the labour market.

We need to recognise that communities raise children in diverse ways with each culture encouraging the kinds of habits and traits that help them to integrate and function within that culture. Families all exist within a larger cultural context – a way of life shared by members consisting of a system of meanings and customs, including values, attitudes, beliefs, morals and laws. It includes physical symbols such as the kind of houses we live in and so on (Bee, 1995). It is shared by identifiable groups and is transmitted through the group from one generation to the other. Recognising the importance of culture on the development of the child is important for a number of reasons. First we need to identify and understand those aspects of development that impact on all children not just through theories and studies based on white, middle class children living within a western culture. Secondly we need to have an understanding of the culture as it impacts on that child. We need to understand the impact of cultural beliefs as part of that environment. We need to consider how different cultural beliefs impact on how people experience their lives.

Paludi (2002) provides a range of examples of difference across cultures, for example in the role of the father and how it is perceived; in children's sleeping arrangements; in the importance attached to 'play'; and in physical development.

> *Differences in height and weight exist between children in economically less developed countries and those in more developed countries.*

> (Paludi, 2002 p.54)

Thus, the impact of where the child lives, the families' income and the education attainment of their parents further define the child's perceived position and status within society, in particular their experience of social exclusion. Particularly for families in low socio-economic groups, children will experience disadvantage in real and crucial ways, including potential disadvantages in relation to health and education.

A research report by UNICEF, the United Nations Children's Educational Fund, titled *The State of the World's Children 2005: childhood under threat* (Bellamy, 2005) provides stark evidence of the numbers of children living in poverty in the world. The report highlights that over 1 billion children are denied the health and protection promised by the Convention on the Rights of Children. Therefore, despite the near universal embrace of standards for protecting childhood, UNICEF shows that more than half the world's children are suffering extreme deprivation from poverty, war and HIV/AIDS, conditions that are effectively denying children a childhood and holding back the development of nations.

In the introduction to *The State of the World's Children*, Kofi A Annan, then Secretary-General of the United Nations, stated that

> . . . for nearly half of the two billion children in the real world, childhood is starkly and brutally different from the ideal we all aspire to. Poverty denies children their dignity, endangers their lives and limits their potential. Conflict and violence rob them of a secure family life, betray their trust and their hope. HIV/AIDS kills their parents, their teachers, their doctors and nurses. It also kills them.

(Bellamy, 2005 p.vii)

Representing one of the first detailed measures of child poverty in the developing world, the UNICEF report (Bellamy, 2005) shows that, worldwide, more than a billion children are severely deprived of basic human needs, and 674 million live in conditions of absolute poverty.

These statistics put some of this information into context:

- number of children in the world: 2.2 billion;

- number of children living in developing countries: 1.9 billion;

- number of children living in poverty: 1 billion = every second child.

The report shows that Britain has one of the worst records in the industrialised world in relation to childhood poverty. The British figures in the report can be seen to be worse than the rates for Turkey, Poland and Hungary, where less relative poverty is experienced. Of 23 countries surveyed, only Italy, the United States and Mexico have a worse record than Britain. The report suggests that Britain is failing children on five key indicators. In addition to the high rate of child poverty there are the high numbers of lone-parent families who also experience poverty; workless households; people on low wages; and people on low benefits. UNICEF says that nearly 20 per cent of young Britons – between 3 million and 4 million children – live in families that are below the official poverty line, judged as household income of less than half median earnings. That compares with 2.6 per cent in Sweden and 3.9 per cent in Norway.

> *Child Poverty in Perspective: An overview of child well-being* (UNICEF Innocenti Research Centre) focuses on the well-being of children and young people in 19 of the world's advanced economies and provides the first comprehensive assessment.
>
> The six dimensions taken to measure the well-being of children – material well-being, health and safety, education, peer and family relationships, behaviours and risks, and young people's own subjective sense of well-being – offer a picture of the lives of children, and no single dimension can stand as a reliable proxy for child well-being as a whole. The Netherlands head the table of children's overall well-being, with the United Kingdom and United States at the bottom.
>
> The landmark report shows that among all of the 21 countries there are improvements to be made and that no single country leads in all six of the areas.

In summary, what we are suggesting is that childhood is a 'social construction'; that is to say that childhood has been formed from a shared perception of what constitutes social order within society, Each individual develops within three contexts: historical, cultural and socio-economic. Whilst each person is unique, these contexts will have an influence and effect on that person's experience and therefore their development.

The developing child

ACTIVITY 3.2

Julie (15) and Shaun (16) have known each other for six months. Both use drugs, particularly heroin and alcohol. Julie is three months pregnant with her first child. Shaun, the father of the child, has recently received a six-month sentence for drug related offences to be served in a Young Offenders Institute. Julie is unhappy and depressed, saying that she does not want to have a baby.

Consider the issues that may impact on the development and give rise to concerns for the unborn child.

The development of the unborn child

We know that even before a child is born the environment will influence them indirectly through the impact and effects on the mother. As a social worker you will need to have an understanding of the relationship and interdependence of a number of inequalities that impact on a person's capacity to parent a child; for example those linked to structural inequalities such as poverty and the consequent impact on other aspects of life. Jowitt and O'Loughlin (2005, pp.66–7) identify a range of such factors including family history; wider family; housing; employment; income; family's social integration; and community resources. You will have been able to identify some of the factors that raise concern for Julie's baby, the mother's own mental health, for example. Julie's depression, and feelings and attitude towards the unborn child are linked to the unborn child's well-being. Children born to mothers who do not want them or who are under stress can give rise to concerns about their development. The mother's general health and nutritional intake will have an influence on the growing foetus. Julie's drug and alcohol use could be linked to increased risk for the unborn child, for example premature birth, low birth weight, vulnerability to illness, and potential disability. Drinking substantial amounts of alcohol while pregnant can lead to impairment of development, potential behavioural difficulties and in severe cases for the baby, fetal alcohol syndrome, a set of symptoms that cause learning disabilities. Babies of mothers who are addicted to heroin are born addicted themselves and will need help in being weaned from the drug. Jowitt and O'Loughlin (2005, pp.61–3) offer a brief review of the possible impact that parental mental health, problem drug and alcohol use or domestic violence may have on children's development. This review is helpfully structured by childhood age-groups. However in any assessment you will need to balance the concerns for the ability of the parents to meet the child's needs with an assessment of strengths; for example the likely impact of problems on their parenting capacity, their family history, their relationship and the range of support networks available to them. For social workers working with a parent where there are concerns for the unborn child, the critical issue is to focus in an assessment on the unborn child's needs (Parker and Bradley, 2007). The primary aim of any plan for the child must be to maximise the opportunities and chances for the parent to care for their child.

The growing child – physical perspective

During the first two years of life the rate and range of development is enormous. Whilst babies are born with a small number of innate reflexes, all other physical movements and skills are learned and improved through practice and interaction with their environment. Children generally show patterns in their development – children grow taller, gain weight and their head circumference increases. Brain growth reflects the expected experiences of the child, for example, the stimulation that they are given through emotional, sensual and linguistic experiences.

All the senses operate at birth with hearing as the most developed and sight as the least developed, although developing quickly, with binocular vision developing at about 14 weeks. They use all of their senses to strengthen their early interactions with others, especially their main carers.

As they develop the baby acquires a relatively predictable range of sensory and motor skills. Motor skills at birth are largely limited to reflexes linked to survival – sucking and breathing. Gross motor skills, such as sitting up and walking, develop from about six months onwards. Fine motor skills, such as picking up small objects, take longer to develop and acquire but gradually the ability to reach, grab and hold is developed. Whilst babies and children may share many patterns in their growth and the skills they develop, there are still many individual differences – you will need to get to know, observe and assess each child. Variations in the development of skills could be attributed to the child's genes, the culture in which they grow up or may relate to development delay linked to disability.

Between the ages of two and six years significant development occurs in children's growth and in their ability in relation to gross and fine motor skills – from a toddler to a five year-old who can run, skip and jump. Children continue to gain weight and height, generally becoming longer, thinner and more active. However there are significant height and weight variations caused primarily by genes but there are also cultural variations due to nutrition when compared to children in other parts of the world. Gross motor skills continue to develop so that the unco-ordinated two-year-old develops into the able five-year-old, using their body in a way that will reflect the ways in which their cultural values have influenced them. Greater control is gained over fine motor skills with confidence and competence emerging as children acquire greater skills.

The intention is to illustrate the different influences on the child's development. These may be attributed to the child's own genes, their temperament, their emotional and social development, the impact of the family, the context in which the family live and the culture in which the child grows up. Each of these cases has limited information and to make an informed social work judgement you would need to gather further information. The critical issue is not to make assumptions. Additionally you need to avoid stereotyping – attributing to, or interpreting traits in, children and adults because of such things as social background, gender, race and culture. However you should be aware of the importance and impact of 'difference', for example culture, as well as the impact of your own values and assumptions on your practice.

One way to monitor and judge growth, related to height and weight, is the use of percentile charts. Centile charts are based on mapping the individual physical growth of weight and height against a set of average standards or 'norms'. The medical professional, particularly Health Visitors, extensively uses them. Children need to be compared not only to the 'norms' of other children but also with their parents, their siblings and their own pattern of growth. Additionally physical development should not be separated from other developments – everything else they are learning.

The centile chart is used to record weight, length and head size. Boys and girls have different charts because their growth pattern is slightly different. The chart has a thick vertical line a quarter of the way along the page. The baby's birth weight is plotted on this line with a dot marking the birth weight. (It may vary if the baby came more than three weeks early.) As the baby grows older the dot marks the place where his/her weight and age come together.

The thick line that goes across the page in a curve denotes the average line; this means that children plotted above the line are above average and those below the line are below average for weight or growth. Most babies double their birth weight by four or five months. Most babies treble their birth weight by one year. If a parent is of Asian origin their baby will on average be lighter and shorter. If they are of African-Caribbean origin the baby will on average be heavier and longer. The baby should have a fairly steady growth, which will show as a roughly curving line usually within the centile lines on the chart.

However, as reinforced in the Early Years Foundation Stage theme 'Learning and develop-ment' (DfES, 2007 p.17) *different children will do different things at different times.*

ACTIVITY 3.3

For each of these examples identify the factors that may have influenced the young child and led to the behaviours:

- *Deanne, a three-year-old girl, was born prematurely to her young single mother. Deanne is developmentally delayed and has frequent episodes of ill-health, resulting in periods in hospital. When she is unhappy she bangs her head repeatedly on the floor. Deanne's mother finds her behaviour increasingly difficult to cope with and is depressed.*

- *Khalid, aged three, and his family are refugees who arrived six months ago from Afghanistan, following the death of his father. He is small and underweight for his age. The two older boys have settled well into their school lives. However his mother is very concerned about Khalid as he is shy and withdrawn, clinging to his mother or two older brothers.*

- *Kieran and Patrick, twin boys aged 4, are described as the 'terrors' of the local nursery school. They are slightly underweight for their age with poor diets, only wanting to eat 'Chips!' They are energetic and lively boys who have poor concentration skills, rarely sitting still; as a consequence they often have bruises or scrapes. Their hand–eye co-ordination is poor. They 'pick' on the other children; for example punching and kicking the smaller children to obtain a toy or any food. Their mother appears timid and shy, finding it difficult to control their boys; their father, who appears to quite dominant, says, 'Boys will be boys'.*

COMMENT

Each of these children are demonstrating behaviours that their parents may need advice and support with from professionals; all of them have a number of apparent needs. Deanne's mother needs support with Deanne's care and in supporting her development. It may be that she would benefit from support from Early Years Services through Children's Centres, such as Portage (an early educational service for families who have a baby or young child (0–5 years) who may need extra support to help him or her learn new skills). It maybe that they would both benefit from a short/respite care break. Khalid appears to suffering from the consequences of his past life and the difficulties in 'making sense' of his current situation. Such things as support for his mother in identifying techniques and resources to help her with Khalid may help, particularly through the support of a person from a similar cultural background. In addition Khalid may benefit from additional support to develop his confidence and integration with other children, through early year's provision such as nursery school and family centres. Kieran and Patrick appear to be influenced by their parent's behaviour and approaches to their behaviour; the focus may need to be on parental advice and guidance. For example, they may benefit from the use of behaviour modification techniques.

The growing child – biological perspectives

The focus of biological theories is that individual patterns and those shared with others are based on inherent patterns laid down in our genes, the control of hormones within our bodies and patterns of growth and development triggered through our brain. Gesell (1928), through studies of twins, advocated that our genes dictate the sequence of our growth, a process he called maturation. Whilst there is no doubt that our genes impact on our growth and development, it is now recognised that a range of other interactions with the environment influence this. Through studies on animal behaviours, for example, the work of Konrad Lorenz (1970), established that some patterns of behaviour were innate, that is to say inborn and that they did not learn the behaviour. Additionally there were crucial periods in the early days of animals and mammals when attachment took place between the child and the mother.

The study of attachment was developed in relation to human behaviour by the work of John Bowlby (1953) who believed that the development of attachment between a mother and a child was innately driven behaviour. We shall return to the crucial issue of attachment shortly. Biological theories offer explanations for some sets of behaviour. You may be able to recognise instinctive behaviours, something done without thinking, in babies, such as physical reflexes. However, although biological explanations offer answers for some aspects of human behaviour, it is a more complex process.

The growing child – cognitive perspectives

Cognitive development is concerned with thinking – the mental activities by which we acquire and process knowledge. It involves a range of processes that we develop – intelligence and learning, memory and language, beliefs and assumptions, facts and concepts, teaching and education. Consequently in any studies of human behaviour an understanding of the development and application of cognitive skills has a critical part to play in developing an understanding of that child or person.

One of the most influential people on the development of cognitive skills was Jean Piaget (1896–1980). His central assumption was that children are active participants in the development of knowledge, adapting to the environment through actively seeking to understand their environment. (You will notice that this contrasts with learning theory, which argues that the environment shapes the child.) The process of adaptation has several important sub-stages – schema, assimilation, accommodation and equilibration.

- *Schemas* are the basic building blocks and are the internal representation of a physical or mental action. Babies have limited schema such as touch, tasting and hearing. By the time they are adolescents they will show evidence of complex mental schema, such as analysis and reasoning. This ability to change is accounted for by Piaget by the following three basic processes.

- *Assimilation* is the process of taking in the new elements of new experiences and information in terms of the schema that the child already possesses.

- *Accommodation* is the process of modifying existing schema to fit new experiences or to create new schemas.

- *Equilibration* refers to the process of balance in which accommodation is consolidated via assimilation.

Piaget identified distinct sets of age-related stages. The first of these stages was identified from birth to two years – the sensorimotor stage. In this stage exploration and learning occur primarily through immediate perception and physical experiences, being largely dominated by their immediate experiences. As they develop objects and acquire such concepts as thinking, memory and language they will move into the next stage.

Between the ages of two and six years is the stage of pre-operational thought, in which the child shows interest and increasing understanding of how the world works and sophistication in their thinking, giving meaning to their experiences. There are several features of this stage:

- egocentric – they have difficulty seeing things from a point of view other than their own;

- centration – they focus their attention on one aspect of the situation having difficulty seeing that a situation may have a number of dimensions;

- lack of reversibility – failing to understand that working backwards can restore whatever existed before or that carrying out a second transformation can negate the first.

There have been critiques of Piaget's theory. One criticism is that his central concept of deductive reasoning is a typical characteristic of modern western society. This focus also denies other aspects of thinking, such as intuition and creativity. Additionally Piaget appears not interested in an examination and explanation of individual differences between children. The process is more complex than Piaget would have us believe. In Chapter 4 we introduce the work of Lev Vygotsky (1896–1934) who places different, but important, emphasis on the development of children's cognitive capacity and skills.

What are the implications of cognitive theories for social workers?

> ### ACTIVITY 3.4
>
> *Michael is five. He has been fostered with the Smith family for the last two years. Michael no longer has contact with his birth family. He is aware that the plan is to find him a 'new family' and you have been asked to talk to him about meeting a family who potentially wish to adopt him. Consider how you might do this taking into account the level of cognitive understanding of a child of his age.*

Social workers need to be sensitive to all aspects and levels of development and the ability of the child to deal with concepts of varying kinds. Working with any child involves building up a relationship – one in which there is trust and commitment. In Michael's case, from a cognitive perspective you will be aware that he is able to use language and symbols as well as actual objects. However he will be 'egocentric' in his views. Children need to be actively involved through discovery. They need concrete representations gradually building up to more abstract reasoning. New ideas need to be built on what children already know. Consequently you will need to view this meeting from Michael's perspective – a focus on him as the key person. You could use paper, pencils and toys to explain the process, that is to say what is going to happen. A family album from the potential adoptive family will help Michael in mentally representing this family. Additionally he will need to know what he needs to do before the meeting and what will happen after the meeting from his perspective.

Child development overview

The summaries below are taken from The Early Years Foundation Stage (EYFS): setting the standards for learning, development and care for children from birth to five. *They relate to the key themes and principles of the EYFS and broad phases of development. The summaries include areas of physical, cognitive, emotional and social development.*

The EYFS recognises that all children are different and to reflect this, age ranges have been overlapped in the EYFS to create broad developmental phases. This emphasises that each child's progress is individual to them and that different children develop at different rates. A child does not suddenly move from one phase to another, and they do not make progress in all areas at the same time. However, there are some important 'steps' for each child to take along their own developmental pathway. There are six broad developmental phases.

Birth–11 months

During this period, young children's physical development is very rapid and they gain increasing control of their muscles. They also develop skills in moving their hands, feet, limbs and head, quickly becoming mobile and able to handle and manipulate objects. They are learning from the moment of birth. Even before their first words they find out a lot about language by hearing people talking, and are especially interested when it involves them and their daily lives. Sensitive care giving, which responds to children's growing understanding and emotional needs, helps to build secure attachments to special people such as parents, family members or carers. Regular, though flexible, routines help young children to gain a sense of order in the world and to anticipate events. A wide variety of experience, which involves all the senses, encourages learning and an interest in the environment.

8–20 months

As children become mobile, new opportunities for exploration and exercise open up. A safe and interesting environment, with age-appropriate resources, helps children to develop curiosity, co-ordination and physical abilities. This is a time when children can start to learn the beginnings of self-control and how to relate to other people. In this period children can be encouraged to develop their social and mental skills by people to whom they have a positive attachment. Building on their communication skills, children now begin to develop a sense of self and are more able to express their needs and feelings. Alongside non-verbal communication children learn a few simple words for everyday things and people. With encouragement and plenty of interaction with carers, children's communication skills grow and their vocabulary expands very rapidly during this period.

16–26 months

Children in this phase are usually full of energy and need careful support to use it well. Growing physical strengths and skills mean that children need active times for exercise,

Continued

and quiet times for calmer activities. Playing with other children is an important new area for learning. This helps children to better understand other people's thoughts and feelings, and to learn how to co-operate with others. Exploration and simple self-help build a sense of self-confidence. Children are also learning about boundaries and how to handle frustration. Play with toys that come apart and fit together encourages problem solving and simple planning. Pretend play helps children to learn about a range of possibilities. Adults are an important source of security and comfort.

22–36 months

Children's fine motor skills continue to develop and they enjoy making marks, using a variety of materials, looking at picture books and listening to stories, important steps in literacy. Self-help and independence soon emerge if adults support and encourage children in areas such as eating, dressing and toileting. Praise for new achievements helps to build their self-esteem. In this phase, children's language is developing rapidly and many are beginning to put sentences together. Joining in conversations with children is an important way for children to learn new things and to begin to think about past, present and future. Developing physical skills mean that children can now usually walk, climb and run, and join in active play with other children. This is an important time for learning about dangers and safe limits.

30–50 months

An increased interest in joint play such as make-believe, construction and games helps children to learn the important social skills of sharing and co-operating. Children also learn more about helping adults in everyday activities and finding a balance between independence and complying with the wishes of others. Children still need the comfort and security of special people. Close, warm relationships with carers form the basis for much learning, such as encouraging children to make healthy choices in food and exercise. At this stage children are becoming more aware of their place in a community. Literacy and numeracy can develop rapidly with the support of a wide range of interesting materials and activities. Children's language is now much more complex, as many become adept at using longer sentences. Conversations with adults become a more important source of information, guidance and reassurance.

40–60+ months

During this period children are building a stronger sense of their own identity and their place in a wider world. Children are learning to recognise the importance of social rules and customs, to show understanding and tolerance of others, and to learn how to be more controlled in their own behaviour. Learning and playing in small groups helps to foster the development of social skills. Children now become better able to plan and undertake more challenging activities with a wider range of materials for making and doing. In this phase children learn effectively in shared activities with more able peers and adults. Literacy and problem-solving, reasoning and numeracy skills continue to develop. Children's developing understanding of cause and effect is encouraged by the introduction of a wider variety of equipment, media and technologies.

Developed from DfES (2007) **www.standards.dfes.gov.uk/eyfs/**

The social and emotional development of infants and children – developing attachments

The relationships that we develop and form with others, especially caregivers, are central to our emotional and social security. Child development takes place, to a large degree, through social relationships.

Communication

A necessary start to socialisation is the existence of communication between children and others, particularly adults. Facial expressions, particularly smiling, are usually the beginning of communication. Although voluntary smiling may begin at around four to six weeks, they begin to be reserved for a social context from around two to three months, with particular smiling for those that they recognise. As babies pay attention to human faces and voices, they learn to distinguish between familiar people and voices, such as a parent. They learn the social consequence of their actions, such as crying and smiling, through the response and importance that is given to them by their carer. Therefore the child is able to give meaning to their behaviour through noting the effect and response on their carers. Babies learn to respond back to the parent through learning about their response. For example, a baby smiling initiates a positive response in the parent, the parent interacts with the child and the baby responds with further smiling. Finally children learn to use their carer for 'social referencing' – gauging a parent's emotional response to a situation before deciding how to interact themselves (Smith and Cowie, 1991).

Research has shown that even before birth babies can identify familar voices (Karmiloff and Karmiloff-Smith, 2001) and it is to those familiar sounds that the newborn child will initially develop attachments.

Attachment

Children need to feel secure in their relationships. An adult, for example a parent, needs to form a positive, emotional attachment to the child to care for them. Early relationships are seen as important as they are viewed by theorists as having a critical role in the person's emotional well-being throughout their life.

Therefore, attachment is central to infants' and children's social and emotional development.

> How we are depends on how we experience (these) early relationships. Warmth, mutuality, support and security are qualities of relationships that tend to produce coherent, well-organised later selves.
>
> (Payne, 2005 p.81)

Attachment theory involves the study of relationships, in particular the critical early relationships of infants and children.

Children use the people to whom they are attached as:

- a safe base from which to explore;
- a source of comfort;
- a source of encouragement and guidance.

Attachment behaviours are patterns of action that keep them in touch with the other person – smiling, crying, laughing, talking and so on.

Traditionally research into attachment was heavily influenced by psychoanalytic theory, in particular Freud who emphasised the importance of the infant–mother relationship. Learning theory explained attachment as operating to satisfy innate needs or drives – the primary drive was the need for satisfaction of basic needs, for example the need for food, the secondary drive was the attachment to the mother in order to meet these needs. Further studies would suggest that the development of attachment is a more complex process.

There are two parts to the development of attachment between a baby and their parents – an initial first part immediately after birth referred to as bonding (usually with the mother) and a second, more important part that develops during the early years of a baby's life.

Bonding

The process of bonding was thought to critically take place usually within hours of birth between the mother and the child. 'Bonding' primarily signifies a bond between the mother and baby, which has been linked to a profound effect on their future relationships with each other. However it may be more useful to some to view this process as 'claiming' behaviour: 'checking out' the baby and beginning to make physical and emotional links with the child. Whilst immediate and close contact is helpful in the beginning of the development of a relationship, studies (Svejda et al., 1980; Eyer, 1992) have shown that it is not essential in the establishment of a long-term positive relationship. It is more helpful to see the process of attachment as a process that could begin during these early days but which continues. Supporting mother–baby contact in the early days can help those mothers who are most at risk of providing poor parenting but only if this support continues in later months. The failure to bond by itself is not an indication of difficulties in parenting or an explanation of later abuse. Though the baby seems to prefer the mother, this does not mean that they have formed a relationship. Early relationships do not have to be with the mother; babies can equally form relationships with their fathers and others.

Attachment during the early years of life

Whilst the early days are not irrelevant the first few months appear to be more crucial in developing a sense of attachment particularly between parents and children. The original concept of 'attachment' has been attributed to the studies developed by John Bowlby (1953, 1969, 1973, 1988). He was highly influential from the mid-1940s to the mid-1970s, shaping research, policies and practice over several decades. Like Freud, Bowlby believed that the root of the development of personality lay in early childhood and that any trauma or failure in these early relationships would permanently shape the development of the child's personality. Drawing on ethological theory, the study of animals and humans within an evolutionary context, he suggested that human evolution resulted in babies having a biological need, or *instinct* to form an attachment. Mothers, whom Bowlby believed were the critical relationship in a child's early life, also had a biological need to be near and protect their children. Therefore 'attachment' is a primary motivational need. The impact of prolonged separation on children was viewed as 'maternal deprivation' – the temporary or permanent loss to a child of their mother's care and attention. He believed that prolonged separation of the child from their mother, especially during the first five years of their life, was a major cause of 'delinquent' behaviour and mental health issues. Additionally this loss of their mother's love appeared to make them incapable of normal emotions, a condition he described as 'affectionless psychopathy' which in turn led to problems in their own ability to parent.

Bowlby's research has had a major impact on the study of attachment. However as research has developed there have been criticisms of some of the early thinking on attachment theory. Children can make attachment relationships to other people, not just their mother. They can also form several attachments. Developing relationships with others is equally important, for example with fathers, siblings and other relatives. The key factor is that the person spends time with them building a relationship. Reliance on one 'exclusive' relationship can itself be damaging, as it does not allow for supportive, healthy relationships with others. Children need to experience stable, reliable relationships. Whilst early experience is important, the idea that this is the pattern for the rest of their lives denies the opportunity to potentially reverse the effect of negative early experiences. The child's outlook on the world depends on how distressing events are handled by others. Children's experiences and development also depend on what happens after the early years. Equally positive experiences in early life do not make a child safe from later emotional damage. Attributing problems in behaviour and in later life to maternal deprivation ('loss') denies the impact of other factors, especially the impact of privation, that is to say, chronic lack of, for example, basic needs, stimulation such as play, the role of others rather than just emotional warmth (Rutter, 1981). The multi-cultural dimensions of relationships need to be taken into account, for example, the different patterns of child rearing and the role of the wider family network.

Bowlby did recognise that the quality and strengths of attachments do vary. Mary Ainsworth, a colleague of Bowlby's, designed an experimental situation, the 'Strange Situation' procedure, which sought to evaluate the relationship that a child has with attachment figures. Ainsworth's (1973) classification demonstrates that infant behaviour can be attributed to secure or insecure attachments.

Table 3.1

Patterns of attachment	Characteristics
Secure (Type B)	Explores freely when their caregiver is present using the caregiver as a secure base. May be distressed at separation. Always greets the caregiver on reunion. If distressed during separation, seeks contact and comfort during reunion, then settles down to continue play.
Insecure-avoidant (Type A)	Explores freely, seems uninterested in the caregiver's presence or departure. On reunion, ignores or actively avoids caregiver.
Insecure-resistant/ambivalent (Type C)	Resists active exploration. Preoccupied with caregiver. Upset at separation. On reunion both resists and seeks contact, showing anger, passivity or clinging. Does not easily return to play.

Table 3.1 Continued

Patterns of attachment	Characteristics
Disorganised (Type D)	Neither plays freely nor responds to the caregiver in any one coherent mode. May cry and then hit; may 'freeze'; trance-like; may move in slow motion or other stereotyped manner; may show fear of parent.
Not classified	Some children fit into none of the four categories.

Patterns of attachment can be affected by a variety of factors. The best predictor of a child's secure attachment is the attention and sensitivity of the carer. Howe (1995) notes that observation of children, for example when tired, frightened or unwell, can support the assessment of the attachment relationship with the main carer.

Table 3.2

Patterns of attachment	Response of carer
Secure	Usually knows the best way to give comfort and care. Caregiver is available and accessible during times of distress and carer is able to contain and regulate distressed state. Inclined to hold and cuddle child as a regular part of their behaviour. Acknowledges their child with smiles and conversation, with a tender-warm voice. Responds to their child's vocalisation. Emotional availability and sensitivity supports the child in the development of sense of self-esteem and self-worth.
Insecure-avoidant	Caregiver uses more controlling co-operative tactics. Rebuffs or is indifferent towards the child. Child is insecure but compulsively self-reliant.
Insecure-resistant/ambivalent	Caregiver is not hostile or rejecting but inconsistent, insensitive and lacking in accurate empathy. Child views self as dependent and poorly valued.
Disorganised	Carer shows little or no sensitivity to the child's emotional needs. Frightening or frightened. Child views self as helpless, angry or unworthy.

(Adapted from Howe, 1995)

Other factors include the impact of family stressors such as low socio-economic status, marital discord. The child's own characteristics may contribute towards the quality of the attachment relationship, for example children who get upset easily.

In developing attachment it is important to be sensitive to the child's needs. Vera Fahlberg (1991) developed two models to understand the development of attachment – the 'arousal and relaxation' cycle and the positive interaction cycle.

- The arousal and relaxation cycle. The child experiences a need leading to displeasure ('arousal'). The caregiver responds to the need and the child is calm ('relaxation'). The child initiates this cycle and their experience of the response leads to trust, security and attachment by the child.

- Positive interaction cycle. The caregiver initiates positive interaction with the child, which produces positive response from the child. This response leads to further positive interaction from the carer and so on. The carer initiates the cycle and the child's experience of this cycle leads to the development of self-worth and self-esteem.

Fahlberg has produced a clear, detailed observation checklist to support the assessment of attachment in her book *The child's journey through placement* (1991).

The case of Denny (below) demonstrates concerns in relation to his attachment. Whilst his behaviour may signify distress at the loss of his main attachment figure, his apparent inability and/or lack of desire to apparently respond to any overtures on the part of his foster carers gives rise to concerns. He appears to have become self sufficient, relying on his own strategies to care for himself. This is further reinforced when his mother visits. She makes no attempt to initiate contact or comfort him. As Howe (1995) suggests different attachment styles and care-seeking behaviours represent different psychological and behavioural strategies developed by children to maximise the care and protection available under particular care-giving regimes. Children actively seek ways of adapting to their world rather than becoming victims of it.

CASE STUDY

Denny, aged 14 months, has been fostered with the Greys for four weeks. He came into care because of concerns about his mother's ability to care for him. He is very independent. Denny feeds himself, refusing to take food from his carers when offered directly – they have to put it in a place where he can reach it himself. The same happens with toys – he will only take toys that are placed where he can reach him. He prefers solitary play. Denny rarely responds to the carers and when attempts are made to cuddle him he goes rigid. When his mother visits he goes to her and offers her a toy. She looks at the toy and gives it back to him. He sits near her. Denny's mother spends a lot of time talking to the foster carers about her problems – with her boyfriend, with friends, with money. Denny does not cry when she leaves but sits quietly staring out of the window.

Why is attachment theory important for social workers?

The nature, form and development of relationships are crucial to social work practice. The assessment of these relationships will play a critical part in your practice. For example, two of the three domains within the *Common Assessment Framework* (CAF) (DfES, 2006a p.17) are:

- how well parents or carers are able to support their child's development and respond appropriately to any needs;

- the impact of wider family and environmental elements on a child's development and on the capacity of their parents and carers.

Attachment theory provides part of a model of analysis in judging the quality of a relationship. This can be essential in knowing when to intervene, or even remove a child, where there are concerns in relation to attachment. Additionally we need to understand the impact of the loss of their attachment figure on the child, for example in order to understand the child's subsequent behaviour. You will need to support carers in developing behaviours which will promote attachment in the child, for example within an adoptive family. Your skills in communication and observation will be essential in assessing and supporting the development of attachment behaviour.

Resilience and vulnerability

In each of these cases we can identify factors that could impact on the children's development. In the case of Rachel we are able to identify factors such as the parents' substance use and dad's mental ill health. Rachel could be said to be demonstrating secure attachment patterns. Sarah has experienced the impact of her parents' break-up and moving to a new area. Sarah may be demonstrating ambivalent or avoidant patterns of attachment. However the children appear to respond differently to the apparent adversity in their lives. How can we explain the different responses from the children? We could say that the teachers' perception of the children may be because of the children's response to liking or disliking school. Certainly in your role as a social worker it is important that you undertake an assessment of the child, to obtain as full a picture as possible from all those involved to help to understand the child and the child's response in a range of situations. (See Parker and Bradley, 2007.) However the teachers' perceptions of the children lead us to ask a number of broader questions.

- What are the adversities – life events or circumstances – that pose a threat to healthy development?

- Are there factors within the environment that provide children with support to safeguard them against adverse experiences?

- Are there factors that may make some children more vulnerable than others to coping with adversity?

- What are the factors that promote resilience – ability in the individual to overcome stressful and difficult situations and function competently and confidently? (Daniel et al., 1999)

CASE STUDY

Rachel, the youngest of four children, is five and has just started school. Her teacher is aware that her parents are long-term substance users. Rachel's father suffers from mental ill-health, which results in him having in-hospital treatment on occasions. The family lifestyle is described as 'chaotic' and Rachel's maternal grandmother provides a lot of support to the family. Her teacher describes Rachel as a happy, outgoing child, who is bright and responsive and mixes well with the other children.

Sarah, the oldest of two children, is five and has just started school. Sarah, her mum and brother have recently moved to the area. Her mother describes this as a 'fresh start' after a difficult marital break-up. She has infrequent contact with her dad. Her teacher describes her as a shy, unhappy little girl who does not mix with the other children.

Adversities that impact on a child

The family environment into which children are born will have the most profound and significant impact on the child. Factors within the family that may influence their ability to respond to the child's developmental needs include the parents' own experience of childhood and parenting style; adverse circumstances within the family and the socio-economic status of the family. Additionally there are children who suffer abuse and neglect, which pose a threat to their healthy development. The *National Service*

Framework (DoH, 2004) specifically considers the impact adult problems can have on children's development.

Protective environments

Protective environments refer to the immediate network of relationships between the individual, their immediate family and their local community. For children this includes one enduring supportive relationship. Additionally a good school experience can support children in overcoming difficult adversities. For the parent, protective environments may be in the form of community support and networks, particularly those that offer emotional support and practical help and advice.

Vulnerability

Factors which promote vulnerability for children include disability, racism, children who appear to have an 'unusual' or 'difficult' temperament. Parental issues which may lead to vulnerability for the child include experiences of their own childhood lacking in affectionate contact with key adults; mental health issues and when parental needs are focused elsewhere, for example through frequent drugs and alcohol use.

Resilience

Despite adversities some children are able to develop reasonably well-adjusted personalities demonstrating resilience and normal development under difficult circumstances.

RESEARCH SUMMARY

Tony Newman and Sarah Blackburn's report describes effective strategies for helping children cope with periods of transition and change through the promotion of resilience. They have identified a number of resilience factors:

The child	The family	The environment
Temperament (active, good-natured)	Warm, supportive parents	Supportive extended family
Female bonding prior to and male during adolescence	Good parent–child relationships	Successful school experiences
Age (being younger)	Parental harmony	Friendship networks
Higher IQ	Valued social role (e.g. care of siblings, helping neighbours)	Valued social role (e.g. a job, volunteering)
Social skills	Close relationship with one parent	
Personal awareness		Close relationship with unrelated mentor
Feelings of empathy		Member of religious or faith community
Internal locus of control		
Humour		
Attractiveness		

They outline the current evidence in relation to research.

- *Evidence from longitudinal studies indicates that a large proportion of children recover from short-lived childhood adversities with little detectable impact in adult life.*

- *An excessive preoccupation with the identification and elimination of risk factors may weaken the capacity of children to overcome adversities.*

- *All interventions in health, education and social care may do harm as well as good. Resilience may be weakened by unnecessary or harmful interventions.*

Continued

- *Where adversities are continuous and severe, and protective factors are absent, resilience in children is a rare phenomenon.*

- *The most common sources of anxiety for children are chronic and transitional events. Chronic problems will usually have more lasting effects than acute adversities.*

- *While self-esteem is a crucial factor in the promotion of resilience, it is more likely to grow and be sustained through developing valued skills in real life situations, than just through praise and positive affirmation.*

- *It is necessary to promote children's ability to resist adversities as well as moderating risk factors.*

- *Resilience can only develop through exposure to stressors. Resistance develops through gradual exposure to difficulties at a manageable level of intensity.*

- *A supportive family is the most powerful resilience-promoting factor.*

- *The acquisition of valued social roles, the ability to contribute to the general household economy and educational success are resilience-promoting factors.*

- *Experiences that promote resilience may not always be pleasant or socially acceptable.*

- *Poor early experiences do not necessarily 'fix' a child's future trajectory. Compensatory interventions in later life can trigger resilient responses.*

They suggest that the factors that promote resilience are:

- *strong social support networks;*

- *the presence of at least one unconditionally supportive parent or parent substitute;*

- *a committed mentor or other person from outside the family;*

- *positive school experiences;*

- *a sense of mastery and a belief that one's own efforts can make a difference;*

- *a range of extra-curricular activities that promote the learning of competencies and emotional maturity;*

- *the capacity to re-frame adversities so that the beneficial as well as the damaging effects are recognised;*

- *the ability, or opportunity, to 'make a difference' by, for example, helping others through volunteering, or undertaking part-time work;*

- *exposure to challenging situations which provide opportunities to develop both problem-solving abilities and emotional coping skills.*

Newman and Blackburn (2002)

Safeguarding children: children in need and children in need of protection

As a social worker you will deal with vulnerable people. Under *Section 17, Children Act 1989*, local authorities are required

> *to safeguard and promote the welfare of children in their area who are in need by providing a range and level of services appropriate to those needs.*

This means that you will be working with families in supporting them in responding to the development needs of their children. Inevitably you will be working with children who are the victims of abuse – physical, sexual, emotional and through neglect.

The Government defines safeguarding as:

> The process of protecting children from abuse or neglect, preventing impairment of their health and development, and ensuring they are growing up in circumstances consistent with the provision of safe and effective care that enables children to have optimum life chances and enter adulthood successfully.

> *(www.safeguardingchildren.gov.uk)*

Chapter 4 of Working Together to Safeguard Children *(DfCSF, 2010) outlines that Local Safeguarding Children's Board (LSCB) should ensure that all staff who work or have contact with children are appropriately trained to understand normal child development and to recognise potential signs of abuse and neglect.*

A concern will be whether the child is experiencing significant harm or impairment. Your intervention will be based on an assessment – *Framework for the assessment of need and their families* (Department of Health, 2000) and possibly the *Common Assessment Framework* (DfES, 2006a). These frameworks are designed to provide a common approach by professionals in deciding if a child is in need and the how best to respond. They identify three systems, which need to interact together to promote the long-term well-being of the child – the child's developmental needs, parenting capacity, and family and environmental factors. Using the *Framework for the Assessment of Children in Need* you will be assessing the child's needs and the family's previous and current ability to respond to the child's needs and sustain this throughout their childhood. Incorporated into the assessment framework is an assessment of the developmental needs of the child. It identifies seven dimensions of developmental need which children need to progress along to achieve a healthy adulthood – health, education, identity, family and social relations, emotional and behavioural development and self-care skills (see Parker and Bradley, 2007).

An understanding of child growth and development will be an essential skill in your work with children who have been abused and in an assessment of their needs. For example in assessing the child's identity, the sense of themselves as a separate and valued being, you will need to be aware of the experience within their families and within the wider community in which they live, for example do they receive praise and encouragement within their families? Do they feel 'accepted' by their community? It will help you to draw on the work of Erikson in assessing this. Assessment of the child's emotional and behavioural development will be supported by consideration of issues in relation to attachment. For example, is there evidence of a warm and positive relationship in which the child is given consistent boundaries?

> *Child development theories are essential underpinning knowledge for social work practice but in the area of child protection are crucial ...*

> (Jowitt and O'Loughlin, 2005 p.59)

REFLECTION POINT

- *What do I know, or can I do now, that I did not know or could not do before I did this section of studying?*

- *Is there anything I do not understand or want to explore further?*

- *What else do I need to know to extend my professional development and learning in this area?*

CHAPTER SUMMARY

Growth and development within early childhood are rapid and involve a complex interaction of 'internal' process supported by 'external' support and stimulation. Understanding the nature of development supports social workers in their practice – in assessment, intervention and review in children's and families' lives. The concept of 'childhood' has undergone a historical process of change. We now recognise the changing nature of childhood and its importance in creating happy, healthy adults, for example through their legitimised rights. However we also need to recognise that many children continue to live in adverse circumstances. We recognise that children from different cultures and children with disabilities may experience their development in a different way from other children. Within Britain today we recognise the continuing impact of poverty and the potential adverse impact this may have on the child and subsequently on them as they grow into adults. Whilst physical and biological changes impact on the child, the area of the development of cognitive skills offers many challenges. The development and sustaining of attachment for babies and children is of critical importance and social work practice has a key role in assessing and supporting its development. We recognise that there are children who may be particularly vulnerable to adversity. However we have also been able to identify factors which promote resilience in children. Finally we have introduced the topic of abuse and recognised that an assessment of a child's development needs will support a wider assessment process. In the next chapter we build on these foundations and examine themes and issues in relation to the middle years of childhood.

FURTHER READING

Bee, H (1995) *The growing child*. New York: HarperCollins.

This book, although examples are based on American children, provides a readable account of child development.

Cleaver, H, Nicholson, D, Tarr, S and Cleaver, D (2008) *Child protection, domestic violence and parental substance misuse.*

The focus of the research is children referred to children's social care where there are safeguarding concerns and evidence of domestic violence and/or parental substance misuse. This can be found on: **www.dcsf.gov.uk/everychildmatters/safeguardingandsocialcare/**

Daniel, B, Wassell, S and Gilligan, R (1999) *Child development for child care and protection workers*. London: Jessica Kingsley.

Based primarily on attachment theory this book is aimed at providing an understanding of child development for social workers, particularly those working in child protection.

Fahlberg, V (1991) *A child's journey through placement*. London: BAAF.

This book takes readers through the stages of development and attachment, providing examples and frameworks to assess children's needs, particularly for those in the looked after system.

Meggitt, C (2006) *Child development: An illustrated guide* (2nd edition). Oxford: Heinemann Educational.

Although this book offers a guide to child development from birth to 16 years, the first 12 parts of Section One are devoted to birth to five years old. This is a very readable text which develops an holistic approach to understanding child development.

Prior, V and Glaser, D (2006) *Understanding attachment and attachment disorders: theory, evidence and practice*. London: Jessica Kingsley.

This book is structured into five parts which include discussion about theoretical perspectives as well as a critical appraisal of attachment theory-based interventions.

www.publications.dcsf.gov.uk

Government policy documents can be found on this website.

www.rip.org.uk

Research in practice is a network of more than 100 Partner Agencies committed to the use of evidence-informed practice to promote positive outcomes for children and families who find themselves in vulnerable situations. This includes reporting on research to support ECM.

www.scie.org.uk/publications/briefings/

SCIE research briefing 5: Short breaks (respite care) for children with learning disabilities
Details of respite care for children with disabilities.

Think Families Toolkit (2009) Available from: **www.publications.everychildmatters.gov.uk**

Think Family is intended to support better outcomes for children, young people and families with additional needs by co-ordinating the support they receive from children's, young people's, adults' and family services. This Toolkit sets out some of the ways in which these practices can be developed. Sections include details of evidence-based programmes and good practice in the areas of parenting programmes, supporting young carers, families with children at risk of offending, families who are workless and have significant barriers to work.

Together for Children www.childrens-centres.org

Together for Children is working in partnership with the Department for Children, Schools and Families to support local authorities in their delivery of Sure Start Children's Centres.

WEBSITES

Chapter 4

Using life course development knowledge in social work practice with older children and their families

A C H I E V I N G   A   S O C I A L   W O R K   D E G R E E

This chapter will help you to begin to meet the following National Occupational Standards:

Key Role 1: Prepare for and work with individuals, families, carers, groups and communities to assess their needs and circumstances.

- Work with individuals, families, carers, groups and communities to help them make informed decisions.
- Assess needs and options to recommend a course of action.

Key Role 2: Plan, carry out, review and evaluate social work practice, with individuals, families, carers, groups and communities and other professionals.

- Interact with individuals, families, carers, groups and communities to achieve change and development and to improve life opportunities.
- Address behaviours which present a risk to individuals, families, carers, groups and communities.

It will also introduce you to the following academic standards as set out in the social work subject benchmark statement:

3.1.1 Social work services and service users.

3.1.4 Social work theory.

3.2.2 Problem solving skills.

3.2.2.3 Analysis and synthesis.

Introduction

In this chapter you will consider life course development knowledge in respect of older children, children in their 'middle years' with particular consideration to social work practice in the context of contemporary policy and legislation. It will start by providing an overview of middle childhood and outlining the context of development. You will explore theories and explanations of development in middle childhood that examine psychosocial processes, biological processes and cognitive processes, in particular aspects of learning. You will examine the role of the family and adults, especially parents and carers in supporting the development of children. The final section in this chapter will demonstrate how an understanding of development needs to be placed in the context of patterns of interactions – the ecological approach.

As discussed in Chapter 3, this book is set within the context of contemporary social work practice and related policy and legislation. Of particular relevance to your learning in this chapter about older children's development and social work practice, is the national strategic development programme *Every Child Matters: Change for Children* (DfES, 2004) and the *Children Act 2004* which supports the implementation of that programme. *Every Child Matters* identifies five key outcomes that are considered to be the most important to children and young people:

- be healthy;
- stay stafe;
- enjoy and achieve;
- make a positive contribution;
- achieve economic well-being.

In the companion reader to this text, Crawford (2006) focuses on each of these five outcomes to facilitate discussion and reflection about what they mean for different aspects of childhood development and social work practice.

Figure 4.1 illustrates how the outcomes and their underlying aims come together in the *Every Child Matters* programme.

Defining middle childhood

The transition into middle childhood is defined as the period of growth and development between the ages of approximately five to 12 years of age. It is suggested that it is qualitatively different from that of young childhood. This is evident through shifts in the child's social world with increased understanding of self and development of complex thinking. There are greater opportunities for independence, greatly influenced by the transition to formal education.

The period of middle childhood is one of relative stability. It is marked on one side by the rapid growth and development of infancy and young childhood and on the other by the beginning of adolescence and puberty. However there are important features of middle childhood. Physical developments allow children to master a range of new skills. The child makes advances in cognitive skills and patterns. Features of personality develop that will support and affect development in adolescence and adulthood. They begin to see the world from others' perspectives. Whilst the family is still important, they learn more about the world and their role within it as they have increased autonomy and independence. Children's social networks expand; they establish relationships with a wider range of others. Friendships become important, particularly same sex friendships. Adults outside the family have a greater influence on the child, for example teachers. Children may become part of wider groups, such as clubs and groups.

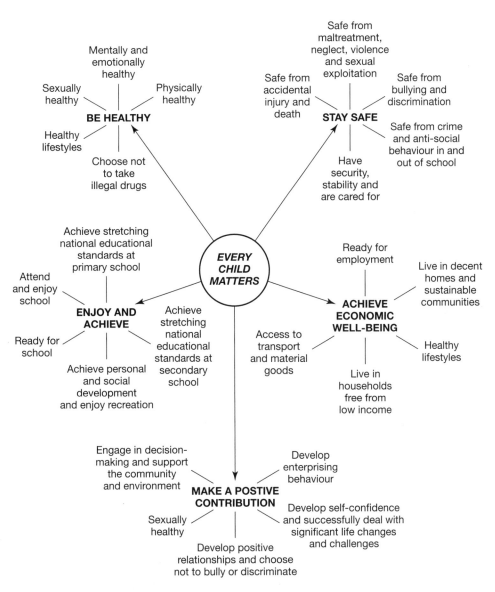

Figure 4.1 Adapted from Every Child Matters: Change for children, *cited in Crawford (2006 p. 14)*

Theories and explanations of development in middle childhood

In this section we shall explore in greater depth theories and explanations of middle childhood. Whilst theorists and researchers appear to give less emphasis to this area, this is an important phase of development in consolidating and developing the abilities and skills acquired in early childhood and in preparation for adolescence. In middle childhood, children become more independent, exploring and gaining an understanding of the wider world of their community. Their lives continue to be shaped and guided by their family and cultural values. Social development is an essential part of the skills that develop in middle childhood, being a unique configuration of social, biological and cognitive characteristics. In all cultures, middle childhood appears to be a universal stage of human development.

Physical development in middle childhood

In relative terms, children in middle childhood grow slower as compared to early years. However they continue to grow gradually and steadily throughout this period. Growth varies depending on genes, gender and nutrition. Typically the majority of school age children become stronger and are healthier.

One of the five outcomes identified in the *Every Child Matters* programme (**www.everychildmatters.gov.uk**) is 'being healthy': enjoying good physical and mental health and living a healthy lifestyle. As you have seen, though, in the previous chapter, children's development is very individual.

However, generally in the middle years of childhood, both gross and fine motor skills continue to develop, especially in relation to expertise, for example sporting abilities and abilities in penmanship. Boys and girls are almost equal in their physical abilities. However cultural influences have a significant impact on differences between sexes. Boys tend to play with other boys in large groups in organised games that involve 'conflict'. Girls form smaller, more intimate groups where fine motor skills are practised (Maccoby, 2002).

For some children their specific needs will only become apparent when they begin school. Some children with specific needs will have benefited from identification in early childhood. However other children, for example those with behavioural or specific learning issues, may not be identified until they begin school.

ACTIVITY 4.1

Jake, five, has Downs Syndrome. As a consequence he has a moderate hearing impairment, speech problems and slow motor development. His mother feels he would benefit from more specialised help in a specialised school. She feels this would give Jake better access to specialist help and appropriate resources and treatment that would support him in developing his physical and cognitive skills. However his father would like him to attend the local primary school; he feels that this would offer Jake the chance to integrate with other children and develop his social and emotional skills.

Consider both of these responses. What are the advantages and disadvantages of each approach? Which approach would you favour? Why?

COMMENT

Certainly both approaches have advantages. It is important that Jake has the kind of specialist support to support his specific needs. It could be suggested that in this approach the focus is on the 'disability'. The other approach focuses on an opportunity for Jake to integrate with the other children, the school community and his local community. It could be suggested that this approach has more of a focus on social integration.

Two theoretical models that represent these approaches are the medical model of disability and the social model of disability. In the medical model the disability is seen as the primary focus with a particular 'pathology' – a scientific approach to the cause and treatment of the 'disease'. The social model of disability considers disability in the context of society, in particular the impact of society's values and attitudes in relation to disability and the physical and social barriers faced by people with the disability. A major problem for children with a disability is that they live in a society that views disability as a 'problem'. In thinking about your approach to the viewpoints in relation to Jake you will have had to think about your own understanding of disability – your attitude and values. Are you able to acknowledge any prejudices and fears that you may hold in relation to disability? Do you recognise the way in which you or others may stereotype disability, for example considering that people with a disability are vulnerable and helpless? In any work with children, young people and adults you will need to take responsibility for understanding the impairment and the impact of that impairment from the individual's perspective. What does the disability mean to that person; what impact does it have on their stage of development? Listening to the child is essential and you have to take responsibility for ensuring that communication is facilitated, particularly if the child may have specific need in relation to communication.

The *National Service Framework (NSF) for Children, Young People and Maternity Services* (DoH, 2004) sets, as one of its principal aims, a requirement that the standards will *give children, young people and their parents increased information, power and choice over the support and treatment they receive, and involve them in planning their care and services.*

The Children Plan (2007) outlines a ten-year plan to improve services for children and *The Children's Plan – Two Years On* describes what has happened two years on from this plan. Both of these documents can be found at http://www.dcsf.gov.uk/childrensplan/

However, the *Every Child Matters* (DfES, 2003) had already identified a number of barriers standing in the way of children with special needs. These include:

- poor co-ordination between health, education and social care for young children with special needs, leading to gaps in support for parents and weaknesses in sharing information between professionals;

- shortfalls in the availability of childcare for disabled children and in specialist advice and support for young children in early years settings;

- difficulties in arranging funding streams so that resources are available to support earlier intervention;

- insufficient information for parents about suitable childcare;

- too much bureaucracy and paperwork associated with the Special Educational Needs (SEN) system.

Aiming High for Disabled Children (AHDC): *Better support for families* (DfCSF and DoH, 2007) is the part of the national service framework that is intended to be the transformation programme for disabled children's services. *AHDC – Best practice to common practice* (DfCSF and DoH, 2009) provides an update on the key developments in the programme since the launch.

Supporting children in education with special educational needs

A 'Statement of Special Educational Needs' describes the special educational needs of a child and the extra provision that is required to meet those needs. Special educational provision is the name used for the extra support a child may need in nursery or school, for example help from a classroom assistant, individual teaching or speech therapy.

The Education (Special Educational Needs) (England) (Consolidation) Regulations 2001 or in Wales the Education (Special Educational Needs)(Wales) Regulations 2002 set out the detailed process of assessment including time limits that the local education authority (LEA) has to follow. The whole assessment process from beginning to end is likely to take at least 26 weeks with strict time limits provided for each stage of the process. The LEA has to obtain advice from: the child's parent (or legal carer); educational advice; medical advice; psychological advice; advice from social services and any other advice they consider appropriate. This may include a meeting with the child. Once the parents/carer has received the Proposed Statement and the formal notice about expressing a preference for a school, a parent/ legal carer has 15 days to express a preference for a school and to make representations to the LEA. Part 3 of the Proposed Statement sets out the objectives which the special educational provision aims to meet (long-term goals); the educational provision to meet the needs and objectives; and the monitoring arrangements (the arrangements for deciding short-term targets and reviewing them, as well as any special arrangements for reviewing the statement). The LEA should normally send the parent/ carer the final statement within 8 weeks of sending the proposed statement.

www.downs-syndrome.org.uk

All the potential problems identified in middle childhood benefit from prevention, early recognition, assessment and appropriate intervention. Each child has unique skills and abilities to cope; all children need support, advice and guidance both at school and at home.

Psychological development in middle childhood

The transition to school coincides with greater independence and capabilities in the child. The interplay of self-understanding and social perception is increasingly evident as the child develops through the middle years.

Whilst psychoanalytical theorists have emphasised the development of personality, there is recognition that in middle childhood this is influenced by increasing competency. Freud refers to this period as the 'latency' period – a period of relative calm with a focus on ego development, particularly social and intellectual skills.

Erikson refers to the stage between six and 12 years as a period of industry (competence) versus inferiority. This is a period when the child seeks approval through the mastering of new intellectual and social skills, such as reading, writing and the formation of friendships. These tasks represent the development of the expected skills of their culture and of society. This has to be balanced with a realistic sense of their limitation to avoid a negative sense of inferiority. If a child is unable to develop these skills then they will develop a sense of inferiority and incompetence; this may be particularly reinforced through the response of others.

ACTIVITY 4.2

Paul, aged eight, is described by his mother Sandra as 'useless'. She says that he cannot be bothered to learn and spends all his time out of the house, usually on his own at the local park. When confronted he is verbally abusive.

Sadie, aged seven, is described by her mother Jackie as 'useless'. She says that she cannot be bothered to learn and has no friends. Sadie is timid and anxious. She spends all her time on her own, usually in her bedroom.

Think about the responses of these children. Write a few sentences that answer the questions below:

- *Using Erikson's model, briefly explain Paul's and Sadie's situations.*
- *Having formed an opinion of Paul's and Sadie's situations using Erikson's approach, what are the implications for the way in which you would work with each of these children as a social worker?*

From the information that you have it is impossible to understand everything influencing these situations, for example, previous influences on the child and family; the context of the child's behaviour. However, whilst both children demonstrate different behaviour, the children's response could be seen as the result of a potential 'failure' to develop their intellectual and social skills. Their individual action, whilst representing two potential examples of 'extremes', could be seen as the response to and the reinforcement of feelings of inferiority. As a social worker you will need to gather further information, which would form a clearer assessment of the child's needs and feelings. For example, you will want to talk to both children's teachers, to gain an understanding of the child's educational ability, for example if they have specific learning needs. You will need to listen to the child – their perception of themselves, their friendships and their feelings about their family. The parent will need support in listening to and understanding their child and the reasons for their behaviour. The parent may need support and guidance in developing strategies and responses that will help to build their child's self-esteem and self-worth. Standard 2 of the *National Service Framework* (DoH, 2004) sets a range of measures for supporting parents to increase the life chances of children.

Cognitive development in middle childhood

Children in middle childhood are ready to learn. Piaget referred to this stage as that of concrete operations (approximately seven to 11 years). Children become less egocentric, being able to take into account other people's ideas, and more logical in thinking through ideas and reaching a conclusion. It is distinguished by the development of an understanding of *conservation* – realisation that weight, mass and volume remain the same despite changes in their shape or physical arrangement; by *decentration* – the ability to focus on more than one dimension of the object at the same time and *seriation* – the ability to order objects according to some identified 'property', such as size. Children acquire the ability to reverse their thinking, as they are able to take into account a number of features.

CASE STUDY

Carly, eight, has been in foster care for six months, following concerns about her emotional and physical neglect. She will be moving to live with a new adoptive family during the next three months. Carly appears to accept this without question. Her social worker, Bill, having undertaken a full assessment of her needs, knows that Carly's early childhood has been marked by frequent moves, inconsistent care and care by a number of people. He recognises that for Carly from her point of view this may be 'just another move'. Her understanding of the concept of family and family relationships is limited because of her early experiences. Bill and her current carers work with Carly in developing a life story book about her past. In addition Bill uses drawings – time lines to help Carly understand her previous life and family trees and network diagrams to help her to 'cognitively' locate herself in her past and future family. He also uses play with dolls and models as an aid to developing Carly's understanding.

Piaget's views were based on the individual – the structures within children's minds and how they gradually become more sophisticated with age. However some developmental psychologists have also explored the social influences on children's development, notably Lev Vygotsky (1896–1934). Like Piaget, Vygotsky saw the child as an active participant in their own development. He differed from Piaget who focused on the content of children's thought, in focusing on functional (practical) aspects. His view was based on the importance of the role of other, more knowledgeable, people. Vygotsky believed that children acquired the means of learning and thinking from the social interaction between themselves and the adults around them. These adults provided the scaffolding (framework) within which a child could acquire greater understanding. Vygotsky placed greater emphasis on language development and that this should be seen in the context of the child's culture and the help and support available within that culture. A central idea of Vygotsky's theory was the 'zone of proximal development'. This refers to the distance between the child's actual development and the level of potential development that they can acquire with support and guidance. Unlike Piaget, who believed that children need to be ready before they are able to learn, Vygotsky argued that adults could and should provide activities for children that were beyond that expected of them – far enough to provide challenge but not so far as to demoralise them.

ACTIVITY 4.3

Consider the case of Carly. Can you identify ways in which Bill is using Vygotskian principles to support Carly's development?

One way in which this is occurring is in the relationship that Bill has developed with Carly – a social interactive relationship that is based on such things as mutual trust, understanding, taking an interest and so on. Rather than assuming that Carly will be able to 'work things out for herself', Bill recognises the need to work together, engaging in mutual activities to develop understanding, with sensitive stimulation by Bill in developing the 'scaffolding' that is required to support Carly's cognitive understanding of her past and future.

Vygotsky places great emphasis on the social interaction of a child's understanding. Consequently as a social worker you will need to have an understanding of the child's race, culture and language and their understanding of what this means to them. You will need to reflect on the past, present and future role and relationships of the adult in the child's life – the role of parents; other adults in the child's life; those of other professionals and in particular your role and relationship with the child.

Social development in middle childhood

In this section we will seek to develop an understanding of how children develop a sense of 'themselves' and how others may view them. In particular we will examine explanations of why children may behave in the way that they do.

The development of self

Young children tend to define themselves through physical characteristics – 'tall', 'short', 'big', 'little'. Children in the middle years increasingly define themselves through social characteristics – for example, 'funny', 'happy', 'sad', and social comparisons – the expectations and reactions of others and what kind of response this generates. This may come as no surprise as children are mixing more with other children and adults, especially within the school environment. A critical part of the development of self is concerned with feelings of self-esteem. Self-esteem is the degree to which children feel accepted and valued by adults and children who are important to them. The development of self-esteem is complex. It is shaped within the child and also by the people around the child.

ACTIVITY **4.4**

Think about the following and try to identify areas in which Richard demonstrates he has low self-esteem.

Richard, aged seven, has had a troubled and turbulent childhood, involving physical and sexual abuse. He has experienced numerous moves in his life. Richard is short and thin for his age. He has been placed with the Jones family for the last three months; plans are in place for the Joneses to adopt Richard. They have found his behaviour difficult and demanding, describing him as 'aggressive' and 'sulky'. At school Richard struggles to read and write as he has missed so much schooling. Although he has additional support he is rude and often aggressive towards his support worker. The other children are scared of Richard so tend to stay away. Richard says that that is okay with him as they are all 'stupid'.

He is good at football but is aggressive when he plays. His teacher says that if he can learn to control his temper on the football pitch he could play for the school team.

According to Susan Harter (1999), self-esteem is based on a balance between what the child would like to be and what they actually think they are. She identified six domains of competence that were important to the child. These are:

- scholastic competence;
- athletic competence;
- physical appearance;
- peer acceptance;
- behavioural conduct;
- general feelings of self-worth.

In the case of Richard you will have been able to identify issues in every area. What matters here is to identify the area that is most important to Richard. In this case we could assume that this may be initially his competency as a footballer. Your role as a social worker and the work of other people who are important in his life would be to help and encourage him in his task; provide emotional support and approval in his achievement and also support in learning that mistakes and failures are acceptable and an inevitable part of learning and can lead to success. The 'behaviours' that Richard exhibits are clear signs of low self-esteem. Children with low self-esteem expect to fail and often show self-defeating behaviour, seeing any success as the result of chance, rather than a result of their own skills and effort. The Joneses will need support and advice in dealing with Richard's behaviour and developing his self-esteem and self-worth. The development of behaviours that promote attachments in the relationship will be crucial (see Chapter 3).

In an extensive study of parent-child relationships and self-esteem, Coopersmith (1967) identified a number of parenting attributes that were associated with boys' high self-esteem. Although his study was based on boys, it is also highly relevant to girls:

- expression of acceptance and affection;
- concern about the child's life and any problems;
- harmony in the home;
- participation in joint family activities;
- availability to give competent, organised help when they need it;
- setting clear and fair rules.

Developing a sense of gender identity

By the time children enter middle childhood they will have developed an understanding of their gender identity and the behaviours associated with this. Differences between boys and girls are sometimes explained by inborn biological differences. Another explanation is that differences that can be observed between girls and boys can be explained through the process of socialisation within their social and cultural settings.

There is no doubt that there is a sex difference determined at birth between boys and girls. They are biologically and physiologically different. These are especially emphasised through puberty. However it would be more realistic to suggest that there is a great deal of variation between children – within sexes and between girls and boys. Studies have suggested some variation between the sexes; for example, girls tend to talk more and in longer sentences in early childhood; boys seem to be better at solving intellectual problems based on numerical reasoning. However these studies are often based on 'averages' and are certainly not applicable to all boys and girls. An alternative view is that differences between the sexes are learned through the roles that are ascribed to them by society. Once they start school children have acquired a sense of being a 'boy' or 'girl'. Most children have been encouraged in activities that are usually ascribed to gender roles – boys involved in physical activities and girls in a more interpersonal world that encourages caring and closeness. During the middle years they learn about more complex ideas of gender roles. While children recognise that individuals can vary in relation to their personal preference, a number of studies identify the 'different' way that girls and boys behave and are socialised into their stereotypical roles.

ACTIVITY 4.5

Denise is 10 and is described as a 'typical girl'.

Liam is 10 and is described as a 'typical boy'.

What kind of behaviours and actions would you expect to see in these children?

COMMENT

We acknowledge that in this exercise we are asking you to stereotype these children and also it does not account for the individual variations for individual children. However it may be that you have been able to identify gender differences. For Denise this would be closer, more intimate friendships and games that would be more 'passive'; she would be neater, more obedient, receiving praise for this kind of behaviour. Liam would tend to be involved in more boisterous games, express himself more aggressively and dominate in games, pastimes and in the classroom. He probably has more freedom in what he is able to do and in relation to travel outside the home.

There are important issues for social workers in gender-stereotyping; limiting behaviour to gender roles can restrict the development of individual identity, skills and competency. Viewing behaviour in terms of gender may result in 'labelling' – 'he's a sissy'; 'she's aggressive'. Boys in particular may demonstrate aggressive, dominating behaviour, finding it hard to express emotions and demonstrate caring actions and skills. Girls may find it difficult to express their individuality and independence. You will recall from Chapter 3 that these are important in developing resilience. As a social worker you will need to support children in expressing their feelings and in developing a positive independent view of themselves. In your work with families, for example through the assessment process, you should be aware of the ways in which the family develop and assign gender roles, for example though a boy 'modelling' the aggressive behaviour of his father; through language and actions which encourage certain behaviours, for example boys to be 'dominant' and girls to be 'passive'. You need to recognise the impact of gender identity on this as being potentially restrictive and stereotypical. Families may need support in identifying the impact that this has on the behaviour of children and the roles within the family. Ways in which you can actively support children are through being a positive role model yourself – modelling behaviours and roles that are non-stereotypical. Other ways include promoting positive images of gender roles through books and play and encouraging non-stereotypical behaviours and activities. You will need to recognise the influence of others, for example, foster carer, adoptive families, residential child care workers, and ensure that you work together in promoting positive role models and images for children.

The influence of the family

It will be clear by now that family actions and reactions (in terms of what they do and do not do), particularly of the main caregivers, have a critical influence on children's growth and development. It is important to recognise that the concept of the 'family' is increasingly being challenged from a stereotypical view of a mother, father and their children. Increasingly children are being raised in different family forms, for example, in lone parent families and reconstituted families. Nearly half the children in England and Wales are not being brought up in traditional families, with the majority being brought up in lone parent families, mostly headed up by the mother. The Office for National Statistics (2005) identified that in 2005, 24 per cent of all dependent children lived in a single parent family, that is nearly one in four children. However, it is also kown that the situation of families is dynamic and diverse.

As a social worker you will play a critical part in assessing, planning and providing appropriate interventions to support families who may be experiencing difficulties. Consequently it is important for you to have an understanding of the role, expectations and values that influence them in supporting the growth and development of their child. See the *National Standard Framework* Standard 2 (DoH, 2004).

CASE STUDY

Ian is 6 and lives with his mother and father. He has recently begun attending the local school, having recently moved into the area with his parents. His teacher has expressed concern about his care and behaviour. Ian is very boisterous and his concentration is poor, finding it difficult to concentrate on any activity for any length of time. The other children avoid him as he is so boisterous and will often punch and kick to get his own way. His physical care has been poor; for example his hygiene is poor and he has had no dental care. He appears to have no sense of danger; for example being unaware of the dangers on the road. You have been asked to assess the parents 'Parenting Capacity' as part of The Framework for the Assessment of Children in Need and their Families (DoH, 2000). What are the kind of questions you would wish to address?

COMMENT

The concerns of Ian's teacher raise a number of questions and would suggest that his mother may need some support; for example you need to understand Ian's history and background and his mother's ability to meet Ian basic needs. The grid 'Parenting Capacity and Thresholds of Intervention' may help you in thinking through areas of concerns and thinking about the range of questions this raises.

Table 4.1 Parenting capacity and thresholds of intervention (adapted from DoH, 2000)

Area of assessment	Expectations	May require intervention if...	Complex needs	Immediate concerns
Basic care	Provision of child's physical, medical, optical, and dental care; provision of food and drink, warmth, shelter, clean and appropriate clothing; adequate personal hygiene.	Basic care is not provided consistently; food, warmth and other basics not always available; parent struggling without support and/or adequate resources; young inexperienced parent(s).	Basic care is frequently inconsistent; food, warmth and other basics not often available; large family with poor coping skills; very young inexperienced parent(s); parent's mental health problems or substance misuse significantly affect care of child/young person; parents have struggled to care for previous child/young persons.	Basic care is rarely consistent; parents have seriously abused/neglected the child/young person; food, warmth and other basics frequently not available; supervision is haphazard; previous child/young persons have been removed from parent's home; parent's own needs mean they cannot keep child/young person safe.
Ensuring safety	Protection from harm and danger; protection from unsafe adults/other children; protection from self harm; recognising hazards.	Haphazard supervision, unaware of child/young person's whereabouts; haphazard use of safety equipment e.g. fireguards; insufficient awareness of dangers to the child/young person; inappropriate childcare arrangements and/or too many different carers; inappropriate frequent visits to doctor/casualty.	Instability and domestic violence in the home; absence of appropriate supervision; inappropriate care arrangements such as succession of carers.	Level of supervision is inadequate given child/young person's age; parent unable to restrict access to home by dangerous adults; chronic and serious domestic violence involving the child/young person.
Emotional warmth	Child's positive sense of being valued and own racial and cultural identity; secure stable and affectionate relationship with adults; adults providing sensitive appropriate response; demonstration of warmth, praise and encouragement.	Inconsistent responses to child/young person by parent(s); child/young person not able to develop other positive relationships; parents struggling to have their own emotional needs met.	Child/young person receives erratic or inconsistent care; parental instability affects capacity to nurture; parents own emotional needs starting to compromise those of the child/young person; some relationship difficulties.	Low warmth, high criticism; parents inconsistent, highly critical or apathetic towards child/young person; parents own emotional experiences impacting on their ability to meet the child/young person's needs; relationships characterised by rejection.

Continued

Table 4.1 Continued

Area of assessment	Expectations	May require intervention if...	Complex needs	Immediate concerns
Stimulation	Provision of encouragement and cognitive stimulation; responding appropriately to a child's language and questions; encouraging play and promoting educational opportunities; encouraging success and ensuring school attendance or equivalent opportunity.	Child/young person spends considerable time alone; child/young person is not often exposed to new experiences; limited access to leisure facilities.	Child/young person receiving little positive stimulation, with lack of new experiences or activities; restricted access, if any, to leisure facilities; child/young person under undue parental pressure to achieve/aspire.	No constructive leisure time activities; no access to leisure facilities; no relevant stimulation or inappropriate for age.
Guidance and boundaries	Demonstrating and modelling appropriate behaviour towards the child; control of emotions and interactions with others; developing in the child an internal model of moral values and conscience; develop appropriate social behaviour; not being over protective regarding exploratory and learning experiences; boundaries to include social problem solving, anger management, consideration for others, effective discipline and shaping of behaviour.	No constructive leisure time activities; no access to leisure facilities; no relevant stimulation or inappropriate for age.	Child/young person has multiple carers, but no significant relationships to any of them.	Child/young person beyond parental control; family life may be chaotic; child/young person has no-one to care for him/her; multiple carers, with no consistency.
Stability	Providing a stable family environment to ensure secure attachments and optimal development; ensuring consistency of emotional warmth to prevent disruption; adaptation by parent to child's developmental progress; maintaining child's contact with significant others.	Child/young person behaves in an anti-social way in the neighbourhood e.g. petty crime; parent/carer offers inconsistent boundaries.	Erratic or inadequate guidance provided; parents struggle/refuse to set effective boundaries; parent does not offer a good role model, e.g. by behaving in an anti-social way; child/young person regularly behaves in an anti-social way in the neighbourhood.	No effective boundaries; child/young person out of control in the community.

Families serve a number of essential functions.

- Meeting physical need by providing such things as food, clothes, shelter.

- Encouraging cognitive development through supporting the mastering of skills, for example academic skills by motivating and guiding their learning.

- Supporting the development of self-esteem through praise and encouragement. Particularly as children become more cognitively aware they become more self-critical. Families need to help children feel loved, competent and assertive in what they do.

- Nurturing relationships with others through encouraging relationships with people such as other relatives, adults and children. They need to provide the time, space and opportunities to achieve this.

- Giving harmony and stability by providing a safe, secure routine, with appropriate guidance and boundaries, that is protective and predictable.

RESEARCH SUMMARY

You may find the following documents helpful in further developing your understanding of issues in relation to parenting capacity:

Social Exclusion Unit (SEU) (2008) Reaching out: Think families. *London: Cabinet Office.*

This document provides an analysis and themes from the Families At Risk Review, *asking: what more can be done to improve the outcomes for families who continue to experience multiple problems. It particularly focuses upon multiple problems faced by parents that have an impact upon the entire family.*

SCIE (2009) Think child, think parent, think family: A guide to parental mental health and child welfare. *London: SCIE.*

This guide is about working with parents who have mental health problems and their children. It provides guidance on policy and practice and makes recommendations for key areas of professional education, workforce development and research. It also provides links to useful resources and contact details of relevant organisations. Available from www.scie.org.uk/publications.

As a social worker you will be assessing the negative and positive parenting capacity of the caregiver and the impact on their child. You will need to take into account the ability of the parent to meet the development needs of the child both in the past, currently and in the future – the development perspective will therefore be key. In addition you will need to put the parents' behaviour and competence in the context of the broader issues within the child's world – the ecological perspective.

RESEARCH SUMMARY

Diane Baumrind (1971) studied patterns of child rearing through a combination of four dimensions:

- *expressions of warmth ranging from very affectionate to quite cold;*
- *strategies for discipline, which may involve explanation, criticism, persuasion and/or physical punishment;*
- *communications, which ranged from extensive listening to demands for silence;*
- *expectations of maturity, how much responsibility and self-control were demanded.*

She identified three specific combinations.

- *The authoritarian parent is high in control and maturity demands, but low in nurturance and communication. They think it is important for the child to learn to behave properly.*
- *The permissive parent is high in nurturance but is low in maturity demands, control and communication. Learning happens best through conversation.*
- *The authoritative parent is high in nurturance, maturity demands, control and communication.*

Maccoby and Martin (1983) have identified fourth and fifth types – the neglecting, uninvolved parent, in which the parents do not seem to care at all and indulgent parents, in which the parents accommodate the child's every whim. Baumrind's studies have come to the basic conclusion that:

- *children raised by authoritarian parents are likely to be quiet, conscientious and obedient, however they can feel guilty or depressed;*
- *children raised by permissive parents lack self-control, especially within friendships and are least happy;*
- *children raised by authoritative parents are likely to be successful, happy, intelligent, articulate and generous.*

The ecological approach

The focus on the last two chapters has been on identifying the different theories and processes as they apply to individual children. Most textbooks written 30 years ago would have emphasised the individual child and in particular the role of the parent in shaping the child. Whilst these are still important, we recognise that the development of the child involves and is influenced by more complex interaction with the 'social' world. This section will focus on bringing together the themes and issues from our study of childhood into a framework that seeks to recognise the influence and interactions between all of the different systems involved in the child's growth and development – the ecological approach. This is particularly important in supporting your practice in assessment. This is the model which underpins the *Framework for the assessment of children in need and their families* (Department of Health, 2000).

You will recall that we introduced the ecological approach, specifically the work of Urie Bronfenbrenner (1979), in Chapters 1 and 2. The ecological approach is based on the principle that the development and behaviour of individuals can only be fully understood in the context of the environment in which they live. The context is made up of a series of interrelated systems that mutually influence and are influenced by each other. You should re-read this section to remind yourself of the different systems within his model.

ACTIVITY *4.6*

Having re-read the explanation of Bronfenbrenner's ecological model, use the model to outline your own systems. Think about how they influence and impact on your own life and how the systems interact.

You may have found this challenging and complex. Thinking about each of the individual systems and their influence on your life is in itself difficult. This becomes even more complex when you have to consider how they interact with each other requiring you to consider and interpret a range of information, facts and personal experiences and opinions. For example you will have recognised and considered the direct and indirect influence of parts of the system, such as those in the macro system. These may not have a day-to-day influence on your life, as the micro system does, but strongly influence the direction and choices within it; for example the political issue in relation to student grants and loans may impact on you. Hopefully it will show you that there is a strong interrelationship between each of the parts that make up 'the system'. System refers to the mutual influences that the different parts (the child, the family, friends, neighbours, community and wider society) have upon one another. The ecological model is based on a systems framework. It can be described as a 'holistic model'; it focuses on the assessment of the ways in which the different parts interact on and with each other; for example the child's developmental needs, the capacity of the parents to respond and the wider environmental context in which this occurs. The other important aspect of the system is the 'chronosystem' – the aspect of time and how this impacts on development.

We are now going to consider the application of Bronfenbrenner's ecological model and how an understanding of child growth and development can contribute to the assessment of the child's needs.

ACTIVITY *4.7*

Using the following case study of Kenny and his family, and using the ecological model, apply theories of development that we have covered so far. A good starting point would be for you to start with Kenny's life course line, noting the key events in Kenny's life. (You will recall you completed your own life course line in Chapter 1.)

COMMENT

Clearly, based on limited information, it is difficult to identify all of the issues and you may have had to make assumptions based on this limited information. You need to talk to a range of people in forming a judgement – Kenny, his grandmother, the school and others. Hopefully you will have identified a number of themes and issues.

CASE STUDY

Kenny, aged 11, is described by his mother Christine, aged 29, as 'difficult, demanding and out of control'. Christine asks for your support in managing Kenny's behaviour, as she fears that as he approaches adolescence she will no longer be able to manage him. Kenny lives with his mother, her partner Ray and their children, Steven, aged six and Bethany, aged four. Christine and Ray have been together for seven years.

Christine describes Kenny as an 'accident'. At the time she was dependent on drugs, earning money as a prostitute to support her addiction. All of her money was spent on drugs. She was living with Greg, Kenny's father, who was dealing in drugs. Kenny was born eight weeks prematurely and was drug-dependent. He spent three months in hospital. Christine visited him infrequently, continuing with her drug use and earning money through prostitution. Kenny was a difficult baby. He cried a lot and was difficult to settle. He was slow to walk and talk. Kenny would be left with a number of different carers, often left in his playpen for hours. Greg has a history of violence and would frequently beat and punch Christine. At the age of two, Christine's mother, Judy, was increasingly concerned about Kenny particularly as Greg was being increasingly abusive towards Kenny, striking him on the face, pushing and shoving him, shouting and calling him names. Judy was concerned with the conditions in the home – the lack of furniture, toys and food in the house. With Christine's agreement, she took Kenny to live with her. He lived with his grandmother for a year during which time he appeared to benefit from the stability and routine. Kenny gained in height and weight, developing his language and play skills, attended the local playgroup where he enjoyed playing with the other children.

After a year and having left Greg, Christine took Kenny to live with her in a flat close to her mother. Christine describes this as a difficult time as she sought to withdraw from the drugs on which she had become so dependent. She was often depressed, resulting in Kenny spending lots of time in his room playing with his toys. Greg would visit on occasions. However their relationship remained volatile. Christine describes her mother as a great support, continuing to help her with Kenny's care. Kenny started school at four. However he found it difficult to settle; he was slow to learn and was unpopular with the other children. With support from the teaching staff, though, Kenny quickly learned to read and write and developed skills as a good footballer. Christine describes meeting Ray as 'the turning point' in her life. Ray, a butcher, and Christine began to live together in his house in another part of the city. Kenny missed his grandmother and did not settle in his new school. However with support from his teachers he began to make progress, showing himself to be an able student. Christine tells you that despite all the problems they have with him he continues to attend school and is in the school football team. However she is concerned that as he moves to senior school this may change. She admits that she does not have much contact with the school and does not bother to ask Kenny anything about how he is getting on.

Kenny dislikes Ray, frequently ignoring him. His mother is caught between the two relationships and admits that she often sides with Ray to attempt to 'keep the peace'. Kenny refuses to join in family activities and now, Christine tells you, they just leave him behind as it 'is easier than getting into a fight'. She says that Ray's job means that they have a nice house in a 'good area' and they have made lots of friends. Christine has a part-time

Continued

job in the local supermarket and tells you that she has made many friends as a result of this job. She does not want Kenny to spoil this, particularly considering the life she used to have. With the birth of Steven and Bethany, Kenny spent more and more time out of the house. By the age of 10, Kenny was mixing with older boys hanging around the local park. They frequently 'dare him' to do things – smoking, annoying the neighbours by shouting abuse at them, hitting other children. Local residents often call the police complaining about the young people hanging about the park and the vandalism that they believe they cause. However one of the local residents has approached the council for support in setting up a football team and skateboard area within the park. The local council are 'sympathetic'. Recently the other boys have been encouraging Kenny to shoplift small items for them. One of the boys stole a car and when Kenny refused to get in the car, they called him 'chicken'.

Within the wider macro-system you may have considered the response of wider society to children and young people and the issue of resources available. You may have considered your role as a social worker in working with children and families and the systems that underpin this. For example, the legal aspects, in this case the duties placed on local authorities and others under the *Children Act 1989*, in particular your duties as a social worker in relation to the *Framework for the assessment of children in need and their families* (2000) and the *Common Assessment Framework* (DfES, 2006a). Additionally you may consider the attitudes of the public to children in trouble with the law, the legal and political response (for example the setting up of the Youth Justice Boards and Youth Offender panels) and the response of agencies to children (for example the work of the Youth Offending Teams, YOT) (**www.yjb.gov.uk**).

Within the exo-system you may have considered the impact of Christine's and Ray's social support, for example friendships and work. Whilst not directly involved, the child may still be strongly affected. In this case you may have recognised the social position that Christine now feels that she has achieved and the network and friends that she has established. When you explored Kenny's life from a chronological perspective you should have noted the potential impact of the different exo-systems in which he lived; for example the impact in early life of the chaotic lifestyle of Christine's (and Greg's) drug use.

Within the meso-system you will have been able to draw on a range of theories and issues in relation to child development. Some are listed below.

- The development of the unborn child – impact of drug use and mother's lifestyle.

- The feeling in relation to the pregnancy and the impact this had following the birth – issues of bonding and attachment, including the impact of these throughout Kenny's life and currently.

- Developmental issues, particularly concerns when under five, for example the development of fine and motor skills.

- Cognitive perspectives – how confident and competent is Kenny in his learning?
  - impact of early life in meeting the different stages;
  - six to 12 years – concerns for ability to grasp the logic of classification and conservation.
- Social and emotional development – communication was poor up to two years of age; influence of grandmother on Kenny's life; issues of resilience and vulnerability.
- Issues in relation to child protection – impact on Kenny's emotional, social and physical development.
- Psychoanalytical theory:
  - impact of early life in meeting the different stages;
  - industry versus inferiority, for example, mother's lack of interest and contact with school.
- Styles of parenting, e.g. Baumrind's study.
- Gender issues – exploring Christine's perception that 'boys will be boys'.
- Behaviour and aspects of social learning theory – issues of 'learned' behaviour e.g. early modelling by Greg.
- Exploration of issues in relation to moral development.

You may also wish to consider what other issues you might need to consider if Kenny's family was from a different culture, for example African-Caribbean. What other issues would you need to consider if Kenny had a disability, for example Down's Syndrome?

REFLECTION POINT

- *What do I know, or can I do now, that I did not know or could not do before I did this section of studying?*
- *Is there anything I do not understand or want to explore further?*
- *What else do I need to know to extend my professional development and learning in this area?*

CHAPTER SUMMARY

The period of middle childhood in developmental terms is one of relative stability, growing gradually and steadily and consolidating and developing the skills acquired in early childhood. They develop a wider view of the world, associated with independence outside of the home, particularly school and the development of friendships. The transition from home to school coincides with the mastering of new intellectual and social skills, taking in of new ideas and dimensions of the world. Through social interaction children draw on and build on their feelings of self-esteem and self-worth. Children experience the socialisation and social behaviour that are linked to their gender roles. Individual behaviour can be attributed to individual temperament but also patterns of learned behaviour and how the world is represented to them. This can be linked to moral development. The family continue to exert important influences on the continuing growth and development of the child. Finally we have attempted to draw together some of the themes and issues from the last two chapters into the ecological model, representing the different interfaces and influences between all of the systems in which the child exists. In the next chapter we explore the world of the adolescent as the transition from childhood to adolescence.

Aldgate, J, Jones, D, Rose, W and Jeffery, C (2006) *The developing world of the child*. London: Jessica Kingsley.

This contemporary text has been written to reflect current national initiatives and acknowledged desirable outcomes for children. The text is structured into three parts: the first offering chapters that explore a range of theoretical perspectives on child development; the second part being dedicated to particular age-related phases of childhood; and the final part being related to direct work with children.

Howarth, J (2009) (ed.) *The child's world: The comprehensive guide to assessing children in need*. 2nd edition. London: Jessica Kingsley.

This contemporary text focuses on assessing children in need and their families and integrates practice, policy and theory to produce a comprehensive and multidisciplinary guide to all aspects of assessment.

Lindon, J (2008) *Safeguarding children and young people: Child protection 0–18*. 3rd edition. London: Hodder Arnold.

This book covers recent developments in legislation and guidance. The book examines the approach to daily practice for professionals taking responsibility for children and young people in early years' provision, schools, out-of-school settings, play and leisure facilities.

Lindon, J (2010) *Understanding child development linking theory and practice*. 2nd edition. London: Hodder Arnold.

This book examines child development making a link between theories and learning and practice.

Every Child Matters: Change for Children www.everychildmatters.gov.uk

This is an extensive website which forms a useful starting point for further study and reading in relation to the contemporary policy agenda for social work and interprofessional practice with children, young people, their families and carers. The site is vast with a comprehensive range of links.

National Society for the Prevention of Cruelty of Children (NSPCC) www.nscpcc.org.uk

The 'Inform' section of this website provides some excellent and up-to-date information and resources in relation to children in need and children who have been abused and their families.

Chapter 5

Using life course development knowledge in social work practice with adolescents

Introduction

In this chapter you will consider human life course development in respect of young people in their teenage years, adolescence.

This chapter will enable you to develop your understanding and ability to critique theories that explain human development, as you will explore a range of approaches for explaining the period of adolescence. The chapter will start by considering how adolescence is defined and experienced in the context of our society. The construction of adolescence in our society can be seen to be partially influenced by political, legislative and policy rhetoic. The whole chapter therefore is set within the context of contemporary strategic developments, the most significant of which is *Youth Matters* (DfES, 2005b).

This document, which focuses on young people ages between 13 and 19 years, builds on the principles of *Every Child Matters* (DfES, 2004). The document uses the term 'teenagers' throughout and proposes a balance of opportunity, support and challenge to ensure successful transition to adulthood.

Through consideration of the transition into adulthood, changing roles and the growth of independence and maturity, you will learn about social development in adolescence. Issues related to physical changes, including puberty, sexuality and growth, will be explored as examples of biological development. This chapter will then look at how behavioural and social learning theories explain human development through the teenage years. There will be a specific section that focuses on theoretical perspectives in relation to the development of behaviour. You will explore moral development. You will briefly consider individual issues in relation to adolescence.

Throughout the chapter you will have opportunities to consider your own thoughts about being a teenager and the importance of each individual's life story within a life course perspective. You will look at how some examples of individual difference, such as gender, race, culture and disability, can impact on an individual's experience of adolescence. Therefore, having developed your understanding of life course development in adolescence from a range of perspectives, the chapter reinforces the view that although there are trends and expected changes within this period of life, there are no pre-determined pathways that lay out predictable ways in which the transition to adulthood will affect all people. The only way of understanding an individual's development and the issues that adolescence may hold for them is to listen to their life-story, as they tell it and perceive it. It is important for social workers to value the individual's own narrative and biographical account.

Defining adolescence

Adolescent development starts with the physical changes associated with puberty, which begin the physical changes to the body. Whilst these are important, it is the critical processes of development of 'self', the search for identity and the development of relationships, for example with friends, and the changing nature of relationships, for example with families, that are a central feature of this period of an individual's life.

The context of adolescence

ACTIVITY 5.1

Let us begin by looking at your experience of adolescence. When did you perceive yourself as beginning adolescence? When did you consider that your adolescence ended? What were you like as an adolescent? Did you perceive it as a happy time? A difficult time? What were the good things about being an adolescent? What were the things that were difficult? Did you have lots of friends? Did you have one particular friend? Did you have a group of friends? Did you have a particular group 'identity'? How did the adults around you help you? What did they get right? What did they get wrong? Do you consider your experience of adolescence is the same/different as compared to adolescents growing up in contemporary society? Why? How does your experience compare with that of other generations, for example your parents' and grandparents'?

Obviously everyone's experience is unique and a wide range of family and social circumstances can influence the experience of adolescence. However, almost certainly, you will have perceived it as a period of immense change. You may have been able to recognise that as adolescence covers a span of some years, there is a significant difference between those experiences and feelings that you had at the onset of adolescence to the experiences and feelings as you neared the end of adolescence. If you had the opportunity to compare your experiences with previous generations, you may have been able to identify similar themes, for example, around friendships and relationships. You may have been able to acknowledge the challenges and opportunities for young people growing up into today's society. Deciding when your adolescence ended will have been very individual, for example it may have been associated with leaving home, getting a job, the start of a relationship.

You have considered changes in terms of transitions or phases within a person's life course development in previous chapters. Adolescence as a period of life is often seen as a whole period of transition, the transition from childhood to adulthood, probably the most challenging and difficult period of life in terms of development. Important biological, psychological and social changes take place. All adolescents confront the same development tasks – adjusting to changes in their bodies and the challenge of their developing sexuality and new ways of thinking, as they strive for their own identity, emotional maturity and independence. Consequently relationships, particularly with the family, will be subject to adaptation and change. However the timing of these changes vary between individuals, influenced by such things as gender, genes and culture. For some young people the challenges of adolescence result in choices, which lead to a number of problems, and some problems peak at this time.

We recognise that the social context of adolescence is considerably different from previous generations. In a traditional society where social change may be slow and the same values are held, for example moral, political and religious values, there may be greater acceptance and integration of these views and values for the adolescence. In some cultures the transition from childhood to adolescence is marked by a rite of passage, a ceremony marking this transition, based on strong cultural cohesion in relation to roles and responsibilities. However we recognise that contemporary society holds many challenges, for example rapid social change, broader values and goals and the expansion of choice in our society. Consequently we need to be familiar with a number of perspectives on adolescence. We need to view adolescence as a series of passages – biological, psychological, social and cultural. The *National Service Framework* (DoH, 2004) Standard 4 relates to 'Growing up into adulthood'. Within this it is acknowledged that:

> *Adolescence is a time when patterns of behaviour and use of services are developed and these tend to be continued during adult life making it an important time to promote engagement with advice and services. Young people want services which are flexible in approach and response to their needs.*

Theories and explanations of development in adolescence

In the first section of this chapter you thought about how you might define your adolescence in terms of the main characteristics or features that it encompassed and how it may be the same and/or different for today's adolescents. Adolescence as a period of development may be considered for a range of different perspectives that focus on biological, psychological and social aspects of development. We shall now explore each of these approaches in more depth, using models from key theorists and case examples. You should note, however, that whilst you will look at each approach separately here, it is important for social workers to take a holistic approach to understanding life course development in adolescence. Therefore, in developing your understanding of this period of life, you should be mindful that an individual's life course development and life experiences are affected by a range of factors, which include their experience of development so far and the social and economic aspects, cultural, historical, psychological, cognitive and physiological influences. Additionally it is important to consider the unique experience of the individual; it is common for adolescence to be 'stereotyped', for example as rebellious and difficult, and defined by its problems.

Biological development in adolescence

ACTIVITY **5.2**

Think about young people in their teenage years, perhaps reflecting on your own teenage years or those of members of your family or friends. List the physical/biological changes that may happen through this period of life.

You may have associated a whole range of physical changes that occur during adolescence. Puberty is the period of rapid changes that occur as the person moves from childhood and begins adolescence. Hormones affect every aspect of growth and development and the level of certain hormones rises naturally during adolescence, primarily causing increased sexual interest and mood swings. A number of physical changes take place. There is a rapid acceleration in growth in height and weight, a growth spurt – a sudden, uneven and unpredictable surge in size of almost every part of the body. This is initially experienced as an increase in weight, followed by an increase in height and strength. There are changes in the body in relation to the distribution of fat and muscle. During puberty proportions of fat rise among girls and decline among boys, while the proportion of weight that is muscle rises in boys and declines in girls. It is important to remember that these are generalisations; for example, females who are 'athletic' may not show such variations. The consequence of this may be that adolescents may appear 'out of proportion' and may appear clumsy and awkward as their bodies change and they come to terms with these changes.

The hormonal changes associated with puberty result in the important changes that are associated with sexual maturity. Adolescents develop sexual characteristics, the gonads (sexual organs), testes in males and the ovaries in females, and there are changes in the genitals and breasts, and the growth of genital, facial and body hair. For girls, menarche, the beginning of menstruation, is a relatively late development, with a great deal of development taking place before the girl begins to menstruate, with the full reproductive capacity not being achieved for several years. It is difficult to predict the age at which individuals may experience the changes associated with puberty. The beginning of puberty can start as early as eight for girls and for boys about two years later. Some individuals will have completed their cycle of changes before others have begun. This is due to individual differences due to genetic factors and also environmental influences. There are variations in the onset of menarche across different countries, for example girls are likely to start menarche earlier in Western Europe than in the African continent. This is influenced by differences in affluence and, consequently, the impact of economic disadvantage, such as poor nutrition and health related issues.

Increases in hormone levels, especially testosterone, cause rapid arousal of emotions – from feelings of 'high' to 'low'. Hormones increase interest in sex and sexual activity. Whilst the erratic, powerful impact of hormones has a significant impact on the adolescent, the social context of their development will also have a significant impact as they are influenced by the cultural context in which they are raised.

ACTIVITY 5.3

Think about your reaction to the following. How would you advise these young people?

- *Jed, aged 15, says, 'I am frightened. I like girls but just as friends. I find that I am sexually attracted to boys. I really fancy Paul but I don't know how to tell him. What if he does not feel the same way? I would be so ashamed.'*
- *Dale, aged 14, has Down's Syndrome. His mother has expressed concern about discussing sex, in particular masturbation, with him.*
- *Jessie, aged 13, tells you about her boyfriend, Brad, aged 17. 'I really love him and he loves me. We want to be together for ever.' She tells you that she wants advice about contraception.*
- *Ali and Sara, both aged 15, have unprotected sex. Ali 'prefers it' and Sara thinks that having a baby would be 'cool' and bring them closer together.*
- *Clare, aged 15, has been with her foster carers for a year. Prior to that she was in a children's home for two years. Clare goes out every evening and despite rules about the time she should come in, ignores these and comes in when she 'feels like it'. The foster carers express concern about her promiscuity. Recently they heard her talking on her mobile, arranging to meet a man and agreeing a price of £25.*

Naturally, individual reactions will vary – you may consider sharing your thoughts with someone else. As a social worker you will need to be prepared to respond to a range of issues and concerns. The critical issue is to be open to the experience and concerns of the young person, listening and respecting their issues, being non-judgemental. There may be conflicts with your personal beliefs, for example a religious belief. You need to acknowledge this and consider how this may conflict with and influence your professional values and practice. Seeking advice, for example from colleagues and other professionals, and discussion in professional supervision, should be used to explore conflicts and difficulties that you have and feel.

There may be a number of other physical changes that you have thought of. However, it is important that you appreciate that whilst many of these biological changes appear to be common-place, that does not mean that as we age these changes can be predicted or are to be considered inevitable.

Social development in adolescence

All societies distinguish between children and adults. The period of transition between these periods associated with adolescence requires the individual to reconsider and redefine themselves and their capabilities and make choices as they encounter their new social status.

The process of development allows for greater autonomy; the development of more mature and independent relationships from their carers and adolescents spend increasing time with their peers, providing the opportunity to make independent decisions, with fewer adults present. The peer group plays an important part in the development of the individual's identity, changes in our self-concepts and self-image. As adolescents have broader intellectual capacity providing new ways of thinking about problems, values and relationships, this gives the opportunity to think about themselves and the persona they are becoming. Erikson (1995) recognised this as the critical crisis of adolescence in the eight stages of development – identity versus role confusion. He believed that the successful resolution of this depends on how the individual resolved the previous crisis of childhood. This period is critical in making sense of the future. Erikson believed the key to this is the interactions that the adolescent has with others – peers, families, institutions, especially school, society. Forging an identity is a social as well as a mental process.

Erikson suggests that the search for identity is ongoing during adolescence and they may experience more than one stage.

- Foreclosure – premature identity formation in which the adolescent adopts parents' or societies' roles and values without questioning them.

- Negative identity – opposite that which is expected, which is taken on as rebellious defiance. Ogbu (1993) identified one version – oppositional identity in which the adolescent adopts and exaggerates a negative stereotype.

- Identity diffusion – a situation in which the adolescent does not seem to know or care what their identity is. Almost every adolescent will experience diffusion at some stage.

- Identity moratorium – a pause in identity formation that allows the young person to explore alternatives without making a choice.

- Identity achievement – the achievement of identity and/or the stage at which the person feels that they are 'unique', through assimilation of past experiences and future plans.

(Steinberg, 1993)

You may recognise these stages in adolescents you know, friends that you knew as adolescents or even yourself. Let us consider the potential implications for your practice.

ACTIVITY 5.4

Think back to the case study of Clare in Activity 5.3. What stage would you describe Clare as being in? Consider how you might support Clare in making alternative choices.

It could be suggested that Clare is undergoing negative identity or identity diffusion. What is clear is that her behaviour is generating significant concern for her well-being and concerns about her feelings about herself. Understanding the impact of Clare's past experiences, particularly her developmental experiences, on her current view of herself is essential in making an assessment of Clare's current behaviour and needs and supporting her foster carers in caring for her. You need to listen to Clare and gain an understanding of her perception, wishes and feelings. You will need to gain an understanding of other people's perception of Clare, for example her teachers, and how they might support her and you. She will need considerable support in building her self-esteem and self-worth and in identifying alternative opportunities to develop other choices to her current lifestyle.

Two important parts of identity development are ethnic identity development (Paludi, 2002) and gender role identity. Between the ages of three and six years children generally think about ethnic difference in physical terms and they do not necessarily see race as a fixed or stable attribute. Between the ages of six and ten years children generally think that race is a matter of ancestry that affects not only appearance but also one's diet, language and leisure activities. Between 10 and 14 years of age, they make the link to social class and are aware of connections for example, between race and income, race and neighbourhood (Rathus, 2008).

RESEARCH SUMMARY

Phinney (1993) describes three stages in the development of ethnicity:

- *Unexamined ethic identity. Lack of exploration of ethnic identity. Existing models suggest that minority subjects initially accept the values and attitudes of the majority culture. This includes internalised negative views of their own group held by the majority.*

- *Ethnic identity search/Moratorium. The initial stage of ethnic identity is conceptualised as continuing until adolescents encounter a situation that initiates an ethnic identity search.*

- *Ethnic identity achievement. The ideal outcome of the identity process, characterised by a clear, confident sense of one's own ethnicity. Identity achievement corresponds to acceptance and internalisation of one's ethnicity.*

You may like to consider the potential impact of these issues for your practice using the case study opposite.

Think about the following and consider how you would respond.

Chris, aged 14, has been in a children's home for a year. Chris' mother is white and his father is African-Caribbean. Another child at the home has been making racist comments and bullying him. Chris expresses confusion and anxiety about feeling that he does not belong anywhere.

Chris will need support and guidance in acknowledging and coming to terms with his emerging sense of self as a person and the impact of his cultural and racial identity. The significance of ethnicity and culture on adolescents' self-esteem, self-concept and emotional development is highlighted by Paludi (2002). As a social worker you should be aware of any low expectations that you may have, for example about children in the looked after system and children from different cultures, and of ways in which you may, even inadvertently, communicate these. You need to ensure that Chris has positive images of his racial origin conveyed to him, not just by you but also by the others around him, for example the staff at the children's home. Racial comments and attitudes need firmly challenging. You may need to consider the environment in which Chris lives, for example the relationships and friendships that he has that promote his positive well-being and image of himself. You could enlist the support of his school in supporting Chris in his interaction with others and in learning about promoting positive images of people from different cultures and ethnic backgrounds. Above all you need to listen to Chris' experience. Using the narrative approach – that is listening to Chris' 'story' – will enable you to make links for Chris between his history and his personal understanding.

Gender, and the development of sexual identity, is a critical part of one's identity. As Cobb (1995) suggests, an individual cannot simply see themselves as a child to which they add sexual feelings and identity but must revise their concept of self. Originally experts such as Erikson and Freud believed that although sexual identity may be confused during puberty, gender identity meant identifying oneself as a heterosexual male or female by adulthood. However later research suggests that sexual orientation and gender identity are much more varied than a simple male–female division. Additionally in contemporary society, the individual has more choices to make as the 'rules' that governed this behaviour are increasingly challenged. Gender is a critical component of one's identity. From birth children are socialised and stereotyped into their gender roles. Boys tend to be encouraged to be strong, brave, logical, and independent, and girls are expected to be gentle, sociable and co-operative. Many of the sexual differences identified in adolescence may in part be due to biological reasons; however they are also due to acceleration in their socialisation into their gender roles. It is suggested that the issue is not one of achieving a mix between female and male qualities and roles but rather achieving 'sex-role transcendence'. This refers to the capacity to look beyond sex-roles and to make use of strengths and talents, regardless of your biological sex (Katz, 1979).

RESEARCH SUMMARY

- *Although the rates have dropped England's teenage pregnancy rate is one of the highest in Western Europe, with over 40,000 under-18 conceptions in 2007.*
- *20 per cent of under-18 conceptions are repeat pregnancies.*
- *Babies of teenage mothers have a 60 per cent higher risk of dying in their first year and have a significantly increased risk of living in poverty, achieving less at school and being unemployed in later life.*
- *Teenage mothers can experience poor emotional health and well-being and are three times more likely to suffer from post-natal depression and experience poor mental health for up to three years after the birth.*
- *Teenage pregnancy is both a cause and result of exclusion, poverty and inequality.*

(Teenage Pregnancy Independent Advisory Group, Annual Report 2008/2009)

Growing up in disadvantaged circumstances (for example, living in social housing and in low income households) was a predictor of young parenthood. In addition, individual childhood attributes such as poor reading ability, having a conduct disorder and having a mother with low educational aspirations for her child were also predictive factors. These five factors combined to increase the probability of having a teen birth from 1 per cent, when none of these risk factors was present, to 31 per cent when all five were present. In males they increased the probability of being a father at age 22 or under from 2 per cent to 23 per cent.

(Berrington, A, Stevenson, J, Ingham, R, with Borgoni, R, Cobos Hernández, MI and Smith, PWF (2005) Consequences of teenage parenthood: Pathways which minimise the long term negative impacts of teenage childbearing)

In a study by Wiggins, et al. (2007) many teenage parents report positive experiences. For some, the pregnancy was either planned or wanted. For others, this was not overtly the case at the time, but in retrospect their teenage pregnancy came to be viewed as a positive occurrence. Much that was negative about the experience of teenage parenthood for the mothers, the fathers and the children resulted from factors related to their socially excluded lives rather than the teenage pregnancy per se.

- *Disliking school is linked to greater risk of teenage pregnancy.*
- *Violence in school and the home is an important risk factor for teenage pregnancy.*
- *Most teenage mothers felt that any sex education they had received at school and at home had been inadequate.*
- *The key factors that characterised the lives of those mothers who had done well were: support from family; having a positive partner relationship; developing a career or having employment they liked; and the passage of time since the birth.*

(Wiggins, M, Oakley, A, Sawtell, M, Austerberry, H, Clemens, F and Elbourne, D (2007) Teenage parenthood and social exclusion: A multi-method study.)

The Teenage Pregnancy Strategy (DfCSF, 2010) outlines the Government's strategic response to these issues.

All these reports are available from:
www.dcsf.gov.uk/everychildmatters/healthandwellbeing/teenagepregnancy

Psychological approaches to development in adolescence

In this section we are going to explore the concept of autonomy. We will explore different explanations for how and why adolescents respond to situations through their behaviour, particularly through an exploration of the concept of autonomy.

The development of autonomy in adolescence is gradual and progressive. Steinberg (1993) identifies three types of autonomy:

- emotional autonomy – aspects of interdependence in relation to changes in the individual's close relationships, for example, changes in expression of affection, interactions and patterns of power;

- value autonomy – changes in the adolescent's concept of moral, political, ideological and religious issues;

- behavioural autonomy – changes in decision-making abilities and changes in conformity and susceptibility to influence, for example from parents and peers.

Thom et al. (2007) discuss the concepts of 'dependence–autonomy' within their chapters which develop a critical analysis of children and young people's development and the impact of risk.

The establishment and maintenance of a healthy sense of autonomy is a lifelong concern from early childhood; for example you may recall that Erikson (1995) identified the development of autonomy as a stage that happens in the second and third year of life, into adult life. Developing autonomy during adolescence is more acute as it involves a range of interdependent processes placing adolescence in new roles and responsibilities, which require choices and decisions. Physical changes associated with puberty require choices about such things as sexuality and the development of sexual relationships. Cognitive changes (for example, the concept of 'formal operation' defined by Piaget) provide the foundation for changes in the adolescent thinking systematically and in abstract terms about social, moral and ethical issue. Critical to this are the friendships and relationships that are formed with others.

ACTIVITY 5.6

Think about the friendships that you had during your adolescence. How were they different from the friendships that you had as a child? What kind of relationships did you have as an adolescent with members of the opposite sex? What kind of relationship did you have with your parents/carers?

COMMENT

Your experience will probably reflect changes in your relationships with friends – closer, more personal and more emotionally expressive. A critical feature will be the development of more intimate relationships. Whilst this is an important concern throughout our lives, during adolescence they became more 'real' as the individual develops greater autonomy outside the family context. You may have been able to identify changes in your relationship with your family, especially as they and you 'adapt' to the different relationships that supported your growing autonomy.

RESEARCH SUMMARY

Harry Stack Sullivan (1953) emphasised the role of friendships in children's development. Sullivan charts a progression of need beginning in infancy with the need for contact and tenderness, the need for adult participation (early childhood), the need for peer and peer acceptance in middle childhood. He identifies three stages during adolescence:

- *pre-adolescence – need for intimacy and validation in same-sex friendships;*
- *early adolescence – need for sexual contact and intimacy, generally with an opposite sex peer;*
- *late adolescence – need for integration into adult society.*

For adolescents all of these stages have the potential to be fraught with anxiety. The challenge for Sullivan is to integrate the individual's need for intimacy with the emerging need for sexual contact. Sullivan views experimentation with different types of relationship as a normal way of handling new feelings, fears and interpersonal needs.

The development of social behaviour

One of the misconceptions is that adolescents demonstrate their independence or 'autonomy' by rebelling against their parents. Autonomy is often confused with rebellion and breaking away from the values and 'norms' of their families. However there is no doubt that the changing relationships within the family can cause conflict and difficulties.

ACTIVITY 5.7

Think about the following. Try to identify the reasons that may be contributing to their described behaviour.

- *Tony, aged 15, is a boisterous, out-going adolescent. June, his mother, describes him as 'out of control' – he never does as he has been told. June says, 'He's going to turn out like his father.' Terry, his father, is currently serving a prison sentence for a violent assault.*

- *Eleanor, aged 14, is a bright and studious child who enjoys reading. Her teacher describes her as an able child, whose intelligence is well above average. Her parents cannot understand Eleanor's ability. 'She certainly does not take after us or our families' they tell you. She spends a lot of time in her room and appears to have few friends.*

- *Shelly, aged 13, gets frustrated and upset when she does not get her own way. She screams, shouts and hits others. Shelly was adopted by the Browns last year.*

- *Blake, aged 14, is quiet and compliant. He has few friends. His teacher has noticed that he is stealing objects from the other children. When confronted he denies everything.*

- *Gill, aged 16, has a learning disability. At school she is described as presenting no behaviour problems. However at home her parents find her behaviour increasingly difficult to manage. When Gill does not 'get her own way' she kicks, spits and throws things. Gill often pinches and punches her brother Shaun, aged nine.*

Understanding the reasons that underlie these behaviours will depend on your perspective. You may have merely attributed them to being a 'normal' adolescent. You may have viewed it as a parent based issue – lack of appropriate response, inconsistent responses or, alternatively, over-control. You may have a view that this is about the genetic make-up of the child, individual personalities, the previous experiences that the young person has had or the behaviour that the young person has seen and learned. You may have viewed it as a combination of all of these factors! As a social worker your response to each of these cases will depend on your assessment of a range of factors. Planning a response and supporting children, young people, parents and others to understand and manage their behaviour is a key role for social workers.

CASE STUDY

Read the following case and identity the motivations expressed by Johnny for taking drugs.

Johnny, 15, says, 'I just like smack, or 'e' when I can't get it, and the buzz it gives me. My mates and I just hang out; there's nothing to do. Drugs make you feel good. Everyone does it around here. No one cares what we do anyway. My Dad's off his head most of the time anyway.'

COMMENT

Clearly there are a number of motivations from Johnny's perception to take drugs, including: influence of peer; feeling of 'fitting it'; boredom; availability of drugs; his father's use of drugs. In the study undertaken by Dillon et al. (2007), they identify three theories that are concerned with the thoughts that influence young people's resilience to involvement in drug using behaviour and subsequently the factors that facilitate them in putting these decisions into practice.

- *Schema theory* (Piaget, 1970) Schema theory suggests that all people have a set of categorical rules or a script that they use to organise their knowledge about a particular concept in order to interpret the world. There appears to be evidence of the young people operating a *'drugs as harmful to self'* schema in order to remain resilient.

- *Self-regulation theory* (Cochran and Tessor, 1996) This theory refers to the internal and external process that allows individuals to carry out goal-focused actions over time, and in different social contexts. There is evidence to suggest that the young people in the current study employed three forms of *approach goals* in order to justify and maintain their resilience.

  1. Ways in which drug use was perceived as incompatible with their career aspirations. Young people suggested that if they were to use drugs this may prevent them from attending classes and, in turn, stop them achieving the qualifications necessary to follow their chosen career path.

  2. Some young people made extensive use of their spare time to play sports, pursue hobbies and work in part-time jobs. As a result, this left them little time to be involved in situations where drug use may take place.

3. The young people who were parents suggested that their role was not compatible with using drugs.

- *Self-efficacy theory* (Bandura, 1977, 1986) Self-efficacy can be conceptualised as people's beliefs about their capabilities of putting their decisions about what they want to do into practice. It is proposed that strong self-efficacy enhances feelings of accomplishment and overall well-being in people (Bandura, 1977, 1986). Young people were successful on two levels:

1. They managed to refuse an offer of a drug.
2. They did not compromise their position within a friendship or relationship, for example.

This provides support for the suggestion of strong self-efficacy resulting in feelings of well-being and mastery.

They sum up resilience and risk factors in a helpful table (see Table 5.1):

Table 5.1 Summary of factors young people identified as facilitating or impeding resilience to drug use

Other people's motivations to use	Contextual risk factors	Factors making it easier/more difficult to refuse offers	Motivations not to use
Following example of others	In trouble with the police/school	Reputation as 'resilient' to drug use	Other people's disapproval
To fit in	Alcohol use	Type of drug offered	Fear of effect on health
Peer pressure	Boredom	Reputation as a smoker or drinker	Fear of addiction
Alleviate boredom	Familial substance use	Age	Alternative sources of support/coping mechanisms
The 'buzz'	Mental health issues	'Happy to be the odd one out'	Current health conditions
Curiosity about effects	Problematic family relationships	Being drunk	Fear of losing control
Ease physical pain			Role as a parent
'To look hard'			Availability of time
To feel more confident			Financial cost
			Personal experiences with drugs

Every Child Matters Change for Children: Young people and drugs (DfES, 2005) guidance sets out how those responsible for delivering children and young people's services and the drug strategy should work together to improve the futures of young people, their families and community.

Understanding and making sense of behaviour must be seen in the context of their development. Theorists take different approaches to explaining why children think and behave as they do.

Temperament

Temperament refers to the individual difference in the basic psychological processes – the apparent in-built tendencies in relation to reactions and behaviours. Children and young people who develop aggressive tendencies tend to have a difficult temperament from an early age. Psychologists studying this area have described key dimensions of temperament. Buss and Plomin (1989) suggest that there are three differences:

• emotionality – variations in the tendency to become distressed or upset easily, with fear or anger;

• activity – variations in tempo, vigour and endurance;

• sociability – variations in the tendency to seek and be gratified by rewards; high level of responsibility towards others.

Thomas and Chess (1977) believe that individuality in temperament is established by the time the child is three months. They describe nine dimensions, which they organise into three types:

• the easy child;

• the difficult child (unhappy, hard to distract, difficult to settle);

• the slow-to-warm-up child (unwilling to be approached or adapt to new experiences).

Theories of temperament argue that individual differences are biologically or genetically determined with studies of twins providing the strongest evidence. They show that identical twins are more alike in their temperament than fraternal twins.

The Big Five are a central group of personality traits that seem to be evident in all humans, no matter what their group or culture. The five-factor model is comprised of five personality dimensions and is held to be a complete description of personality:

• openness: imaginative, curious and artistic attitude; welcoming new experiences;

• conscientiousness: organised, deliberate and conforming impulses;

• extroversion: outgoing, assertive and active behaviour;

• agreeableness: kind, helpful and easy going feelings;

• neuroticism: anxious, moody and self-punishing thoughts.

This is often referred to by the mnemonic OCEAN.

(Quoted in Berger, 2003 p.205)

These studies are not conclusive – individual differences in temperament should be seen as tendencies and may influence experiences. Temperament could be weakened or strength-ened by the child's experience, for example the reactions of their caregiver. Some traits may be regarded as appropriate and encouraged in the child, for example physically active boys and quiet, sedate girls. Children described by adults as having a difficult temperament, such as irritability and being hard to comfort, could be affected by a more punitive reaction to their behaviour. However temperament does not inevitably determine personality, rather it may suggest a bias towards certain patterns. A difficult temperament can be modified over time with appropriate caregiving. Thomas and Chess (1986) describe the concept of 'goodness to fit' to explain how temperament can change. Goodness to fit refers to the fit between the child's behaviour and their caregivers' expectations and behaviour towards the child. For example if a parent has an expectation of a sociable, happy child they may have difficulties adapting to a difficult child. Additionally they may not have the resources to draw on to support them, for example coping skill and social support. Consequently the parents' behaviour may reinforce the child's undesirable behaviour. Where parents are able to respond patiently, caringly and positively to this behaviour the child is able to progress well with their development.

Socialisation within the family

Children and young people learn from the modelling and communication of values within their family. Children need opportunities to participate in helping activities in which they learn how to co-operate, share and receive positive encouragement and praise for their actions. They imitate the behaviour of adults, particularly of those with whom they have a positive relationship. This includes values such as fairness and caring (Oliner and Oliner, 1988). Consequently if parents are punitive, the expectation is that young people are more likely to model this. Additionally parents who are inconsistent in administrating and following through on discipline are more likely to have aggressive and difficult children.

ACTIVITY 5.8

Do you have a view on smacking? Do you believe that children should never be smacked? Or do you think that a smack is an appropriate measure of discipline? What is your view on the following article:

Leader, Sunday 4 May 2003 Observer

'As we report today, the Government wants to make it illegal throughout the United Kingdom for childminders to smack children in their care. The antiquated defence of "reasonable chastisement" will no longer be admissible – except for parents. We welcome the belated recognition that this 140-year-old justification for hitting young children has left Britain with one of the worst child-cruelty records in Europe and has offered carte blanche to sadists and abusers. But it is feeble of the Government not to take the argument to its logical conclusion and outlaw the hitting of children by anyone.

Social workers and police have long complained that the "reasonable chastisement" defence prevents them from intervening in cases of parental abuse, from which, shockingly, one child a week still dies in the UK. In Sweden, in the ten years following a ban on smacking, not a single child died as a result of parental physical abuse.

Striking other adults (whether "reasonable chastisement" or not) is unlawful. Why then do we persist in finding it acceptable to visit violence on children? It is time for an outright ban. Hitting children is never right.'

The impact of parental discord, for example being exposed to verbal and physical violence, will have an impact on children's behaviour. Research demonstrates the impact of domestic violence on children (Hester and Pearson, 1998; Mullender et al., 2000). These reports show that children are aware of and responsive to domestic violence to a greater degree than had previously been thought. Although many develop coping strategies, their social, emotional and educational development may be hindered where processing of their destructive experience is not facilitated.

A number of studies have identified the overlap of domestic violence and child abuse.

- The domestic violence perpetrator may also be directly abusive to the child.

- Witnessing violence to their mothers may have an abusive and detrimental impact on the children concerned.

- The perpetrators may abuse the child as a part of their violence against women.

Children (even within the same family) may be affected in quite different ways due to age, gender, temperament and so on may act as mediating factors. Factors which may eliminate any harm to children and young people include:

- Ensuring the safety of the mother.

- Focusing on safety and quality in deciding on and arranging child contact.

- Listening to children and counselling support.

- Primary prevention – in schools.

(Holt et al., 2008)

RESEARCH SUMMARY

SCIE Research briefing 25: Children's and young people's experiences of domestic violence involving adults in a parenting role *(June, 2008) Worrall, A, Boylan, J and Roberts, D*

- *Professional understanding of, and responses to, domestic violence should be informed by the perspectives of children and young people.*

- *Practitioners need to recognise that domestic violence may be a cause of a range of physical, emotional and behavioural difficulties for children and young people.*

- *The complex relationship between domestic violence and safeguarding children requires respectful and sensitive handling.*

- *Children and young people aware of domestic violence have the right to be listened to and need help to understand what is happening.*

- *Some children and young people cope well despite their experiences of domestic violence.*

- *Work with perpetrators, though controversial, is an important aspect of reducing domestic violence and its impact on children and young people.*

www.scie.org.uk

As a social worker you will need to take into account the impact of all of these factors, especially the role and attitudes of the carers, in your assessments of children who are at risk of abuse and/or may be in trouble, for example with the law.

The impact of socio-economic status, for example poverty, adds to the stressors for families and may mean that there are limited resources, both physically and emotionally, to support and engage children in their development.

Increasing research is being undertaken into the impact of television and video games on the levels of violence demonstrated by children and young people. Some research suggests that it has an impact on children's behaviour; other research contradicts this view.

RESEARCH SUMMARY

Research carried out by Dawson et al. (2007) into why people play video games and what impact they think playing games has on them has been published by the British Board of Film Classification (BBFC). This qualitative research project consisted of interviews and discussions with people who play games and involved video games players ranging from children as young as seven through to players in their early 40s; parents of young games players; games industry representatives; and games reviewers. The interviews were carried out in Edinburgh, Birmingham, Leeds, Newcastle upon Tyne, Radlett in Hertfordshire, Croydon and Greater London.

The following is an extract taken from parts of the report, where the findings have been analysed in respect of the impact of violence in games on the players' behaviours.

> *A few gamers fear that the violence in games may have regrettable effects on some people's behaviour, principally people who become obsessed with games and spend too much time playing them.*
>
> > 'If someone's got that violent side in them they'll sit and play computer games with violence in them for hours and hours and it's not going to do them any favours.'
>
> *It is sometimes argued that playing violent games can make a player aggressive in the short term, again particularly if he plays 'too much'.*
>
> > 'I would say that your emotional mood definitely changes when you play a violent game. If you're not winning you can get quite aggressive.'
>
> > 'I don't like (violent) games because my brother plays them and it makes him really aggressive. There's this boy who lives near us... and he plays like 18 games, for 18s and over. Before he played them he was all right but since he's been playing them he's become a bit aggressive. It's really changed him quite a bit.'
>
> > HOW WAS HE BEFORE?
>
> > 'He was normal. He would get angry if someone made him angry but he wouldn't try to punch them... He used to be quite good at work and he used to really like maths and now he doesn't.'
>
> *It is generally only boys and men who are regarded as being at any sort of risk in this way, but one young girl in this sample seemed to say that playing games made her feel aggressive.*
>
> > 'When you're playing one of those (violent) games you're so controlled that you think it's like real... I've played it before, not like a really old one, just like a 12 one, and you do switch off the rest of the world and just focus on the telly. When I stop playing it it's all weird and you feel like punching someone.'

Continued

It sometimes seems to be suspected that playing too much, becoming obsessed with video games, might tip someone over the edge into violence.

> 'You get some people that get too into it. You get problems and they go out and do something stupid in real life...You hear about it on the news. They go out on a killing spree... It frustrates me because it's not the computer game's fault.'

A few gamers put the counter argument – that games can provide a safe outlet for aggression that might otherwise find unfortunate expression in real life.

> 'If you're in a mood and want to hit someone, then you can play the game and it releases you.'

Most gamers have a robust conviction that only people with some exceptional propensity to be violent are susceptible to influence by the violence in video games. People who commit violent acts are not ordinary gamers but 'idiots' and 'nutters'.

Dawson et al., (2007, pp.78–9)

The whole of the research report from which the extract is taken can be downloaded at www.bbfc.co.uk. You may be interested to read the whole report or other parts of it, but for the purposes of this chapter it is sufficient to develop your understanding and ability to critique the different influences on the development of young people in contemporary society.

ACTIVITY **5.9**

Having read the research summary above, reflect upon your views of this issue.

Consider not only video games, but the greater role of the media and internet communication; how significant do you believe the impact of these issues is on the social and behavioural development of young people?

It can be seen that there is little doubt that the various new technologies have some form of influence on young people's lives and their experiences. However, to what extent and to what effect, can be debated. In the research extract, you can read of different views from people who are themselves gamers, so there is a range of perspectives. With respect to developing as a social being, one of the most influential developments in recent years is arguably the widespread, extensive use of mobile telephones, text and internet communication facilities. Young people have new, different and innovative ways to communicate with each other, to source information and to be listened to, for example, the internet provides a wide range of ways in which young people can voice their views, source information and express their ideas.

Behaviourism and social learning theory

We have introduced the basic concept of behaviourism and social learning theory in Chapter 2. The focus in this section is to apply some of these principles to an understanding of children's behaviour. The focus of the approaches to a young person's behaviour is to study what is actually going on in the situation. The basic principles are that children learn new behaviour through modelling – copying the action of others. This behaviour is strengthened by reinforcement, which increases the likelihood that the behaviour will be repeated. Positive reinforcement refers to a positive addition to the situation, such as praise, a hug or a reward.

Negative reinforcement refers to the removal of something unpleasant or unwanted from the situation.

In behaviourist terms, this is not the same as punishment; punishment is the removal or denial of something pleasant from the situation. For example, Karl's mother may have said that he could not have any sweets that day if he does not clean his room. This may have prompted Karl to clean his room. This may work in the short term. However, behaviourists would argue that this might have unintentional emotional effects such as frustration and anger, for example an outburst of temper. Consequently it may increase rather than reduce the unwanted behaviour.

CASE STUDY

Sophie, aged 13, has been fostered by the Green family for the last six weeks. She has been subject to emotional and physical neglect by her parents. Sophie finds it difficult to sit at the dinner table. She eats her food as fast as she can and constantly gets up from her chair. Recognising that Sophie has not had any pattern at mealtimes, Jonathan and Pauline, the foster parents, talk to Sophie about her experience of mealtimes and the importance of them as an opportunity to be together, within their family. Sophie admits that her experience of mealtimes in her family is non-existent – there was no pattern to mealtimes and you had to 'grab' food when it was available. They agree that they will support Sophie building up a pattern of sitting at the table. The first week she must sit on her chair for five minutes building up to staying at the table for the whole meal. Each day that she achieves her goal the Greens say she can have a small treat, with a week's achievement resulting in a bigger reward. Additionally they ensure that she is encouraged and praised privately for sitting at the table.

Cognitive-developmental approach

The cognitive explanation of children's and young people's behaviour is concerned not only with what is actually happening but also with their understanding and mental representations of what is going on. They are also concerned within everyday interactions in their social environment – with other children and with key adults in their lives.

CASE STUDY

Karl, aged 14, is told to go and clean his room. He whines and moans as he does it, deliberately creating more mess. His mum persists in telling him to clean his room. She eventually gives in, lets him go and cleans the room herself. Karl has learned that whining works in avoiding unpleasant tasks.

Children and young people are treated differently for a whole range of reasons. In this case it may be because of Susan's age and the parents' expectations and response to her gender. However Peter is aware that the quality of interaction between himself and his parents is different. He recognises that he is treated differently from his sibling. Differences in treatment are an important ingredient in the child's developing internal model of self and contribute towards difference in behaviour between children in the same family.

CASE STUDY

Susan, aged 13, comes in late. Her parents talk to her about the importance of time keeping and how concerned they were about her. Peter, aged 15, remarks, 'That is different from what you would say to me! I would get shouted at and grounded for a week!' 'Well, that is because you are just trouble and always doing things to annoy us,' replies Dad.

Moral development

Moral development is concerned with the development of values relevant to how we treat other people and how we get treated. Children's and young people's behaviour needs to be grounded in an expectation that they are able to grasp and manage moral issues in their social world. In the first eight years of their life children develop a network of social relationships with people – their family, other adults and children. They develop different relationships based on their expectations and the constraints of different settings and different people.

Babies are born morally neutral. As they begin to be more mobile they begin to discover the rights and wrongs of situations. This is based on adult approval or disapproval as they do not understand the adults' moral judgement. For example, when a toddler is urged 'not to touch' an ornament, they do not grasp the adult's moral judgement but rather that the adult will disapprove. Initially children will learn through direct observation about 'rules' and move on to understand general principles abut tasks and situations. As their experience develops their judgements move from being definite and fixed into being more qualified – 'ifs', 'buts' and 'what ifs'. They move from seeing everything from their own viewpoint to taking a broader perspective. By five and six years children have a clear understanding and working assumption about how the social world works.

Piaget (Birch, 1997) emphasises the cognitive aspect of moral development believing that a child's moral development is linked to their stage of cognitive development. He concludes that there are two broad stages of moral development.

- Stage 1: heteronomous morality or moral realism. Rules are seen as strictly to be complied with. An act is judged on the consequence rather than intention. It is 'naughtier' to break several cups rather than just one.

- Stage 2: autonomous morality or moral relativism. This occurs around the age of seven or eight. Rules are established and are maintained through negotiation within the social group. Intention and consequence are linked.

Subsequent researchers have used different methodology in testing children's and young people's moral thinking, which have confirmed Kohlberg's three levels. However they have also identified the potential impact of two other features – the impact of culture as it affects moral judgement and differences in morality relating to gender. Some critics believe that Level 3 thinking in particular reflects liberal western intellectual values. Some cultures, for example the Turkish culture, place great emphasis on the community and community values. Consequently this could be considered as a higher form of moral thinking than the individualism emphasised by Kohlberg (Walker et al.,1995).

Carol Gilligan (1982) believed that Kohlberg overlooked significant differences in approach attributed to gender as his very research was based on male values; for example, he only used boys in his original research. Gilligan argued that there were two distinct orientations towards morality – a morality of care, which females are more likely to orientate towards, and a morality of justice, which males are more likely to orientate towards.

- Morality of care – the tendency for females to be reluctant to judge rights and wrongs in absolute terms because they are socialised to be nurturing.

- Morality of justice – the tendency of males to emphasise justice over compassion, judging right and wrong in absolute terms.

RESEARCH SUMMARY

Lawrence Kohlberg (1976) studied the moral reasoning of children and young people building to develop a stage model of moral development. He proposed three levels of moral development, with two stages in each.

Level 1:   Pre-conventional morality (middle childhood).

Stage 1: Punishment and obedience orientation. Children keep rules in order that punishment may be avoided.

Stage 2: Instrumental morality. Children follow rules when it is in their immediate interest to do so. Although they are able to consider others, it is only when the results are favourable to themself.

Level 2:   Conventional morality (approximately 13–16).

Stage 3: Mutual expectations within relationships. Being good is worthwhile for its own sake.

Stage 4: Social systems and conscience. The source of morality is placed in a wider social, 'societal' context.

Level 3:   Principled or post-conventional morality (approximately 16–20).

Stage 5: The social contract. Rules may not be absolute but take into account the good of the many rather than individual wants. Moral and legal viewpoints may conflict with each other.

Stage 6: Universal ethical principles. Individuals have developed a personal system of moral principles, which guide personal beliefs and actions.

Gilligan raises an important debate about the 'voices' of men and women. Why should the experience of the definition and routes to morality be different for men and women? How do we ensure that both of these 'voices' are placed alongside each other in order to develop an integrated approach to justice and care?

Individual difference in adolescence

You will be aware that as a social worker you need to have an understanding of 'normal' child growth and development. This will allow you to compare, contrast and assess the development of a child with whom you will be working with that of the average child. Additionally it will help you to judge the role of others, especially parents, in their development, for example their ability to meet the demands of the different stages of development, their ability to respond to the competing demands of parenting, their values and attitudes and the impact that this has on the child and so on. Throughout this and previous chapters we have attempted to identify issues which may specifically impact on the individual's experience of adolescence – issues of gender, issues of race and culture and disability. Drug and alcohol use is increasing among young people. For the majority of young people this may be experimentation associated with peer culture and peer pressure. For others it may be a more serious issue. Young people who use substances may demonstrate low self-esteem and self-worth, rebelliousness and lack of aspiration in relation to academic achievement. You will also need to consider and work with children who present with more challenging behaviour and you will need to work with children who present with emotional issues. A distinction needs to be made. There are those young people who present with a range of anti-social behaviour, such as criminal activity, aggression, defiance and refusal to comply, for example, with authority. These behaviours may be labelled as conduct issues. Other young people may present with emotional issues, such as depression and anxiety. A distinction needs to be made between those that might be associated with developmental issues and those that may be more serious. For example, a small proportion of young people will present with psychiatric disorders such as suicide attempts associated with depression, schizophrenia, anorexia or bulimia nervosa.

RESEARCH SUMMARY

Beinart et al. undertook a survey of 14,000 students in English, Scottish and Welsh secondary schools in order to assess their involvement in crime, drugs and alcohol misuse and other anti-social activities. The survey describes 17 major risk factors and six protective factors.

Risk factors	Protective factors
Poor parental supervision and discipline	*Strong bonds with family, friends and teachers*
Family conflict	*Healthy standards set by parents, teachers and community leaders*
Family history of problem behaviour	*Opportunities for involvement in families, schools and the community*
Parental involvement/attitudes condoning problem behaviour	*Social and learning skills to enable participation*

Continued

Low income and poor housing

Recognition and praise for positive behaviour

Low achievement beginning in primary school

Aggressive behaviour including bullying

Lack of commitment including truancy

School disorganisation

Community disorganisation and neglect

Availability of drugs

Disadvantaged neighbourhood

High turnover and lack of neighbourhood attachment

Alienation and lack of social commitment

Attitudes that condone problem behaviour

Early involvement in problem behaviour

Friends involved in problem behaviour

(Beinart et al., 2002)

CHAPTER SUMMARY

In this chapter you have explored human life course development in respect of adolescence, focusing on the use in practice of human growth and development theories and knowledge. The chapter started by putting adolescence into the context of the society in which we live and considering the way the term is socially constructed in our society.

The chapter then worked through a range of theories that explain human development during adolescence. Exploration of social development in adolescence included consideration of the transition into adulthood, changing roles and the growth of independence and maturity. Biological development focused on physical, bodily changes such as puberty, sexuality and growth. You also looked at learning theories that explain development in adolescence as shaped by predictable processes of learning.

Whilst considering your own thoughts about being a teenager, you have considered examples of individual difference, such as gender, race, culture, disability and difficult behaviours and how these issues can impact on an individual's experience of adolescence. Throughout the chapter, you have developed your understanding of the range of influences that impact on a person's experience of adolescence. However, you have also seen the importance of recognising that whilst there are certain expected changes within this period of life, there are no pre-determined pathways that lay out predictable ways in which people will experience or behave in their adolescent years. This then reinforces the importance of developing an understanding of the individual's perspective and the meanings they attach to their life events and the impact this has had for them. The significance of personal biographical accounts cannot be underestimated.

FURTHER READING

Daiute, C, Beyont, Z, Higson-Smith, C and Nucci, L (2006) *International perspectives on youth conflict and development*. New York: Oxford University Press.

This text may be of interest as it will widen your studies to take account of difference in an international context. This editied volume of essays considers the social, political and economic contexts of youth conflict across 14 countries on seven (sic) continents. The range of international authors introduce case studies and use research to examine social practice embedded in local, national, and international processes, through analysis of young people's participation in armed conflict, fighting, and social exclusion in the context of ther local environments. Whilst this text will expand your reflections on youth development, it is simply a very intresting and informative read.

Kroger, J (2007) *Identity development: Adolescence through adulthood* (2nd edition). London: Sage Publications.

Kroger presents an overview and analysis of general theoretical orientations to the question of what constitutes identity; including narrative; psychological; and sociocultural approaches. The book also describes key biological, psychological, and contextual issues due in each phase of adolescence and adulthood.

WEBSITES

The National Youth Agency www.nya.org.uk

According to the information provided on their website, the National Youth Agency (NYA) was founded in 1991 and is funded primarily by the Local Government Association and relevant government departments. Their aim is to support those involved in young people's personal and social development, to promote young people's voice, influence and place in society, thus enabling all young people to fulfil their potential within a just society. The website provides a range of resources including publications and information about policy development.

Chapter 6

Using life course development knowledge in social work practice with adults

Introduction

In this chapter, and in Chapter 7, you will consider human life course development in respect of adults. The material has been separated into two chapters, the first being dedicated to considering adults in their early and middle years, with Chapter 7 developing these ideas to consider life course knowledge as it relates to older adults. This chapter will begin by exploring what we mean by adulthood. The chapter will then develop your knowledge and understanding of the significance of life course development and life transitions in adult life and the implications for social work practice. Drawing on theories, illuminated by case examples including situations where adults experience a range of disabilities, the chapter will discuss how adult life course development can be explained. The value of the person's first-hand account of their life, their own explanations and meanings will also be considered. Following the life course perspective described in Chapter 1, you will consider how life transitions present opportunities for growth and development or conversely potential crisis points in people's lives.

Social work practice with adults and older people, and hence your learning about life course development in this chapter and Chapter 7, is set within the context of key policy and practice developments. Of particular importance here, amongst other initiatives, is the government White Paper *Our health, our care, our say: A new direction for community services* (DoH, 2006a). This White Paper was preceded by a Green Paper titled *Independence, well-being and choice: our vision for the future of social care for adults in England* (DoH, 2005). Within these strategies and consultation documents, seven outcomes for social care with adults are outlined. These are:

- improved health;
- improved quality of life;
- making a positive contribution;
- exercise of choice and control;
- freedom from discrimination or harassment;
- economic well-being;
- personal dignity.

The parallels with the strategic programmes for children and young people discussed in earlier chapters of this book are perhaps not surprising as overall these all relate to the lives of people and how they are experienced. *Building a safe and confident future: Implementing the recommendations of the Social Work Task Force* (DfESF, DoH, DfBIS with SWRB, 2009 p.20) suggests:

> In adult services, social workers are essential to the delivery of personalised services and to achieving better outcomes with adults of all ages who need services, support or protection. Social work is focussed on supporting independence, promoting choice and control for people facing difficulties due to disability, mental health problems, effects of age, substance misuse, and other circumstances.

The Future of Social Work in Adult Social Services in England (March 2010) proposes social work skills will continue to be important to assessment, care planning and review, but social workers may do more direct social work with a stronger therapeutic element. Listening, empowering individuals, being alert to conflict, safeguarding needs and the capacity of individuals, being sensitive to diversity and putting people in control should be part of the behaviours of all staff and services, from the first contact. The future of social work includes:

- The development of social work and interpersonal support: working alongside and led by people using services and their families, including services for people who fund their own social care.

- A focus on social work and safeguarding rights: having an important role in community development work and promoting social cohesion, for example where disabled, mentally ill or substance misusing people are victims of hate crime.

- Working with families; helping to break the cycle of generations of individuals trapped in abusive relationships, crime, substance misuse, poor health, unemployment and other factors.

These documents, and others we will refer to, are hugely influential in our understanding of adulthood and in influencing the language, assumptions and principles that are articulated through these documents.

What do we understand by the term 'adult'?

Before we can study the life course development of adults in detail, we need to consider what we mean by the word 'adult'. In the previous chapter you considered adolescence as the transitional stage before adulthood, you will now think about how we define the point at which a person is deemed to have reached adulthood.

ACTIVITY 6.1

Let us presume that you consider yourself to be an adult. Write down the point in your life when you feel that you made this transition. Now list the factors that you believe made you an 'adult' as opposed to being a child or an adolescent.

COMMENT

You may have considered a number of factors as being important. Perhaps you have listed a certain birthday or a particular life event like leaving home or something more difficult to define like a feeling of having developed your own sense of individuality, however that may be defined.

It is likely that you thought that age was a factor. For example, in Britain the law permits various activities once the individual reaches certain ages. At the age of 16 a person can legally consent to sex, they can also get married with parental consent and can leave full-time education. However, the right to vote or purchase alcohol is not legally granted until the age of 18. In our society people often celebrate their twenty-first birthday with the notion of getting the 'key to the door' as a particular transition point into independence. In other countries these events may be permissible at different ages, for example in Spain you can legally purchase alcohol on reaching your sixteenth birthday, yet in Canada that right is not legally permissible until the age of 19.

Adulthood can also be linked to physical and biological changes. From this perspective we could define adulthood as the time when physical growth is complete and the individual has moved through puberty and is able to reproduce. However the rate and point at which individuals reach physical maturity will vary greatly and may be difficult to determine.

Another aspect of being an adult could be defined in terms of psychological development. Yet recognising and measuring emotional, personality and identity development, in order to decide upon whether a person has reached adulthood, is also fraught with difficulties.

Whether you choose one or more of these areas to help define adulthood will depend upon your own perspective. What is clear is that the point at which we become an adult is contested. In social work practice, we need to be mindful of the ways in which individuals construct their own sense of self and the points along the life course at which they would locate themselves. We also need to be mindful of the ways in which laws, policies and agency remit affect how people are responded to and, indeed, whether or not they receive a social work service. However, for this chapter we shall consider early and middle adulthood within an age-frame of approximately between 18 and 65 years.

Stages of development through adult life

Separating the life course into easily definable segments is not straightforward. However, there are theories and models that explain adult life in terms of stages of development or tasks through which individuals progress. In Chapter 2 of this book, we introduced you to Erik Erikson's model of life stages (Erikson, 1995). We are going to explore this further, alongside other models that consider adult life in stages, namely those developed by Havighurst (1972) and Levinson (1978).

ACTIVITY 6.2

Think about adult life in our society, in particular your life and those of other adults known to you. Write down the answers to the following questions.

- *Do you think of adult life as divided up into segments or stages of some kind?*
- *If so, what are these stages?*
- *How would you identify and define the stages of adult life? For example, when does one part of adulthood start and another end?*

COMMENT

We cannot guess how many stages you have identified, but it is likely that you have used some age-related divisions, perhaps considering young adulthood, middle age and older age adulthood as main categories, with possibly more stages in between.

Erik Erikson's 'eight stages of man'

Erikson's theory arises from a psychosocial perspective on human life course development. He describes 'eight stages of man' that represent a process of personality and identity development. Erikson's theory was developed from the concepts first described by Sigmund Freud (1949). Freud put forward a psychoanalytic theory to explain the development of personality through childhood stages of psychosexual development. Erikson took this a stage further, in that his theory covers the whole of life and incorporates the influence of the social context of people's lives, thus taking a psychosocial perspective.

Erikson's model explains human development as the process of forming our identity, our thoughts, emotions and personality, through the interaction between the individual, the

---

RESEARCH SUMMARY.

Eric Erikson's (1902–1994) eight stages of development:

- *first year;*
- *second and third years;*
- *fourth and fifth years;*
- *six to 11;*
- *adolescence;*
- *young adulthood (20s and 30s);*
- *middle adulthood (40 to 60s);*
- *late adulthood.*

Young adulthood   **Middle adulthood**   Late adulthood

Young adulthood   **Intimacy versus isolation**
(Age 20–30 years)

Erikson describes this life stage challenge as forming intimate relationships with other adults. The struggle in this stage is to experience intimacy, yet retain a sense of your own identity. Successfully negotiating this challenge enables the individual to experience love and commitment to others, whilst unsuccessful movement through this stage may lead to isolation and the forming of superficial relationships with others.

Middle adulthood   **Generativity versus stagnation**
(Age 40–60 years)

This stage of life presents the challenge of contributing to society, being productive and creative. Thus this stage is linked with parenting, employment and occupation. Erikson stresses the importance of progression and the need for individuals to have contributed to the progression and future of society. The favourable outcome is stated as having the ability to be concerned and caring about others in the wider sense, however, the unfavourable outcome is the individual may not grow or develop himself or herself, becoming bored and over-concerned with themselves.

Eric Erikson's stages of psychosocial development in adulthood

---

Jeanette is a single parent with two children, both under five years of age. She is 21 years old and lives with her children in a flat within a multi-storey complex. Largely due to lack of money, but also difficulties securing childcare, Jeanette seldom goes out or socialises without her children. She has a number of friends, many of whom she has met through the local nursery; they are also single parents. Jeanette has very little contact with her mother, although she lives close by, as they fell out when Jeanette first became pregnant. Jeanette has never known her father, who left the family home when she was a baby. Things have become increasingly difficult for Jeanette, she is gradually getting into worsening debt to a local money lender and feels that she has no one she can discuss her problems with. Jeanette is considering turning to prostitution.

society and situations in which they live. He suggests that people confront a series of developmental challenges or conflicts, each occurring at particular and predictable times or stages in their lives.

In negotiating each stage or life crisis, the challenges could be successfully or unsuccessfully met, leading to favourable or unfavourable outcomes. Erikson refers to this balance as a *favourable ratio* (Erikson, 1987). Where the outcome of moving through a life stage is unfavourable, the individual will find it more challenging to meet the trials of the next stage. Erikson states that at each of the developmental stages, it may be necessary for individuals to return to unsettled earlier points in their lives. This is similar to crisis theory as discussed in Parker and Bradley (2007).

Unlike many other theories, Erikson's model covers life from infancy to old age, although the crises associated with these ages may be experienced repeatedly at different chronological periods in an individual's life. For the purposes of this chapter though, we will explore the two of Erikson's stages that relate to early and middle adulthood. We shall look at the last of Erikson's stages in the next chapter.

Jeanette is in Erikson's young adulthood life stage, within which Erikson describes the challenge of 'intimacy versus isolation'. As we have discussed above, Erikson stresses the significance of each life stage in preparing the person for the next stage and that where the person has experienced difficulties in negotiating one stage, they may revisit that point later in their lives. In Jeanette's situation, some of her difficulties may arise from her adolescence or even childhood experiences, for example where issues of attachment to her father may have been unresolved. Furthermore, Jeanette's pregnancies during adolescence could be interpreted, using Erikson's model, as her way of attempting to meet the challenge of adolescence by developing her own identity and role in society. It could be argued, therefore, that Jeanette is now seeking to reduce the isolation she feels by considering forms of relationships that may also provide financial reward. Additional aspects of this case study that you should consider are the needs of Jeanette's children and whether she is able to meet their needs, not only in terms of basic, practical resources such as food and warmth, but also in respect of their emotional and support needs. In other words, is Jeanette, in her current situation, able to adequately parent her children? This is not a straightforward issue and would require detailed assessment of Jeanette and her family's situation.

Ivy is a 44 year-old, single woman who lives alone. Her parents died ten years ago. She has a younger brother who lives some distance away and has a young family and busy career. Ivy has a progressive physical illness and experiences episodes of severe pain and difficulties using her limbs. She finds that some days are worse than others, but on bad days her mobility and ability to take care of herself are substantially impaired. Through an individual budget (DoH, 2006a), Ivy employs a team of care staff to meet her needs in her own home. Throughout her adult life, she has successfully controlled and managed all of her own affairs. For a number of years Ivy has been very active within a national voluntary organisation, campaigning for the rights of disabled people. Lately she has stopped attending the meetings and has not been responding to telephone calls. She does not readily engage in conversation with her care staff and appears low-spirited. When one member of the care team insisted on questioning Ivy about what was the matter, she angrily responded 'I think I'll give up and go into residential care!'

ACTIVITY **6.3**

Consider Ivy's current life situation. Explain the significance of events in Ivy's life using Erikson's model of life stages. You could do this by answering the following questions.

- *Which of Erikson's stages is Ivy likely to be in?*
- *What might be the conflicts and challenges facing Ivy at this time?*
- *What might be causing the difficulties that Ivy faces?*
- *In what ways is Erikson's model helpful in explaining Ivy's situation?*
- *How would your understanding of Ivy's situation, using Erikson's approach, help you to think about social work practice with her?*

We would suggest that Ivy is in the 'middle adulthood' stage. Erikson describes meeting the challenge of the conflict between 'generativity versus stagnation' as crucial to success at this stage of life. You may have thought that Ivy is facing a number of challenges at this point in her life. Her physical health may be declining as the progressive nature of her illness, alongside age-related changes, exacerbate her impairments. Ivy is also reaching other physical changes of middle adulthood, such as the menopause. The impending reduction of reproductive ability will lead to role and identity dilemmas, as Ivy will need to consider that she may never have children. Furthermore, Erikson's definition of 'generativity' extends beyond parenthood, to include productivity and developments for future generations. Ivy may feel disheartened that after many years of work and campaigning her efforts have effected little change. Thus her self-identity, role in society and the meanings she attaches to them are being challenged and redefined.

Erikson's theory leads us to think about whether Ivy has moved successfully through previous life stages. In other words, to look at whether there are outstanding or unresolved issues from an earlier point in her life. So, for example, during her young adulthood, how did Ivy meet the challenges of 'intimacy versus isolation'? It appears from the information that we have that she is isolated and self-absorbed within her experiences. She does not appear to have any intimate relationships or attachments. Therefore, according to this model, it could be seen that Ivy had not been able to successfully meet the challenges of young adulthood.

You may have felt that this model was helpful in suggesting explanations for the difficulties Ivy faces. You may have thought that the model was less helpful as it restricted your ability to consider specific issues that may have been relevant, in that Ivy may have a very close relationship and be in regular contact with her brother.

Your thoughts on this activity so far would all impact upon your assessment of Ivy's situation. Having applied Erikson's model to help you understand the issues for her, you were asked to think about the implications for social work practice. One of the areas of work would be to help Ivy identify, clarify and express her strengths, expectations and limitations (See National Occupational Standards for Social Work, Key Role 1). For example, the whole principle of the individual budget scheme is to support and empower individuals (DoH, 2006a). Using the flexibility of this approach Ivy may need assistance to change how she uses the budget to meet her current needs. The apparent concerns she has in respect of her self-identity and role in society need to be explored so that Ivy can express her needs and preferred options. Within this book we have stressed the value of taking a biographical or narrative approach to understanding the service-user's life course. In respect of Ivy's situation, her first-hand description would bring out issues about previous life stages and her perspective on the relationships she has, for example with her brother.

Daniel Levinson's 'seasons of life'

We shall now consider a different theory of adult life development that was formulated by Daniel Levinson (1978). This theory was developed following research with men aged 35 to 45, although studies with women have since been undertaken. In his book *The seasons of a man's life*, Levinson states that adulthood involves distinct 'seasons', as seen below. He saw some of these stages as being transitional phases of change, whilst others require tasks and decisions to be made.

The transitional phases of change are 'early adult transition', age 30 transition, mid-life transition, age 50 transition and late adult transition. Each of these periods of life is seen as the process of passing from one stage to another. Adaptation and planning for change are key activities that take place within the transition phases. Between the transitional phases, Levinson describes stages of stability and consolidation such as entering the adult world, settling down, entering middle adulthood and culmination of middle adulthood. These life stages are typically periods where the individual reappraises their past life, and strengthens their role and identity, establishing firm foundations for the next phase of life.

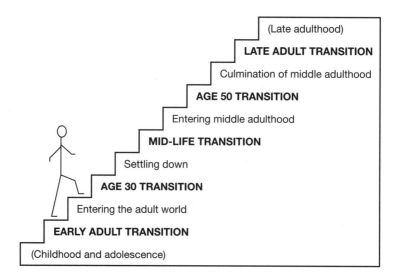

Figure 6.1 Levinson's seasons of life

(Adapted from Levinson, 1978)

CASE STUDY

Marcus is 43 years old; he is married and has two children. His son is 17 years old and has just left school and joined the armed forces. His daughter is 19 years old and is in her first year at university. Marcus was born and spent his childhood in Jamaica, moving to England to study when he was in his early twenties. Marcus' father was taken ill and died in Jamaica four months ago. Shortly afterwards his mother had a stroke, resulting in some long-term impairments. As Marcus is her only family, she has moved to England to live with Marcus and his wife.

Using Levinson's model, Marcus could be seen to be in the stage of entering middle adulthood, which Levinson describes as a transitional phase, characterised by change. Levinson used the popular term 'mid-life crisis'; this term is often linked to some of the challenges and responses apparent in the middle years of adulthood. Marcus is experiencing a number of changes and new challenges in his life, through which he will need to reconsider his own identity and role. On the one hand his children are becoming independent and his role as father may need to take a different approach. At the same time, however, his identity and role as 'son' has also changed. He may previously have visited his mother for holidays, but will not have lived with her for many years. His relationship with his mother will change due to her level of dependency and their new living arrangements. Additionally, Marcus may have to renegotiate roles with his wife, in order to encompass the evolving changes in their family situation. For Marcus, successfully having moved through previous stages in life will also be significant, for example how his relationship with his mother and later his children developed through other stages in his life.

Therefore, Levinson's model could be seen to be helpful in explaining the situation that Marcus is experiencing. However, given that Levinson based his theory on original research that was undertaken with only male participants, you should consider whether the model would be as useful if Marcus were female, for example. Levinson's work has been criticised for only being relevant to white, middle class males (Bee, 1994), with the later studies that included women being considered as only providing weak support for the model. In the case study here, however, the transitional issues of change, challenge and role adjustment facing Marcus could be described and explained using Levinson's model if this case study were based upon a female.

Robert Havighurst's developmental tasks

We shall now look at a third staged model of life development, as proposed by Robert Havighurst (1972). Like Erikson, Havighurst divided the whole life course into stages with the additional concept of 'developmental tasks'. He defined these as tasks that occur during life and need to be successfully achieved if the person is to move on to succeed in completing later tasks. Failure in the tasks will lead to unhappiness, disapproval by society and problems with later tasks. You will note some similarities with Erikson's approach to life stages and 'crises' in this respect.

RESEARCH SUMMARY

Havighurst's developmental tasks

Robert Havighurst describes six life stages and related 'developmental tasks'. Two of these are stages of adult life, each has a number of 'developmental tasks' associated with that phase.

- *Infancy and early childhood.*
- *Middle childhood.*
- *Adolescence.*
- *Early adulthood.*

    Development tasks are:

  - *selecting a mate;*

  - *learning to live with a marriage partner;*

  - *starting a family;*

  - *rearing children;*

  - *managing a home;*

  - *getting started in an occupation;*

  - *taking on civic responsibility;*

  - *finding a congenial social group.*

Continued

- *Middle age.*

    Development tasks are:

    – *achieving adult social and civic responsibility;*

    – *assisting teenage children to become responsible and happy adults;*

    – *reaching and maintaining satisfactory performance in one's occupational career;*

    – *developing adult leisure time activities;*

    – *relating to one's spouse as a person;*

    – *accepting and adjusting to the physiological changes of middle age;*

    – *adjusting to ageing parents.*

- *Later maturity.*

According to Havighurst's model, Marcia has not been able to achieve the developmental tasks in early adulthood, such as managing a home or starting a family. Additionally she is now not able to engage in many of the tasks of middle age, such as achieving adult social and civic responsibility. Havighurst would therefore suggest that Marcia's failure to complete these tasks would result in unhappiness and disapproval by society. Marcia, though, has many friends and lives a settled and seemingly contented lifestyle.

CASE STUDY

Marcia is a single, 50-year-old woman who has a learning difficulty. She has lived in a small residential care unit for many years. With regular support, encouragement and guidance, Marcia can meet her own daily self-care needs. However, she cannot read or write, she is unable to appreciate danger and needs a great deal of support with practical tasks such as money management. Marcia attends a local day centre, where she partici-pates in adult education classes. She has a number of good friends at the centre, as she has been attending for a long time.

Therefore, it could be argued that Havighurst's model cannot adequately help us to understand Marcia's life course. This may be because it lays out expectations that apply to all people, assuming a particular path of fixed events and tasks along the life course. These assumptions of what might be considered 'a normal life course' can result in the devaluing and oppression of individuals who deviate from that course and are therefore seen as different. The government White Paper *Valuing people: a new strategy for learning disability for the 21st century* (DoH, 2001) sets out new national objectives for services for people with learning disabilities. Central to the principles in the White Paper is enabling people with learning disabilities to have their voices heard and that planning of services should start with the individual and take account of their wishes and aspirations. It can be seen, therefore, that Marcia's voice, her views on her life so far and her personal hopes and goals are paramount when looking at her situation and life course development.

A central component of the *Valuing people* White Paper (DoH, 2001) was the introduction of person-centred planning (PCP) in order to ensure that support is tailored to meet the individual aspirations and needs of people with learning disabilities. In research to evaluate the impact of the introduction of PCP, findings indicate that

> PCP represents a positive step in the direction of delivering individualised support to enhance the quality of life of people with learning disabilities

> (Institute for Health Research, 2005 p.122)

Critique of staged theories of adult development

The strengths of these psychosocial staged approaches to explaining human development are that they can help to provide reference points for the descriptions people give of their life experiences and to our understanding of their life course. However, they are criticised for the following:

- Not incorporating difference and diversity. These theories are culturally specific, in other words, it does not always make much sense if you attempt to apply these models to adults that are not from western cultures. Furthermore, other areas of difference, such as sexuality and gender, are not easily explained, these models were developed mostly from a male perspective. So, for example, in Erikson's stage of young adulthood (intimacy versus isolation), theories of homosexuality and the social significance of stigma and oppression are not integrated.

- Being too fixed and deterministic. Life stage models are seen as being fixed, simplistic and determined, whereas in reality, it is not possible to divide real life neatly into stages. Erikson's model was popular and influential in the mid-twentieth century. However, it is criticised for being set in a particular time in history with no acknowledgement that things will change over time, in different societies and across different cultures. In other words, life stages or transitions are socially constructed and value-laden. The models suggest there are universal experiences that all people encounter. However, in reality, whilst human biological and physical changes are relevant, the meaning and significance of these transitions will vary considerably. Anthony Giddens (1991), a sociologist, lays out a compelling argument that modern society is continually changing and that people pursue many different paths through their lives. According to Giddens, it is no longer possible to draw on traditional ideas of previous generations and we have to work out our identities for ourselves as we go through life.

- Reinforcing socially constructed expectations. These models thus reflect many of the expectations and values of our society and culture. In this way, by reinforcing these expectations people who move through their lives in different ways can be left to feel as if they have failed, for example, if they continue to live with their family of origin beyond their mid-twenties, or if they are not in a mature sexual relationship in adulthood.

It is important to remember, therefore, that whilst theories of human development can be particularly useful from a social work perspective, when considering an individual's life experiences and the meaning they put on their life and own development, the stages outlined in the models are socially, culturally and historically defined. In other words, life stages are not fixed and accepted universally.

Life events as transitions

One of the common themes across these models is that they consider life in stages, often with an age-related dimension. The theorists then explain how each stage or period of transition is moved through and the impact this may have on the person's life development.

In Chapter 1 of this book we introduced the concept of transitions as phases or stages within a person's life course when people move through life events. We also explored how different people may experience the same life event, yet their response and subsequent development through the transition will be different. Therefore, it is important for social workers to understand the potential impact of transitions within a person's life course in order to help us work with people at different times in their lives.

The theoretical models that we have explored so far in this chapter have provided a framework for describing and predicting certain transitions that might be expected as part of the life course. However, as we have seen, these theories suggest fixed life-cycle stages that form a common experience for all adults. They do not, then, easily account for unexpected life events that may have social or personal significance nor do they consider the impact and challenges of multiple life events.

Challenges and opportunities

Transitions are processes of change within the life course, they demand personal change and often result in role readjustment. In this way, transitions present considerable challenges and opportunities for growth and development. In order to inform social work practice, it is necessary to understand the influences and factors that enable individuals to adapt and cope with changes in their lives to positive effect.

All transitions or life events have the potential to be stressful and challenging, even those that we might plan for and welcome. In order to determine some indication of the potential challenges and stresses in your life at the time, using the Holmes and Rahe Social Readjustment Rating Scale on p.119, you should add together the total of all the units related to the life events you have experienced in the past 12 months. Where this figure is over 300, it is said to imply that you have a significantly increased chance of major health breakdown in the following two years.

This model, as with the other theories explored in this chapter, presents an explanation of people's reactions to transition as being predictable and universal. It also suggests only the negative perspective of stress and challenge, without the potential for growth and development being reflected. Furthermore, whilst the Social Readjustment Rating Scale considers the cumulative effect that major life events may have, it does not account for the fact that the influence upon our development depends not only upon the life event but also on social, physical and psychological factors.

The Holmes and Rahe Social Readjustment Rating Scale

In the mid-1960s researchers Holmes and Rahe concluded that an accumulation in a 12-month period of life-changing events scoring 200 or more on a scale (see below) could increase the risk of stress and ill health. Holmes and Rahe developed a tool to identify, rank and score the accumulative potential stressors in a person's life. The Social Readjustment Rating Scale lists 43 life events; these are the top 12.

Rank	Life event	Life change units
1	Death of spouse	100
2	Divorce	73
3	Marital separation	65
4	Jail term	63
5	Death of a close family member	63
6	Personal injury or illness	52
7	Marriage	50
8	Fired from job	47
9	Marital reconciliation	45
10	Retirement	45
11	Change in health of family member	44
12	Pregnancy	40

Adapted from Holmes and Rahe (1976)

ACTIVITY **6.4**

Consider the Holmes and Rahe Social Readjustment Rating Scale for yourself. Have you experienced any of the life events listed in the extract given, over the past 12 months? Do you feel that this grading of stressful events reflects your own experiences or the experiences of adults known to you?

The staged models of life course development introduced earlier in this chapter suggest that each period of transition has to be, in some way, successfully negotiated or undertaken in order to develop and move on through further life stages. In this section of the chapter we are going to consider other factors that may affect the outcome of a person's move through a period of transition, in particular the importance of individual and personal resources and the influence of societal factors.

Personal resources

Personal resources can take many different forms. They may be characteristics within the individual or more tangible resources that are available, from outside of the individual. Individual characteristics would be a personal, psychological or inner strength, resilience and confidence that may enable that person to cope with and adapt to changes in their life. As we have discussed in previous chapters, the development of this strength of personality may have arisen through the individual's life course and the experiences of previous life events. This would support Erikson's approach to life stages in that, according to his approach, the successful completion of each stage prepares the person for subsequent challenges. Another factor to consider is the extent to which the individual has control over their own lives and decisions they make. Léonie Sugarman (1986) describes research into personal resources and their effect on effective coping mechanisms. She states that:

> A cluster of personality characteristics has been identified as being associated with more effective coping, including self esteem, self efficacy, mastery, internal locus of control [i.e. the extent to which an individual believes she can influence events], self confidence and flexibility.

(Sugarman, 1986 p.156)

Another factor to consider at this individual level is the person's access to physical, external resources. These may be financial resources, material assets or social support networks. Léonie Sugarman (1986) describes the latter as:

> ...interpersonal networks in which the individual is embedded.

(ibid. p.148)

These support networks may include close family, friends, people in the community, mutual or peer support systems or professional and voluntary support. The extent of the person's access to internal, emotional and psychological resources and external, material resources can shape how they move through life transitions. Further potential influences are factors in society, which may make transition and life development more challenging for certain individuals. We have considered how the person's own interpretation of what is going on in their lives is an important factor in shaping their response to change. Their interpretation, however, and the perspectives of those around them, will have been formed in the context of the society in which they live and their previous life experiences. In other words, the meaning they put on their own lives will be influenced not only by their own values and experiences but also by the values, views and expectations of society at that time. This is particularly significant for individuals who experience care needs, impairments or oppressions and discrimination in our society. In summary, therefore, the way in which a transition is experienced and the extent to which it is successfully negotiated will depend upon the individual's access to resources, their interpretation of what is going on, their previous experiences of transitions in life and the social construction of the transition.

ACTIVITY **6.5**

Think about a life transition that you have experienced, it may be moving your family home, changing a job or school, for example.

Do you feel that you moved through this transition successfully? If so what were the resources you used to enable you to negotiate this life event?

Whatever life transition you chose to consider, you will have had access to resources of some kind. This is likely to have been a mixture of personal resources, such as inner strength, self-esteem, confidence, and external resources like social networks, friends, family, financial resources and mutual help. The significance of specific resources and their influence on your passage through the transition will be very personal and dependent upon the many factors discussed above.

ACTIVITY **6.6**

Reflect upon your learning about the concept of transitions and their impact on the life experiences and development of adults. As just one example, consider how the impact of transitions, for example moving house or starting a new job, might impact upon an adult who is physically disabled.

As you have seen, the impact of transitions will be different for all individuals and that impact will be influenced by a range of issues. However, there may be some additional potential complexities for people who experience particular needs within our society. So, for example, a person who is physically disabled and moves house may need to rearrange different support services or adaptations in the home. Taking up a new job may mean specific assessments and arrangements for equipment or specific support services. All of these things often take time and can be complex to set up, adding to the potential for stress and anxiety. For further discussion and examples, Crawford (2006) cites recent research into the difficulties faced by disabled people making transitions in their lives. You may find your notes on this activity useful as you read the next section of this chapter.

In this section you have explored life events and transitions. This is particularly relevant to social work practice, in that social work service-users are very likely to experience a number of such challenges. Sometimes people access social work services as the result of complex transitions in their lives or it may be that as service-users they experience transitions as a result of the service they receive. For many people, both of these situations will apply.

Building the National Care Service (HMG, 2010) outlines the government's proposal to develop a National Care Service by 2015. The National Care Service will be for all adults in England with an eligible care need, free when they need it, whoever they are, wherever they live and whatever condition leads to their need for care but also start to respond to rising expectations and demographic pressures. This, they suggest, is related to such issues as: demographic changes; changes in technology; changing expectations; and economic conditions. They therefore propose that a care service should ensure that care and services should include the following elements:

- Be universal – supporting all adults with an eligible care need within a framework of national entitlements.

- Be free when people need it – based on need, rather than the ability to pay.

- Work in partnership – with all the different organisations and people who support individuals with care and support needs day-to-day.

121

- Ensure choice and control – valuing all, treating everyone with dignity, respecting an individual's human rights, personal to every individual's needs and putting people in charge of their lives.

- Support family, carers and community life – recognising the vital contribution families, carers and communities play in enabling people to realise their potential.

- Be accessible – easy to understand, helping people make the right choices.

RESEARCH SUMMARY

Personalisation has been a central theme for all government policy, particularly for adults in need of care and support. Personalisation means starting with the person as an individual with strengths, preferences and aspirations and putting them at the centre of the process of identifying their needs and making choices about how and when they are supported to live their lives.

Personalisation means:

- *tailoring support to people's individual needs;*

- *ensuring that people have access to information, advocacy and advice to make informed decisions about their care and support finding new collaborative ways of working (sometimes known as co-production) that support people to actively engage in the design, delivery and evaluation of services;*

- *developing local partnerships to co-produce a range of services for people to choose from and opportunities for social inclusion and community development;*

- *developing the right leadership and organisational systems to enable staff to work in creative, person-centred ways;*

- *embedding early intervention, re-ablement and prevention so that people are supported early on and in a way that's right for them;*

- *recognising and supporting carers in their role, while enabling them to maintain a life beyond their caring responsibilities;*

- *ensuring all citizens have access to universal community services and resources – a total system response.*

(Carr (2010) Personalisation: a rough guide. Adults' Services Report 20)
Available from: www.scie.org.uk

In December 2007, Putting people first (HM Government, 2007) proposed that all social care users should have access to a personal budget, with the intention that they can use it to exercise choice and control to meet their agreed social care outcomes. This includes access to such things as Individual Budgets. Individual Budgets (IBs) are designed to bring about independence and choice for people receiving care or support. It gives them a full understanding of the finance that is available, in order to empower them to take control and make decisions about the care that they receive.

Continued

RESEARCH SUMMARY *continued*

For an evaluation of the pilot of IB's see: *Glendinning, C, Challis, D, Fernandez, Jacobs, S, Jones, K, Knapps, M, Manthorpe, J, Moran, N, Netten, A, Stevens, M and Wilberforce, M (2008)* Evaluation of the individual budgets pilot programme: Final report. *Social Policy Research Unit, University of York.*

Available from: php.york.ac.uk

The impact on life course development of having a disability

In this section you will explore how the experience of having an impairment or disability in adulthood can change your life course and affect how you move through transitions.

Cree and Davis (2007) state that, for individuals who experience a physical or learning disability:

> *identity differs markedly from those around the individual and is characterised by difference, stigma, exclusion, loss of power and the denial of citizenship. It is then sustained through diagnosis and the social welfare and economic arrangements that are made for disabled people by the society in which they live.*

(Cree and Davis, 2007 p.108)

We have already found that staged models of life development can be seen to be problematic, in that they do not incorporate issues of difference. So, as an example, we shall look in more depth at the period of becoming an adult. Each of the models explored earlier in the chapter includes a stage of becoming an adult and gaining some independence, as part of identity and personal development. For Erikson, the period of 'young adulthood' was characterised by the conflict between intimacy versus isolation, for Levinson, 'entering the adult world' required the development of life goals, and for Havighurst 'early adulthood' required the completion of development tasks such as getting an occupation and selecting a mate.

These notions of independence, leaving the family of origin and setting out in occupational pathways are potentially in conflict with the possible need for ongoing care and support that may characterise physical, learning or mental health difficulties. The expected transition of 'leaving parents' may be delayed or may not happen at all. The challenge of developing meaningful, intimate and physical relationships may be hampered or not 'allowed', particularly where individuals with learning difficulties or several physical and sensory impairments have difficulties expressing their own wishes and feelings and may be deemed vulnerable or at risk.

In respect of outcomes for adults who have particular needs, the White Paper *Our health, our care, our say* (DoH, 2006a) proposes a range of new services to support independence, for example joint health and employment support accessible through local services. The following case study has been taken from the White Paper.

CASE STUDY

Seventeen-year-old Joseph Tomlinson from Wigan has a severe learning disability. Joseph has the same aspirations as any other 17-year-old but faced barriers in achieving them. Now thanks to In Control, a new scheme being pioneered in Wigan, funded by social services, the local authority, the Learning Skills Council and Independent Living Funds, Joseph can attend the local college, go to the gym and live an ordinary life. His mum Caroline explains how In Control has revolutionised Joseph's life.

Before the pilot started Joseph went to a special school, a good hour away, and had lots of different carers and found that lack of continuity really difficult. At one point I had 46 different people coming through the house! It was also extremely expensive and Joseph really wasn't receiving the benefit. We were totally dependent on whatever support was prescribed for him. In Control means people who need support are given both the money and the freedom to choose and buy the services they need, so it has enabled us to choose the services that Joseph needs.

We decided that Joseph needed to be able to do the same things as other young people of his age and that it was very important for him to have continuity of care, so that the same people stayed with him. Although we could have used an agency, we decided to employ a team of personal assistants to support him directly. There are six of them altogether and the assistants support him throughout the day inside and outside college, during the week and at the weekend. It has raised the quality of his life phenomenally – before this scheme started he wouldn't have been able to do three quarters of the things he does now, like go away for the weekend or go to the gym. If we do something as a family he can come with one of his supporters. He is so much happier. Most importantly he has continuity in the people who work with him, they are people he has chosen to be with.

DoH (2006a, p.101)

There are also separate but related issues in respect of the development of individuality, self-image and sense of personal identity. Young adults with learning difficulties and physical disabilities can in particular have problems being accepted with the status of adult, this can be compounded by the use of language which denies adult status – 'mental age of three'. All of these issues can potentially be more apparent where the person lives in supported care environments, such as residential care, as issues of safety, segregation and stereotyping may be more evident.

So having a disability could significantly alter a person's opportunities for growth and development through their lives, further supporting the argument that prescriptive, staged models of development are not able to explain life development for all adults. Added to this, as you have seen, the presence of a disability can impact upon a person's ability to cope with transitions. Of course, the onset of a disabling condition would, in itself, be a life event or transition.

The value of taking the narrative approach when working with adults who experience disabilities is again evident. The individual is the only person who can truly know and explain what having those impairments means to them and their life. The person's own account of their life history will be unique and as such, will facilitate the valuing of difference and diversity.

CHAPTER SUMMARY

In this chapter you have explored human life course development in respect of adults in the early and middle years of adulthood, focusing on the use in practice of human growth and development theories and knowledge. We examined the problematic nature of the term 'adult' before looking at three examples of theories that take a staged developmental approach to explaining human life course and identity development. Using case examples we considered the significance of transitions in adult life and evaluated the models in this context. Taking a life course perspective we examined how life transitions present opportunities for growth and development or conversely potential crisis points in people's lives. The significance of the resources available to the individual in determining their passage through the transition was discussed before looking at the potential impact of disability on an adult's life development.

The following chapter develops these themes further, as it sets out knowledge in respect of older adults. The chapter will consider older age in terms of opportunities for growth and development and will address issues related to ageing, older age and how it is constructed in our society. By developing the themes introduced in this chapter, particularly the significance of transitions in later life, you will develop an understanding of effective ageing and end-of-life issues.

FURTHER READING

Brown, K (ed.) (2006) *Vulnerable adults and community care*. Exeter: Learning Matters.

This book is one of the series of post-qualifying texts published by Learning Matters. However, the content is also relevant and accessible to social work students and practitioners from other disciplines. The book will be useful to your studies of this chapter and Chapter 7, particularly, because it is so steeped in professional practice issues with adults, in helping you to make the connections between theoretical life course perspectives and the reality of practice,

Race, D (2002) *Learning disability – a social approach*. London: Routledge.

This book looks at how people's lives are affected by services. The book has been strongly influenced by the real-life experiences of adults with learning disabilities and will therefore be of particular interest in exploring how the narrative approach can impact on an evaluation of services.

Sugarman, L (1986) *Life span development: concepts, theories and interventions*. London: Methuen.

Léonie Sugarman's text, despite being written some years ago, remains a relevant and important text for students of human life course development. It is particularly useful for further reading related to this chapter, as it has specific chapters dedicated to *adulthood* and *life events, transitions and coping*.

WEBSITE

Department of Health www.dh.gov.uk/en/Policyandguidance/

The policy and guidance section of the Department of Health website is a useful starting point for looking at the policy context of adulthood, with particular relevance to social and health care, in our society today. The site offers a range of downloadable reports and bulletins, all of which will have further references that might direct your additional reading.

Chapter 7

Using life course development knowledge in social work practice with older adults

A C H I E V I N G   A   S O C I A L   W O R K   D E G R E E

This chapter will help you to begin to meet the following National Occupational Standards:

Key Role 1: Prepare for and work with individuals, families, carers, groups and communities to assess their needs and circumstances.

• Work with individuals, families, carers, groups and communities to help them make informed decisions.

Key Role 2: Plan, carry out, review and evaluate social work practice, with individuals, families, carers, groups and communities and other professionals.

• Interact with individuals, families, carers, groups and communities to achieve change and development and to improve life opportunities.

Key Role 5: Manage and be accountable, with supervision and support, for your own social work practice within the organisation.

• Manage and be accountable for your own work.

Key Role 6: Demonstrate professional competence in social work practice.

• Research, analyse, evaluate and use current knowledge of best social work practice.
• Work within agreed standards of social work practice and ensure own professional development.

It will also introduce you to the following academic standards as set out in the social work subject benchmark statement:

3.1.1 Social work services and service users.
3.1.4 Social work theory.

Introduction

In this chapter you will consider human life course development in respect of older adults. The chapter will start by exploring what we mean by the terms 'older adults' and 'old age' and considering where these meanings originated from. The chapter will then develop your knowledge and understanding of the significance of life course development in later adulthood. You will explore theories and explanations of development in later adulthood that examine social, biological and cognitive processes. Some of the theories introduced in Chapter 6 will be revisited and their relevance to life course development in later life will be considered.

Using a range of case studies you will examine the concept of successful ageing and what this means for professional social work practice. As shown in earlier chapters, practice is embedded within a social, cultural, policy-driven context. In particular, as with the previous chapter, social work practice with older people is informed by key policy and strategic developments. As with Chapter 6, the government White Paper *Our health, our care, our say: A new direction for community services* (DoH, 2006a) is of particular relevance here. The White Paper could be seen as an overarching strategy, as there is a range of other, more specific areas of policy and legislation that impact upon the lives and experiences of older people, for example *The Mental Capacity Act 2005*. Underpinning these developments has been the *National Service Framework (NSF) for Older People* (DoH, 2001) and the more recent publication of *A new ambition for old age: Next steps in implementing the National Service Framework for Older People* (DoH, 2006b) which sets out the priorities for the second phase of the government's ten-year NSF for Older People. As stated in previous chapters, these documents are extremely significant. It could be argued, for example, that our understanding of later adulthood is, in some ways, influenced by the terminology chosen, assumptions made and principles espoused in the policy agenda.

Throughout the chapter you will have opportunities to consider your own thoughts about growing older and the importance of each individual's life story within a life course perspective. Again, building on your reading in earlier chapters, you will look at the impact of life transitions in later adulthood, considering how such events may present challenges and opportunities for older people. This part of the chapter will incorporate discussion about end of life issues.

Defining 'later adulthood'

In order to explore life course development in the later stages of life we need to have a clear understanding of the different terms that are used to describe people who may be considered to have reached this stage of life. You considered the term 'adulthood' in Chapter 6 and reflected on how difficult it can be to agree a firm definition of this notion. The concept of 'later adulthood' is no different. As stated in Chapter 6, as social workers we need to appreciate how each individual understands themselves, their identity, their own lives and place in society. We need to consider whether they would see themselves as an older person and what meaning this has for them. We also need to consider how our society, its laws, policies, expectations and agency requirements can affect how older people are responded to.

ACTIVITY 7.1

Write down your first thoughts in response to these questions.

- *So far, we have used the terms 'later adulthood' and 'older people' to describe people who are considered to be in the later stages of adulthood. Write down any more words or phrases that you have heard used.*

- *Name some people that you know and would consider to be at this stage in their lives. Think about these people and write down what it is about them that makes you consider them to be defined in this way.*

You may have thought of many different words or phrases that are used to describe older adults, for example 'people who are ageing', 'old aged', 'senior citizens', 'old age pensioners', 'elders' or 'elderly people'. As you will see from the title of this chapter, we have chosen the term 'older adults'. You may also have identified a number of different features that would lead you to think of a person as an older adult. As with other stages of life, a common starting point is to think of chronological age, for example, you may have thought that anyone over the age of 65 years could be described as an older adult. Linked to this, you may have listed some social aspects of ageing, such as being a person who has retired from employment, or who can receive certain entitlements such as a pension or travel pass, due to their age. You may also have listed some biological changes, perhaps some of the more visible changes such as hair or skin changes or aspects of ability. Finally you may have included changes in people's ways of thinking or understanding as they grow older, with issues about the life they have lived and their life coming to an end being prevalent. These ideas would reflect aspects of cognitive changes associated with ageing. Through this chapter you will explore each of these perspectives in more detail as you consider some theoretical perspectives on development in older adulthood.

Whatever range of responses you may have made to Activity 7.1, we feel sure that you will agree that most people have a common understanding of what is meant by 'older adults' and who might be included in that group. In other words, the meanings of these terms are taken for granted in our society. In earlier chapters of this book you have been introduced to the concept of 'social construction'. The 'social construction of old age' refers to the way in which meanings, interpretations and images that emerge from our society affect our understanding of older age. These meanings and images that are entrenched in the structures of society, our history, culture and language, become so powerful that people see them as 'fact'.

In this chapter we will challenge the assumptions that arise from the way in which society gives meaning to ageing. We shall do this by demonstrating that older adults are not one homogeneous group, but are diverse individuals, who have made many life choices, having moved through distinct and very different life courses, therefore reinforcing the importance for social work practice to take account of how individuals think of themselves and the meanings they attach to their own lives.

CASE STUDY

Margaret lives with her husband Charles in the south of England. Margaret is 72 years old and Charles is nearing his 75th birthday. Margaret and Charles have one daughter who lives near them; she is a single parent of two children aged seven and nine years. Margaret retired from a nursing career ten years ago, Charles retired shortly after his wife, having worked in engineering for most of his working life. As their daughter works full-time, Margaret and Charles enjoy spending a lot of time taking care of their grandchildren. They take them to and from school and care for them during school holidays. Margaret likes the children to call her 'Peggy', rather than Grandma, whilst Charles is happy for his grandchildren to call him 'Gramps'. When the children are at school, Margaret and Charles take pleasure in participating in a variety of voluntary activities and hobbies. Charles enjoys swimming at the local sports centre and is a governor at the school his grandchildren attend. Margaret works in a voluntary capacity at the Citizens' Advice Bureau and also delivers meals-on-wheels twice weekly. Margaret also likes going to yoga classes one evening a week.

Margaret and Charles are both within the chronological age group that could be defined using the words you have explored. In terms of the social aspects of ageing, Margaret and Charles have both experienced the transition of retirement and would be entitled to any benefits linked to their age. It is also likely that Margaret and Charles are aware of some of the physical changes of ageing. However, it is apparent that this couple have a positive outlook on their lives. It is possible that they would not describe themselves as 'older people' or in any way dependent or vulnerable.

Therefore, the danger of constructing one definition of older adulthood is that it does not allow for individuality. Margaret and Charles do not neatly fit the stereotypical meanings attributed to being an older person in our society. Such definitions imply beliefs about later life and how an individual older person should look, behave and live in our society.

ACTIVITY 7.2

We all expect to grow into older adults. Think about the following questions and write down short answers to each one.

- *When you think about your own life and prospect of growing older, what is your attitude towards this time of life? In other words, do you think your life as an older adult will be enjoyable? Is it something that you look forward to or are fearful of?*
- *How do you think your attitude and thoughts have been developed?*
- *Complete the following sentence, with at least six different endings:*
  'Getting older means . . . '

COMMENT

It is probable that your responses to the first part of this activity have been developed by thinking about the lives of older adults you know, perhaps your grandparents, neighbours or friends, or you may have thought of older adults in the media, politicians and soap-opera actors. It would be useful to ask the older adults in your family what growing older means to them. You will have completed the sentence in a range of ways, some of which may be similar to the examples below, but the ways in which older adults themselves would complete the sentence are the most meaningful.

- 'Growing older means freedom from work and more opportunities.'
- 'Growing older means being able to take time to do things and enjoy companionship.'
- 'Growing older means having less hair and more wrinkles.'
- 'Growing older means having accumulated a wealth of life experiences and knowledge.'

Thus, some people will think about later life with some excitement, as an opportunity to have time for yourself, time to travel or relax. Others may have expressed some concerns about growing older, as the experience is something of an unknown and it may seem to be a long way off.

Your responses to this activity will not only have been shaped by your experiences, but also by the expectations and meanings that society has given to later life. In other words, as stated earlier, the experience of being an older adult is socially constructed and through this older adults become stereotyped. Furthermore, the generalisations about older adults may lead to negative assumptions about development in older age and consequently older adults being devalued in our society. Such negative generalisations often include concepts of physical weakness, loneliness, vulnerability, depression, lack of cognitive ability and overall dependency on other people and society. Through the discussion, activities, case studies and examples as you progress through this chapter, we will challenge these notions and demonstrate that later life is a time of opportunity for growth and development.

Thus it can be seen that

> chronological age has a powerful effect on how we are perceived, the expectations of others and the opportunities that may be available to us.

> (Crawford and Walker, 2004 p.10)

Negative generalisations like those mentioned above can result in discrimination against individuals on the grounds of their age; this is called 'ageism'. This can refer to discrimination at any age, but the social construction of old age and the negative connotations mean that ageism in respect of older age is particularly prevalent in our society. Prejudice and inequality related to older adulthood can be seen at a number of different levels, from the attitudes and behaviours of individuals, through to the structural policies and cultural beliefs in our society.

At a structural level, chronological age is the determining factor for a number of socially and legislatively determined transitions, for example the age of retirement or holding a driving licence. Therefore an age limit is being used to justify access or exclusion of individuals from a service, facility or entitlement. This is discriminatory and is an example of ageism. Within the area of health and social care, the government have recognised that ageism exists and needs to be eradicated. *The National Service Framework for Older People* (DoH, 2001) is an example of a national programme that sets out to develop, change and improve health and social care services for older people.

The National Service Framework for Older People (2001) Standard One

Rooting out age discrimination

Aim
To ensure that older people are never unfairly discriminated against in accessing NHS or social care services as a result of their age.

Standard
> NHS services will be provided, regardless of age, on the basis of clinical need alone. Social care services will not use age in their eligibility criteria or policies, to restrict access to available services.

> (Department of Health, 2001 p.16)

In the foreword to *The National Service Framework for Older People* (2001) Alan Milburn, Secretary of State for Health, states that *services sometimes fail to meet older people's needs – sometimes by discriminating against them…*

The NSF sets out a programme of action and reform to address these problems and deliver higher quality services for older people.

(Milburn, 2001)

Additionally within the White Paper *Our health, our care, our say* (DoH, 2006a) one of the principal outcomes for social care with all adults is freedom from discrimination and harassment.

ACTIVITY 7.3

Do you think there should be an upper age limit set for any of the following?

- *Retirement.*
- *Receiving certain state welfare benefits.*
- *Holding a driving licence.*
- *Receiving social care services in your own home.*

Write down the reasons for your response to each point.

COMMENT

A non-ageist response to all of these points would be that there should not be any upper age limit set. The reason for this is that eligibility for each of these entitlements could be more equitably determined through an assessment of individual need or ability.

The state retirement pension is paid to people who have reached a set age and meet certain criteria in respect of National Insurance contributions; the pension age is currently 60 years for women and 65 years for men. However, Parliament has passed legislation to equalise pension age at 65 years for men and women, although this will not affect people born before April 1950. Again, chronological age is the deciding factor on eligibility, whilst not everyone would wish or need to start drawing their pension at the same age. There are, however, complex regulations that allow for a certain amount of deferment in when the person claims their pension. Added to this, the government drive to root out age discrimination in employment includes looking at ways in which the age of retirement could be made more flexible, but this will require primary legislation to change Revenue and Customs rules, occupational pension rules and current restrictions related to deferring a state pension.

The majority of drivers can hold a driving licence from 17 years of age and it remains valid (with certain exceptions for specific medical reasons) until they are 70 years old. However, on reaching their 70th birthday drivers are required to complete two sets of paperwork and pay a fee to renew their licence. Further renewal is then required, using the same process, every three years thereafter. This condition appears to be solely based upon chronological age and effectively puts in place a different process, with additional requirements, for holding a driving licence where the individual is aged over 70 years.

The National Service Framework for Older People cites examples of age discrimination in aspects of social care:

> *In some localities the eligibility criteria for non-residential services mean older people have had to demonstrate higher needs to qualify for services compared with younger adults.*

(Social Services Inspectorate, 1999, and Netten and Curtis, 2000, cited in *NSF for Older People*, 2001 p.17). The framework goes on to state that:

> *In social care assessed need should be matched to fair eligibility criteria for access to help and support.*

Another aspect of life in which older adults may be considered to be disadvantaged due to the policies and structure of society relates to financial security. Later adulthood is often characterised by stereotypical images of poverty and social exclusion. However, within our society there is substantial variation in amount and sources of income and also living standards. Patterns of income distribution in later adulthood most usually continue to reflect the distribution of income throughout the life course, although inequalities can be seen to become greater with increasing age. So, for example income differences that have been identified in relation to gender, disability and ethnicity continue to be evident in later adulthood, but the disparities become greater.

So far in this chapter we have stressed the uniqueness of each older person and their situation. We have also highlighted the ways in which attitudes, ideas, concepts and beliefs about later life might be developed. Added to this, the whole of this book has been underpinned by social work values, the importance of listening to the perspectives of individuals and the narrative tradition. For social work practice with older people and for developing an understanding of their life course, the narrative, biographical approach is particularly valuable and enables us to gather some appreciation of their 'chronosystem', in other words, the influence of their life course and the history of their growth and development (see Chapter 2). As stated by Cree and Davis (2007, p.8), *The narrative turn builds on the oral history and life history tradition*. So consider this poem written by Roy Barker, aged 80 years, which is about his life growing up in Doncaster.

Where we live

Doncaster town or Donny to proper folk
Been a good place to grow up in
From the time of gaslights flicker to neon brightness
Milk in jugs home made bread
To sliced loaf tightly packed
Pantomime at Christmas black and white pictures that moved
To television in living colour
Seeing a man taking a step on the moon
Whilst eating crisps – sat on the sofa in the room
Going to work on yu bike – Now busy roads full of cars
Remember club trips tu Cleethorpes on train

Now it's planes that land and take yu tu Spain
Oh! and wine that makes yu dizzy
Who now – gets their beer in a jug carried home – from the landlord's pub
Have yu noticed now that coals not burned
The sky is clearer up above
Doncaster built mainly on level ground
Better than Sheffield – wi all its ups and downs
Sunny Donny is the place of memories sweet
Parkinsons – Nuttalls – Do you still recall the taste?
Mmm!!!

Roy Barker, aged 80, as cited on the Age Concern Internet site at www.ageconcern.co.uk

---

ACTIVITY 7.4

Roy's poem is, at the same time, amusing, poignant and informative. What were your initial thoughts, given the little bit of information you have here, about Roy's story? Does this tell you very much about Roy and his life course so far?

COMMENT

Of course, this is a very short poem, but it does tell you some things about Roy's background, his thoughts and his experiences. It certainly highlights the range of changes and developments that Roy has experienced and been part of through his lifetime so far. It is also useful to consider that 'stories', narratives or biographies do not always have to be in oral form – they do not always have to be heard through interviews or discussions, there are other very effective ways of 'listening' to people and enabling them to express themselves. As the chapter moves on to consider different ways in which later adulthood is theorised or explained, you may find it useful to remember Roy, or perhaps return to his poem, as a real example.

Theories and explanations of development in (later) adulthood

In the first activity of this chapter, you thought about how you might define later adulthood in terms of the main characteristics or features that it encompasses. We commented that your responses might have come from a range of different perspectives that focused on social, biological or cognitive aspects of growing older. We shall now explore each of these approaches to ageing in more depth, using models from key theorists and case examples. You should note, however, that whilst you will look at each approach separately here, it is important for social workers to take an holistic approach to understanding life course development for older adults. *The lifecourse is central to any understanding of ageing* (Phillips et al., 2006 p.32). Therefore, in developing your understanding of later life, you should be mindful that an individual's life course development and life experiences are affected by a range of factors, these include social and economic aspects, cultural, historical, psychological, cognitive and physiological influences.

Social development in later adulthood

In Chapter 6 you examined Erik Erikson's (1982) theory of the 'eight stages of man', the eighth and final stage being 'late adulthood'. As with the earlier life stages, Erikson theorises that late adulthood is a developmental challenge or conflict, which can be successfully or unsuccessfully met, resulting in favourable or unfavourable outcomes.

Late adulthood *(aged 70+ years) Integrity versus despair*
Erikson describes this last life stage crisis as one of integrity versus despair, the struggle in this phase being to experience a sense of wholeness and acceptance of one's own life and the choices that were made, without harbouring regrets or feelings of having inadequately fulfilled life's expectations. Successfully negotiating this challenge by reaching a stage of self-acceptance and comfort with one's life enables the individual to come to terms with death.

Late adulthood

Figure 7.1 Erikson's stages of psychosocial development in late adulthood

Erikson describes the demands of later life as requiring the individual to look back over their life experiences and draw them together into a form of self-acceptance that he calls 'ego integration'. Where the individual feels that they have not had a successful life, they may sense some regret about not being able to 'turn the clock back' and do things again. Such regrets, according to Erikson, lead to 'despair' and ultimately a fear of the end of life.

From the information you have on Henry's life, it is not possible to know about his whole life course and whether he has moved successfully through the previous life stages described by Erikson or whether there are outstanding issues for him. Henry's behaviours could be seen as the result of feeling angry and discontent with his life. Perhaps the loss of his wife, the subsequent change of role and feelings of having no purpose or worth in life could result in the bitterness and contempt that are exhibited. The move to sheltered accommodation may also have been a difficult transition for Henry, as this happened shortly after his wife's death. Henry also has to adjust to his changing physical capabilities, which potentially threaten his independence and the self-identity that he has known. The apparent dependency on one individual, and the unreasonable behaviours described, may be explained through difficulties at earlier lifestages, which may be exacerbated now. For example, having no contact with his family means he is not aware of their development and contribution to society, this being a key element of 'generativity' at the middle adulthood stage.

The implications of this knowledge for social work practice are immense. The most significant concept though would be for social workers to work to encourage and enable the development of 'ego integrity'. This can be achieved by valuing the individual, their experiences and their own interpretation of their life events, through active listening. Therapeutic work through reminiscence and biographical approaches to life reviews can help the person to integrate past life experiences and enable them to form a realistic acceptance of their life course. We have also noted that Henry may have a low self-esteem and feel he has no purpose in life. Therefore, enabling him to seek a purpose or role in life could be beneficial. At the same time, considering ways to increase and maintain Henry's independence would be valuable in restoring his feelings of self-worth.

There is some disagreement amongst theorists, however, as to the value of maintaining activity or conversely reducing activity, in later adulthood. In this context, the term 'activity' is taken to have a wide meaning, encompassing not only physical activity, but also mental activity, involvement, engagement and interactions within society. The two approaches to the debate on the value of activity in later adulthood are 'disengagement theory' and 'activity theory'.

CASE STUDY

Henry Jones (aged 85 years) was widowed ten years ago and shortly afterwards moved into a bungalow, in a supported housing complex, where he now lives. Henry has two children, both of whom have families and careers, they live about 60 miles away from him. Henry is finding it increasingly difficult to care for himself. He needs regular assistance with practical tasks and is starting to have problems attending to his personal needs. Since the death of his wife, Henry appears to have gradually alienated all of their friends and family. He is considered by many to be difficult, demanding, often angry and sometimes extremely rude to people who have offered support and friendship. Following many minor disputes and difficulties, his family no longer visit him. Henry has also rejected support services from a range of carers as, for one reason and another, he has disapproved of or disliked each service. Now the only support that Henry will accept is from the housing support warden. The warden visits regularly and, due to Henry's increasing level of need, finds that he is becoming gradually more dependent upon her, to the extent that her support role is far beyond that which a warden would usually undertake. An example of this is that Henry will telephone the warden frequently at her home, when she is off-duty, or has left his home only minutes before. These calls are not usually urgent matters and could have waited until the next planned call.

ACTIVITY 7.5

Think about the challenges that face Henry. Write down a few sentences that answer the questions below:

- *Using Erikson's model, how would you briefly explain Henry's situation?*
- *Having formed an understanding of Henry's situation using Erikson's approach, what are the implications for the way in which you as a social worker would work with Henry?*

Henry's life situation could be seen to demonstrate some elements of disengagement theory (Cummings and Henry, 1961). Henry has distanced himself from previous friends and family and appears to reject most opportunities to interact with people. Henry appears to be isolated and to have chosen to withdraw from active involvement in earlier social roles and networks. From the perspective of disengagement theorists, these behaviours are not indicative of physical change or impairment, but demonstrate a change of emphasis to focus on other tasks that are prioritised. This corresponds with Erikson's later adulthood challenge, where the importance of focusing on reviewing one's life and reaching a point of acceptance and 'ego integration' is seen as paramount at this stage of life. Disengagement theory attempts to dispel the negative myths of ageing as a period of loneliness and reducing ability, by reframing these notions as natural, appropriate and purposeful processes that enable the individual to move through later adulthood success-fully. Thus, according to this approach, by reducing social and emotional interactions and becoming increasingly preoccupied with themselves, the older adult is thought to be able to increase their satisfaction with life. Crawford (2006, p.121) discusses Hunt's (2005) analysis of disengagement theory when applied to transitions in later life, particularly 'the contemporary social and economic outcomes of retirement'.

Disengagement theory, however, is directly opposed by activity theory. According to the views of activity theorists, the more active, occupied and involved the older adult is, the more likely they are to be satisfied with their life. Activity theory proposes that older adults should maintain either the same or substitute activity patterns that they established in middle adulthood.

The case example of Margaret and Charles from earlier in this chapter provides a useful example of how older adults might continue to be active in a broad sense as they develop in later life. So Margaret and Charles have substituted the activities, commitment and involvement in their careers with their roles and activities as grandparents and volunteers and their participation in leisure pursuits.

Critics of disengagement and activity theories would highlight the constraints posed by the structural expectations of society. For example retirement and institutional care could be seen as mechanisms that enforce disengagement and do not enable continued activity. Disengagement theory is then accused of providing a political tool in that it legitimises such policies. On the other hand activity theory could be seen to promote the involvement of older adults in voluntary activities, which again can be argued to be a useful political mechanism for maintaining the high number of unpaid, yet productive citizens in the economy.

In the light of this debate it is interesting to note that in *Our health, our care, our say* (DoH, 2006a) one of the core principles is 'Improving health', which is related to encouraging people to exercise, be active and contribute to society.

Biological development in later adulthood

Throughout the life course, increasing age is associated with certain physical bodily changes. Such biological developments are associated with normal expectations of the ageing process.

ACTIVITY 7.6

Think about people you know who are becoming older adults, perhaps your parents or grandparents. List the physical or biological changes that they may be experiencing.

You may have associated a whole range of physical changes with increasing age. Perhaps you noted some of the more familiar age-related physical changes such as sensory changes. So you may have noted that as people grow older, they may need to have their sight corrected with spectacles, despite not having needed spectacles earlier in their lives, or have a more complex prescription than previously required. You may also have included a possible reduction in hearing ability. Changes related to the person's joints or bones, such as osteoporosis or arthritis, that gradually impact upon their ability to do certain physical tasks, is another area that you may have covered.

There may be a number of other physical changes that you have thought of. However, it is important, that you appreciate that whilst many of these biological changes appear to be commonplace, that does not mean that as we age these changes can be predicted or are to be considered inevitable.

The common aspect in any of the physical changes that can be linked to later adulthood is that they are related to changes taking place within the cells of the body, most usually degenerative changes.

RESEARCH SUMMARY

The Hayflick Limit

Dr Leonard Hayflick, a biologist, researched the biology of ageing. He suggested, following laboratory tests, that human cells can divide or repair up to a maximum of 50 times before they degenerate and die. This led to the concept of there being a maximum capacity for cell regeneration, known as the Hayflick Limit. This biological approach presents a form of cellular clock, ticking away, that has been individually programmed into the person's physical make-up. The Hayflick Limit puts human lifespan at a maximum of 120 years (Hayflick, 1977).

These notions of cellular clock, physical degeneration and progressive age-related changes can be used to support ideas of increased frailty and dependency in older age, with no possibility for growth and development. It is for this reason that biological perspectives should not be taken in isolation. Such changes are not universal, in that they do not affect all individuals in the same way through a predictable pathway. Other aspects of people's lives also impact upon and interact with their individual development, for example social, environmental and psychological factors.

This example of the marathon runner is a powerful illustration of the potential for physical development and renewal in later life. However, whilst only a small minority of people, at any age, are physically active to this degree, the majority of people in later life do lead active lives.

So far, in this section of the chapter you have mostly considered visible biological changes in later adulthood. However, another change that faces some older adults is deteriorating intellectual ability.

CASE STUDY

At 80 years of age Michael Aimable ran and completed the London Marathon 2007. He is a dedicated runner and through his running supports the Muscular Dystrophy Campaign. He is a regular London Marathon runner, having taken part in events since the 1980s. Michael did not take up running until 1980 when he was 54 years old. Since then he has notched up an incredible 90 marathons and 132 half marathons. That's well over 4,000 miles in the last 26 years, and that's not counting all the other races, plus an average of 40 miles a week of training. A former cipher operator in the Army for 22 years, he caught the running bug after he decided on the urgent need to lose weight. I was 15 stone and overweight. I was getting violent pains down my left arm and heart and I knew I had to do something. It took me a month to be able to run a mile, and then one day a friend said they would give me five pounds if I did a half marathon for charity. It was a blessing in disguise.

www.muscular-dystrophy.org/index.html

Severe loss of memory associated with other changes, such as personality change, and problems related to overall functioning, is termed 'dementia' and is given a biological or medical interpretation. Dementia is then described as a symptom of a disease, such as Alzheimer's disease or Parkinson's disease. There is considerable debate, though, as to how dementia can be explained. On the one hand, it is seen as a clinical disease, linked to the biological ageing process, which comes about due to changes in the cells in the brain, and is therefore a diagnosable and treatable pathological condition. The contrasting view suggests that a biological interpretation alone is not comprehensive and that social, environmental and individual or personal factors can be significant. Tom Kitwood (1993) has written about and researched dementia, he states that *it is being realised that a purely technical frame has had its day*. Kitwood develops the notions of *malignant social psychology* and *personhood* as he argues that dementia results from the interplay between cell deterioration in the brain and the interpersonal, psychological and social environment. Kitwood's work provides a strong incentive for social work practice that offers a person-centred approach, that actively acknowledges the individual's perception of their life and their situation (Kitwood, 1993).

Marshall and Tibbs (2006) add to this by developing a 'citizenship approach' to dementia which understands that *people with dementia are fellow citizens who make a contribution to society as well as receive services* (p.16).

RESEARCH SUMMARY

A joint publication by the National Institute for Health and Clinical Excellence and the Social Care Institute for Excellence (November, 2006) Dementia – Supporting people with dementia and their carers in health and social care *states that dementia is a progressive and largely irreversible clinical syndrome that is characterised by a widespread impairment of mental function. As the condition progresses, people with dementia can present carers and social care staff with complex problems including aggressive behaviour, restlessness and wandering, eating problems, incontinence, delusions and hallucinations, and mobility difficulties. It is estimated that there are 700,000 cases of dementia in the UK and approximately one million people caring for people with dementia.*

It made the following recommendations.

- *People with dementia should not be excluded from any services because of their diagnosis, age or coexisting learning disabilities.*

- *Health and social care professionals should always seek valid consent from people with dementia.*

- *Health and social care managers should ensure that the rights of carers to receive an assessment of needs as set out in the* Carers and Disabled Children Act 2000 *and the* Carers (Equal Opportunities) Act 2004 *are upheld.*

- *Health and social care managers should co-ordinate and integrate working across all agencies involved in the treatment and care of people with dementia and their carers.*

- *Care managers and care co-ordinators should ensure the co-ordinated delivery of health and social care services for people with dementia.*

- *Memory assessment services should be the single point of referral for all people with a possible diagnosis of dementia.*

- *People with dementia who develop non-cognitive symptoms that cause them significant distress or who develop challenging behaviour should be offered an assessment at an early opportunity.*

- *Health and social care managers should ensure that all staff working with older people in the health, social care and voluntary sectors have access to dementia-care training that is consistent with their roles and responsibilities.*

- *Acute and general hospital trusts should plan and provide services that address the specific personal and social care needs and the mental and physical health of people.*

Available from: www.scie.org.uk

If you wish to develop your understanding of issues in relation to dementia, SCIE have developed an excellent web learning resource available at www.scie.org.uk

Cognitive development in later adulthood

In this section you will look at age-related intellectual and cognitive changes in later adulthood. As with the biological changes discussed earlier, it is important that you appreciate that ageing does not automatically correspond with a significant decrease in cognitive functioning or intelligence.

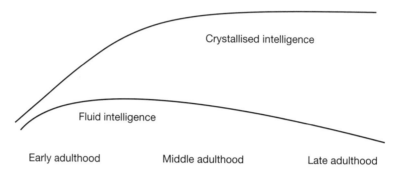

Figure 7.2 Crystallised and fluid intellectual abilities as they develop in the adult life course

Intelligence can be described as encompassing a range of cognitive abilities or thought processes. These are sometimes known as crystallised and fluid abilities. Crystallised intellectual abilities refer to the individual's knowledge that has been acquired over the life course, usually familiar material and general knowledge. Fluid intellectual abilities relate to the ability to reason, analyse, evaluate and process complex information. Older adults are thought to be less proficient with tasks that require fluid intellectual abilities, whilst retaining the crystallised abilities. However, these are generalisations and there are differences in intelligence across individuals that may demonstrate age related effects, life course events, social or cultural differences.

Cognitive abilities can also be described as the result of the interaction between information from the senses, concentration, short-term memory, long-term memory, learning and recall.

Thus, whilst certain cognitive processes may decline with age, ageing, by itself, does not result in significant decreases in intelligence. It is a myth that older adults become less intelligent with age. The possible changes to cognitive processing described above are not universal characteristics and many older adults can develop ways to compensate for any difficulties that they do experience, for example writing things down in order to remember them. Furthermore, individual difference in cognitive ability at any age is enormous. As with the other areas you have looked at in this chapter, cognitive development in later life is interrelated to many other aspects of life, including general physical health, social and environmental factors. As a social worker, therefore, it is important to consider the most effective ways in which to enable the older adult to maximise their cognitive abilities by attending to all of these interrelating factors.

RESEARCH SUMMARY

Baltes' life course model

Professor Paul Baltes (1987), a German researcher, proposed that intelligence develops in relation to biological, social and cultural forces. Biological influences on intelligence include the brain cell development that occurs throughout the life course.

As an individual ages, the capacity to read, execute calculations, draw abstractions, and make judgements develops in relation to biological and social experiences. Baltes' life course model also suggests that intelligence becomes increasingly diverse over time. The majority of older adults can read, perform calculations, draw abstract inferences and exercise independent judgement. However, the performance of these intellectual abilities is much more varied than it would be within a group of children.

(Baltes, 1987)

CASE STUDY

Jack Ward from Nottinghamshire was 75 years of age in 1999; he was married and had five grandchildren. On leaving school, Jack was unable to read or write and later was diagnosed as having dyslexia. Jack's wife Audrey taught him to read and write and encouraged him to attend night school. Jack worked in the government's Property Services Agency, but on retirement took up academic studies. In November 1999 Jack received a PhD from Sheffield Hallam University after carrying out research into heat pumps at the school of engineering. Dr Ward was, at that time, the oldest person to achieve a PhD at the university.

(BBC News Online, 1999)

Dr Curtis Sparkes spent his adult life fascinated with engineering, developing, building and inventing various devices. When he was in his very early 20s he achieved a Higher National Certificate in Mechanical Engineering, but it was some 60 years later in his early 80s that Dr Sparkes was awarded a Masters degree and two years later a PhD in the History of the Machine Tool Industry.

(UMIST News, 2002)

Significance of transitions in later life

Throughout this chapter you have looked at some of the ways in which development and change in later adulthood can be explained and understood. In previous chapters you have also considered changes in terms of transitions or phases within a person's life course development. You will now look at how transitions and life events impact on a person's development in later adulthood.

As social workers it is important to appreciate that each individual will experience transitions in a different way. Even where the life event or transition is something that is common to many people in our society, for example retirement, each person will respond and adjust to that change in a unique way. Furthermore, all transitions, whether predictable and expected or sudden and unplanned, present considerable challenges and opportunities for the individual, their growth and development. Therefore, social workers who work with older adults need to understand not only the changes that may occur in later adulthood, but also the variety of factors that influence how people adapt to such changes in their lives.

In earlier parts of the chapter you have seen how older adults may experience a range of changes in their lives, some of these are physical and psychological changes, others are related to the expectations and rules of society and some changes are transitions or personal events that impact on the person's life. In this section, you will look at different ways of explaining how people adjust to these changes in later adulthood.

As you have seen, the model of life development proposed by Erik Erikson (1982) suggests that later adulthood presents a challenge between integrity and despair. Erikson's approach is to argue that individuals can move successfully through transition at this stage in their lives, if they develop a measure of self-acceptance and feel fulfilled with the life they have lived. Thus, by presenting life stages as challenges to be negotiated and met successfully or unsuccessfully, Erikson's approach provides a way of explaining how individuals might grow older 'successfully'.

ACTIVITY **7.7**

Think about the phrase 'successful ageing'.
- *What does 'successful ageing' mean to you?*
- *Write down your own definition of 'successful ageing'.*

COMMENT

The term 'successful' is a subjective one, in that your interpretation of success will be different to another person's perspective. However, you may have felt that there are many potential areas of life that can impact on whether you feel that you are ageing 'successfully'. Aspects such as having good physical and mental health, being independent, feeling content and happy, having enough money, suitable accommodation, having friends, family and social outlets may all have featured in your thoughts. The term 'successful ageing', as used in the literature and research related to later adulthood, originally arose from the work of Rowe and Kahn (1987).

RESEARCH SUMMARY

Successful ageing

Doctors John Rowe and Robert Kahn based their ideas on studies of groups of people as they moved through middle adulthood into later adulthood. They propose that there is great variation in how people experience ageing and that an understanding of 'usual' or 'pathological' ageing will help us to develop preventative strategies with older adults, so that they are more likely to achieve 'successful ageing'. Rowe and Kahn suggest three measures that will enhance the quality of life in later adulthood:

- *avoid disability and disease;*
- *maintain high cognitive and physical functioning;*
- *stay actively involved with life and living.*

(Rowe and Kahn, 1987)

It can be seen that Rowe and Kahn connect the concept of 'successful ageing' to being free of disease or ill health. This is a biological approach, as described earlier in this chapter. From this perspective, health promotion strategies, good diet and exercise would be seen as important ways in which to enable the body to successfully adapt to the changes of later adulthood. However, this viewpoint can be seen as very restrictive, in that it does not take account of the many other aspects of the individual's development that impact on how they experience transitions, as we have seen from Activity 7.7 above. It could also be argued that this biological perspective would disadvantage individuals who experience impairment or disease.

Successful ageing from a broader perspective could be seen to be described through the seven outcomes for social care with adults, formulated through work with adults of all ages and now being developed and implemented by means of recent national policy initiatives (DoH, 2005, 2006b). The outcomes are: improved health; improved quality of life; making a positive contribution; exercise of choice and control; freedom from discrimination or harassment; economic well-being; and personal dignity. Within these ideals you may perceive many parallels with earlier discussions in this chapter in relation to successful later adulthood.

The following case study is taken directly from a brief guide to the government's White Paper *Our health, our care, our say: a new direction for community services* (DoH, 2006a). You will see how a number of the outcomes are evident in this short extract.

CASE STUDY

Doreen Shepherd, 68, moved into Reeve Court Retirement Village in Rainhill, St Helens, Merseyside, 18 months ago, and takes a keen part in the activities on offer.

I'm very happy that I moved to the village, *says Doreen.*
There's lots to do. I belong to the choir, the knitting group and the discussion group. I've made lots of friends here and feel very secure.

While Reeve Court was being built, the managing company, Extra Care Charity Trust, worked in partnership with the local authority to find older people who would benefit from this active, independent environment.

There are lots of people in residential and nursing care homes because there's nowhere else for them to go *explains manager Lesley Blowers,* when, with the right support, they could live independently. While we were building the village, we gave people information about it because, together with the local authority, we wanted to give older people a choice. Social services identified people in residential care who they thought would benefit from the environment we offer.

(DoH, 2006a p.17)

It is clear that issues of choice, control, quality of life and access to resources have been significant in Doreen's situation. We do not know any more about the types of resources that may have been available to Doreen in making the decision to move to Reeve Court, but in Chapter 6 you read about the different types of resources that individuals may be able to draw upon to support and assist them as they move through life transitions. The availability of internal, emotional, psychological resources and external, material resources remains significant in determining how individuals will experience transitions in later adulthood. Also in Chapter 6 you read about how the experience of having an impairment or disability in adulthood can change your life course and affect how you move through transitions. Again, the issues remain relevant in later adulthood. It may be helpful for you to reread pages 123–4 of Chapter 6 at this point.

End-of-life issues

One area of life course development that is most often associated only with later adulthood relates to end-of-life issues. That is not to discount that people may die at any age from a range of causes, but that in the later stages of adulthood the end of life becomes expected. You have already seen how Erikson's model considers that individuals who move successfully through the later stage of adulthood will be prepared for the end of life and will face their death without fear. You have also explored how biological approaches to human development, such as the 'Hayflick Limit' describe a 'cellular clock' putting a time limit on human life (Hayflick, 1977).

A discussion about end-of-life issues in respect of human life course development provides the opportunity to draw together many of the themes that have been raised throughout this chapter. Death is, in pure terms, the end of biological and physical functioning of the body. However, end-of-life issues raise a complex, interacting range of emotions, meanings, interpretations and beliefs both at a personal level and in a wider societal context. Therefore, for social work practice the individual's perspective on nearing the end of their life, their response to the issues that this raises for them and the effect on their life are the paramount concerns. The way in which each individual perceives the prospect of the end of their life will depend upon a range of influences in their lives. A person's values, outlook and beliefs are constructed through their life experiences and through cultural and societal expectations.

The attitudes, values and beliefs of the society and culture in which people's lives develop, and in which they are currently living, will strongly influence their thoughts about what the end of their life means to them. In our society, death in later adulthood is likely to take place in an institutional setting, either in hospital, residential or nursing care or in a hospice.

Thus dying and death could be seen to be part of a professionalised process, which is managed and controlled by the professionals, their theories, perspectives and interests. The logical conclusion of this view is that the individual older adult has, in these circumstances, little control over the process of their own death. This is, however, not necessarily the case as, particularly with the growth of the hospice movement philosophy, practitioners work towards user empowerment, enabling choice and control in all aspects of one's death.

RESEARCH SUMMARY

Age Concern, citing sources such as the National Statistics of Deaths in England and Wales in 2001 *and* Deaths: place of occurrence and sex by underlying cause and age group, 2002, *state that:*

> The main places of death for older people in England and Wales are, in descending order of prevalence, hospitals, care homes, own home and hospices. There is some research evidence concerning the decisions that people would prefer to make about care at the end of their lives. Most studies have found that around 75% would prefer to die at home. People who are recently bereaved, and therefore have experience of death, are slightly more likely to prefer in-patient hospice care. There is a clear inverse relationship between where people say they want to spend the last period of their lives and where they actually die. There is significant variation across European countries as far as place of death is concerned, with some of the highest rates of deaths in hospital occurring in England and Wales. This suggests that the organisation of services plays an important role in determining the options that people can consider.

(Age Concern, 2005 p.5)

It can be argued that death is an unmentionable subject in our society; it is both denied and stigmatised. Within the medical doctrines, for example, methods for prolonging human life and curing disease are dominant, although, as stated above, with the growth of the hospice movement, goals of pain control and dignity in death have become recognised and valued. In our language too, we could be accused of avoiding or denying death. We allude to death, but choose euphemisms such as 'passing on' and 'passing away', rather than being open, acknowledging and discussing death as an inevitable element of life itself.

Death is construed in some parts of society as a punishment. This is reinforced through some religious writings that connect death and dying with sin and retribution. However, many religious teachings also suggest that death is another significant transition, a transition from physical life to another form of life, where one's spirit lives on, 'life after death'. Religion and culture also provide the structure and meanings to the way in which death is ritualised. Thus funerals, burials and the grieving process take place within a social and often religious context that gives meaning and importance to death as a life event.

Thus social, cultural and religious beliefs and expectations impact on the community, family and social networks of the individual, as much as they do on the individual themselves. The death of any one person usually results in the roles and identities of those around them having to be renegotiated and changed. In other words, the death of one individual can be a major life event or transition for the friends and relatives that they leave behind them. In this way, the older adult's perspective on death will be influenced by the behaviours and attitudes of those for whom they care. At a personal level, death is frequently related to loss, not only loss of bodily functions, but loss of opportunity to achieve certain things.

All of this means that for social care practice it is vital that the individual's perspective, wishes and feelings are fully understood and acted upon. Advance care planning (ACP) is a process of discussion between an individual and their care providers irrespective of discipline. If the individual wishes, their family and friends may be included. With the individual's agreement, this discussion should be documented, regularly reviewed and communicated to key persons involved in their care. The notion of ACP is the focus of a recent Department of Health publication *Advance care planning: a guide for health and social care staff* (DoH, 2007).

CASE STUDY

Eleanor Jacobs is 79 years old; she was widowed some 35 years ago, when her husband died after a long and painful progressive illness. Eleanor has four children but she has lived alone for many years. Eleanor's eldest daughter, Maria, married an Australian man and settled in Auckland over 15 years ago. It is ten years since Eleanor saw her daughter, although they speak on the telephone and Maria writes long letters regularly. Maria has two children that Eleanor has never seen. Eleanor's other children live within easy travelling distance from their mother and visit occasionally. However, Thomas and Benjamin, her sons, have never had a good relationship with each other and more latterly Eleanor is aware that they argue about their responsibility to her and her care needs. She also believes it is very likely that they have argued about their possible shares of an inheritance after her death. Ann is the youngest child and Eleanor has always felt close to her. Eleanor has tried on several occasions to talk, with Ann, about planning her funeral and what will happen after her death. Ann finds this distressing and very difficult and always closes down the discussion by smiling jokily and saying 'Don't be silly Mum, you're not going to die, you'll live on forever!' However, in the past year Eleanor's health has deteriorated rapidly and she has become more acutely aware that the end of her life may not be far away. Being alone for long periods has given Eleanor plenty of opportunity to think about her death. The thoughts are gradually filling her with dread, anxiety and distress as she finds she is unable to discuss or plan for the end of her life with those close to her.

It can be seen, therefore, that each person's perspective on the end of their life is influenced by a complex interaction between the social and cultural images and ideologies through which they have lived their lives. The images may depict a process within which the individual has little control, added to this there may be connotations of punishment, denial and stigma. It would, then, seem reasonable for individuals to develop a fear of death. However, older adults do not often express fear of death, although some describe a concern about the manner in which they might die. Citing evidence from a range of writers and research, Moyra Sidell explains that most older people have reached *some stage of acceptance*, which reminds us of Erikson's notion of ego-integrity (Sidell, 1993). Perhaps this relates to death being inevitable and expected in later adulthood and thus people are prepared for the end of their life.

The White Paper *Our health, our care, our say* (DoH, 2006a) also acknowledges end-of-life issues. This has led to The End of Life Care Programme (EOLC), which aims to improve care at the end of life for all people. More information, including a helpful range of downloadable documents, can be found at www.endoflifecare.nhs.uk.

Diversity in later adulthood

Throughout this chapter you have considered life course development in later adulthood from a range of perspectives, yet the overriding theme has been that whilst there may be trends and patterns to growing older, there are no predetermined pathways that lay out predictable ways in which increasing age will affect people. The only way of understanding an individual's development and the issues that later adulthood may hold for them is to listen to their life-story, as they tell it and perceive it. In other words, to value the individual's own narrative and biographical account.

In this way, you will be able to appreciate the impact of life transitions for the individual and take account of differences between older adults. Life course development happens across the whole of life, being a gradual and progressive accumulation of influences, crises, transitions and growth, each of which can in turn be seen as processes of social, biological and cognitive development. Each older adult's experience of late adulthood, therefore, is not only moulded by the complex interactions of their current life, but is also influenced by their own life history and their subjective interpretation of it. For example, the experience of being an older black woman in contemporary British society may hold many challenges, but each older black woman will deal with those challenges differently, dependent to some extent upon how she experienced and thinks about her life as a black woman.

REFLECTION POINT

- *What do I know, or can I do now, that I did not know or could not do before I did this section of studying?*

- *Is there anything I do not understand or want to explore further?*

- *What else do I need to know to extend my professional development and learning in this area?*

CHAPTER SUMMARY

In this chapter you have explored human life course development in respect of older adults, focusing on the use in practice of human growth and development theories and knowledge. We examined the problematic nature of some of the words used to describe this stage of human development and considered how late adulthood is constructed in our society, before looking at some approaches that explain human life course development in late adulthood. You have looked at the significance of transitions for older adults and considered how access to resources may influence their experience of life changes. This incorporated studying the concept of successful ageing and end-of-life issues. Throughout the chapter we have presented older adulthood as an opportunity for growth and development.

FURTHER READING

Crawford, K and Walker, J (2008) *Social work with older people*. 2nd edition. Exeter: Learning Matters.

This book will help you to develop a distinctive focus on social work practice with older people. It is written in the same format as this book with interactive activities and case studies throughout. This book would prove a useful supplement to further developing your understanding of later adulthood.

Gubrium, J and Holstein, J (eds) (2003) *Ways of aging*. Oxford: Blackwell.

This book presents a compelling collection of ten original essays on the experience of ageing and through the biographical approach taken, demonstrates diversity and uniqueness in growing and being older.

McDonald, A and Taylor, M (2006) *Older people and the law*. Bristol: The Policy Press.

This paperback book is unique in addressing the legislative context of practice with older people. As such, this offers useful, accessible underpinning knowledge to further your understanding of the context of growing older in our society.

Ray, M, Bernard, M and Phillips, J (2009) *Critical issues in social work with older people*. Basingstoke: Palgrave Macmillan.

This text highlights the importance of informed and critical practice in social work with older people.

WEBSITE

Age Concern England www.ageconcern.co.uk

Age Concern is a federation of about 400 independent charities working together with and for older people, locally, regionally and nationally. On their website you will find a wealth of information and research for students and for older people themselves and their carers. You will find that the section headed 'Policy' is particularly helpful in providing statistical information, government policy, Age Concern commissioned research. Age Concern has networks across a wide range of related research organisations.

Conclusion

The content of this third edition of *Social work and human development* meets the core elements of the requirements for social work education as outlined in the Department of Health's prescribed curriculum for competence, knowledge and understanding of human growth and development, incorporating the development of skills and knowledge relevant to interprofessional working, values and ethics. The early chapters of this book also relate to the *Common core of skills and knowledge for the children's workforce* (DfES, 2005a), specifically the area of expertise titled 'Child and young person development'. The book is primarily written for student social workers who are beginning to develop their skills and understanding of the requirements for practice, in their first year or level of study.

The book also set out to meet subject skills identified in the Quality Assurance Agency academic benchmark criteria for social work. These include understanding the nature of social work and developing knowledge and understanding under the following headings:

- social work services and service users;

- values and ethics;

- social work theory;

- the nature of social work practice.

Furthermore, this book aimed to enable you to meet the requirements of the National Occupational Standards (NOS) set for social workers. Within the Standards the importance of working with individuals, families, carers, groups and communities to achieve change and development and to improve life opportunities is clearly stated.

In the language of the NOS social workers must:

- prepare for work with people and assess their needs and circumstances;

- plan, carry out, review and evaluate in social work;

- support individuals to represent needs, views and circumstances;

- manage risk;

- be accountable with supervision and support for own practice;

- demonstrate professional competence in social work practice.

This book will have given you a firm grounding in and understanding of theories and models related to social work and human life course development. In essence, this book has developed your knowledge and understanding of human development throughout the life course and its importance to social work practice.

Book structure

This third edition preserves the same overall logical structure as the first edition. However, the authors have supplemented each chapter with additional links to current policy agendas and developing legislative frameworks. Furthermore there is additional and updated *Further reading* at the end of each chapter to include annotated references to recent texts and internet resources.

Through an interactive approach with additional diagrams, activities, case studies and updated research information, this third edition set out to help you reflect, evaluate and progress your learning

The chapters within this book will have developed your understanding of a range of explanations of human life course development and their impact upon social work practice. Additionally research and theory summaries have been included to reinforce your developing knowledge and understanding.

Within the chapters of this book you have been encouraged to start by examining your own views and perspectives and to think about the origins of these. The book has taken a whole of life course approach, drawing out the concept of taking a biographical, sometimes called a narrative, approach. This is about listening to the first-hand interpretation of individuals and their constructions of their own life course. Unit 2 of Key Role 1 of the NOS sets standards for social work that encompass:

> *work with individuals, families, carers, groups and communities to enable them to analyse, identify, clarify and express their strengths, expectations and limitations.*

Understanding and adopting the biographical approach to understanding an individual's life course development will enable you to meet key elements of the criteria for this standard. Additionally, you have learnt about other key elements of the prescribed curriculum, such as knowledge of child development and legal intervention to protect.

Each of the seven chapters of this book has concentrated on a different aspect of human development through the life course. In Chapter 1, you explored the reasons why knowledge and understanding of human development throughout the life course are important to social work practice. This included consideration of the importance of recognising the impact that your values and life events can have upon your practice. The requirement to *reflect on your own background, experiences and practice that may have an impact on the relationship* is a criteria within Key Role 1, Unit 1 of the NOS for social work in respect of preparing for social work contact and involvement. Within this chapter the concept of life-events and transitions was introduced and the links between practice and public inquiries into social and health care was made. In this chapter you will have considered the role of social work practice in working with individuals through transition periods in their lives. The broad overview of a range of theoretical approaches to human life course development and the significance of knowledge from other disciplines, provided within this chapter, created the links to the later practice-focused chapters.

Chapter 2 concentrated on an introduction to theoretical models for understanding development across the life course. This chapter, as required by the social work subject benchmarks, offered an outline of research-based concepts and critical explanations from the theoretical approaches commonly used by social workers and other professionals when working with people in a variety of settings, across the whole life course. The connections, similarities and differences between the theories were considered, using the case study approach to enable you to compare and contrast models and apply them to social work practice situations. The knowledge that you have acquired through this chapter is outlined in the NOS for social work Key Role 6, element 18.3, which states that as a social worker you must:

research, analyse, evaluate, and use current knowledge of best social work practice

and:

implement knowledge based social work models and methods to develop and improve your own practice.

The chapter reinforced the importance of listening to the individual's perspective on their life course and understanding the range of theories that attempt to explain the complexities of human life course development. Having introduced a range of perspectives and developmental theories in this chapter, the remaining chapters of the book developed these ideas further as they focused on specific phases in the human life course.

Chapter 3 examined life course development knowledge in social work practice with infants, young children and their families, setting out knowledge in respect of early child development. Through an exploration of pre-natal, peri-natal and neo-natal periods of life development you considered the relative importance of hereditary factors and environmental factors in determining an individual's development. Human life course development knowledge and its use in social work practice with children in need and children in need of protection were considered in this chapter. The chapter also developed your ability to critique theories that explain human development taking a cognitive approach and theories taking a biological or physical perspective. This chapter will have helped you work towards meeting the NOS, particularly Key Role 2, Unit 5:

interact with individuals, families, carers, groups and communities to achieve change and development and to improve life opportunities.

The chapter covers the requirements of element 5.3, that social workers:

apply and justify social work methods and models used to achieve change and development and to improve life opportunities.

Chapter 4 examined life course development knowledge in social work practice with older children and their families. The NOS Key Role 2 sets the standard for social workers to:

plan, carry out, review and evaluate social work practice, with individuals, families, carers, groups, communities and other professionals.

After studying this chapter you will be able to address Unit 9, element 9.2 of this key role, which relates to:

behaviour which presents a risk to individuals, families, carers, groups and communities; identifying and evaluating situations and circumstances that may trigger the behaviour.

The chapter will assist you to develop your understanding and ability to evaluate and analyse theories that explain human development taking a systemic approach. The Department of Health *Framework for the assessment of children in need* was used to explore this approach. The chapter also discusses the role of the social worker in supporting children to express their views and feelings and to develop a positive sense of self-identity and independence.

In Chapter 5 you looked at life course development knowledge in social work practice in respect of young people in their teenage or adolescent years. The chapter considered issues related to the transition to adulthood and the particular significance that this may have for young people with disabilities. Social work practice in supporting young people and their families to understand and manage behaviours is considered within this chapter. Again, this chapter will have linked to a range of the NOS for social work, specifically relevant across this chapter were Key Roles 1, 5 and 6 in respect of:

professional competence in social work practice

with:

work with individuals, families, carers, groups and communities to assess their needs and circumstances.

Theories that explain human life course development taking a behavioural and social learning approach were explored and critiqued in this chapter.

In Chapter 6, life course development knowledge in social work practice with people in early and middle adulthood was examined. In particular, the significance of transitions in adult life was considered, drawing on situations related to adults experiencing physical disability, adults with learning difficulties and adults who have caring responsibilities. The chapter looked at how transitions present opportunities for growth and development or conversely potential crisis points. Within this chapter you considered factors that may affect the outcome of a person's move through a period of transition, in particular the importance of resources, or support networks, and the influence of societal factors. Amongst other areas of the NOS covered in this chapter, Key Role 2, Unit 7 which:

supports the development of networks to meet assessed needs and planned outcomes

was particularly relevant. Each of the elements within Unit 7 of Key Role 2 refer to the social work role in supporting the development of networks and recognising their contribution when assessing individual need and planning intervention. Chapter 6 also developed your understanding and ability to critique theories that explain life course development in stages or phases.

The final chapter examined ways in which an understanding of the theories of human development are necessary to effective social work practice with older people and their families. Late adulthood was considered as an opportunity for growth and development, with issues related to ageing and how this is constructed in our society being addressed. An exploration of the significance of transitions in later life enabled you to consider effective ageing and end-of-life issues. Social work practice in palliative care settings is considered within this chapter. The theoretical approaches in this chapter built upon the models examined in Chapter 6 and considered their application in explaining life course development in later adulthood. As with all chapters in this book, this final chapter will have helped you to meet a range of elements of the NOS for social work, as outlined at the beginning of the chapter.

Professional development and reflective practice

This book has provided an introduction to human life course development and social work practice. It set out to develop your knowledge and skills by assisting you to take a critical approach, to reflect on your work and participate in the development of your learning, through the interactive approach taken in the book. We would now encourage you to look back over the chapters, reflecting and reviewing your progress by charting and monitoring your learning. Reflecting about, in and on your practice and your learning is not only important during your social work education, it is considered key to continued professional development. This continuation of your development and lifelong learning includes keeping up to date, ensuring that research informs your practice and that you continually improve your skills and values for practice. The importance of professional development is clearly shown by its inclusion in the National Occupational Standards (Key Role 6, Unit 19) and is reflected in the General Social Care Council (GSCC) Code of Practice for Employees.

By taking responsibility for your learning and reflecting on your progress, you will always be in a position to consider your further learning and developmental needs. At this stage in your learning, you will have developed an appreciation of the knowledge you have gained, your understanding and ability to apply this learning to practice and hence, your future learning needs. The appreciation of your own learning will prepare you for further development as you work through the other books within this series *Transforming Social Work Practice*.

Appendix

Subject benchmark for social work

The content, structure and delivery of the social work programme leading to a degree level qualification should enable social work students to demonstrate that they have met the National Occupational Standards for Social Work (GSCC, 2002) (see Introduction) and the Social Work Subject Benchmark Statements (QAA, 2008). This Appendix provides a brief summary of the key areas in relation to the Benchmarks to support you in understanding the relevance of them for social work learning, teaching and practice.

Preface.

The Preface outlines subject benchmarks as . . . *a means for the academic community to describe the nature and characteristics of programmes in a specific subject or subject area. They also represent general expectations about standards for the award of qualifications at a given level in terms of the attributes and capabilities that those possessing qualifications should have demonstrated.*

1   Introduction.

The benchmark statement reaffirms the generic knowledge and skills required for the award of a social work degree as the preparatory qualification for practice across settings and 'client' groups and the complex and rapidly changing context of social work.

2   Context for social work education.

This sets out the political and regulatory context of social work education and practice at the time of writing these benchmarks (2008).

3   Nature and extent of social work.

The *Subject Benchmark Statement* for social work as an applied academic subject at honours level sets out expectations concerning:

- The subject knowledge, understanding and skills of an honours graduate in social work.
- The teaching, learning and assessment methods employed in their education.
- The standards expected of them at the point of graduation.

4   Defining principals.

At honours level, the study of social work involves the integrated study of subject-specific knowledge, skills and values and the critical application of research knowledge from the social and human sciences, and from social work (and closely related domains) to inform understanding and to underpin action, reflection and evaluation. Honours degree programmes should be designed to help foster this integration of contextual, analytic, critical, explanatory and practical understanding. As an applied academic subject, social work is characterised by a distinctive focus on practice in complex social situations to promote and protect individual and collective well-being.

4.6 Social work is a moral activity that requires practitioners to recognise the dignity of the individual, but also to make and implement difficult decisions (including restriction of liberty) in human situations that involve the potential for benefit or harm. Honours degree programmes in social work therefore involve the study, application of, and critical reflection upon, ethical principles and dilemmas. . . . this involves showing respect for persons, honouring the diverse and distinctive organisations and communities that make up contemporary society, promoting social justice and combating processes that lead to discrimination, marginalisation and social exclusion. This means that honours undergraduates must learn to:

- Practise in ways that maximise safety and effectiveness in situations of uncertainty and incomplete information.

4.7 The expectation that social workers will be able to act effectively in such complex circumstances requires that honours degree programmes in social work should be designed to help students learn to become accountable, reflective, critical and evaluative. This involves learning to:

- Work in a transparent and responsible way, balancing autonomy with complex, multiple and sometimes contradictory accountabilities (for example, to different service users, employing agencies, professional bodies and the wider society).

- Acquire and apply the habits of critical reflection, self-evaluation and consultation, and make appropriate use of research in decision-making about practice and in the evaluation of outcomes.

5 Subject knowledge, understanding and skills.

Subject knowledge and understanding

5.1 During their degree studies in social work, graduates are expected to acquire, critically evaluate, apply and integrate knowledge and understanding in five core areas of study.

5.1.1 Social work services, service users and carers, which include:

- The social processes that lead to marginalisation, isolation and exclusion and their impact on the demand for social work services.

5.1.2 The service delivery context.

5.1.3 Values and ethics, which include:

- The moral concepts of rights, responsibility, freedom, authority and power inherent in the practice of social workers as moral and statutory agents.

5.1.4 Social work theory, which includes:

- Research-based concepts and critical explanations from social work theory and other disciplines that contribute to the knowledge base of social work, including their distinctive epistemological status and application to practice.
- The relevance of psychological, physical and physiological perspectives to understanding personal and social development and functioning.
- Social science theories explaining group and organisational behaviour, adaptation and change.
- Models and methods of assessment, including factors underpinning the selection and testing of relevant information, the nature of professional judgement and the processes of risk assessment and decision-making.
- Approaches and methods of intervention in a range of settings, including factors guiding the choice and evaluation of these.
- User-led perspectives.
- Knowledge and critical appraisal of relevant social research and evaluation methodologies, and the evidence base for social work.

5.1.5 The nature of social work practice, which includes:

- The characteristics of practice in a range of community-based and organisational settings within statutory, voluntary and private sectors, and the factors influencing changes and developments in practice within these contexts.
- The nature and characteristics of skills associated with effective practice, both direct and indirect, with a range of service-users and in a variety of settings.
- The processes that facilitate and support service user choice and independence.
- The place of theoretical perspectives and evidence from international research in assessment and decision-making processes in social work practice.
- The integration of theoretical perspectives and evidence from international research into the design and implementation of effective social work intervention, with a wide range of service users, carers and others.
- The processes of reflection and evaluation, including familiarity with the range of approaches for evaluating service and welfare outcomes, and their significance for the development of practice and the practitioner.

Subject-specific skills and other skills

Social work necessarily involves the development of skills that may be of value in many situations. Some of these skills are specific to social work but many are also widely transferable. What helps to define the specific nature of these skills in a social work context is: the context in which they are applied and assessed; the relative weighting given to such skills within social work practice (e.g. the central importance of problem-solving skills within complex human situations); the specific purpose of skill development; and a requirement to integrate a range of skills.

5.3 All social work honours graduates should show the ability to reflect on and learn from the exercise of their skills. They should understand the significance of the concepts of continuing professional development and lifelong learning, and accept responsibility for their own continuing development.

There are five areas of skill development identified:

Problem-solving skills

5.5.1 Managing problem-solving activities. Honours graduates in social work should be able to plan problem-solving activities, i.e. to:

- Think logically, systematically, critically and reflectively.

- Plan a sequence of actions to achieve specified objectives, making use of research, theory and other forms of evidence.

- Manage processes of change, drawing on research, theory and other forms of evidence.

5.5.2 Gathering information.

5.5.3 Analyse and synthesise knowledge. Gathered for problem-solving purposes.

5.5.4 Intervention and evaluation. This includes building and sustaining purposeful relationships with people and organisations in community-based, and interprofessional contexts; being able to make decisions, set goals and construct specific plans to achieve these, taking into account relevant factors including ethical guidelines.

Communication skills

This includes being able to communicate clearly, accurately and precisely (in an appropriate medium) with individuals and groups in a range of formal and informal situations.

Skills in working with others

Working effectively with others includes involving users of social work services in ways that increase their resources, capacity and power to influence factors affecting their lives; being able to consult actively and co-operatively with others and being able to develop effective helping relationships that facilitate change; acting within a framework of multiple accountability; and challenging others when necessary, in ways that are most likely to produce positive outcomes.

Skills in personal and professional development

This includes advancing their own learning and understanding with a degree of independence; taking responsibility for their own further and continuing acquisition and use of knowledge and skills; and using research critically and effectively to sustain and develop their practice.

ICT and numerical skills

This includes being able to communicate clearly, accurately and precisely (in an appropriate medium) with individuals and groups in a range of formal and informal situations).

7.3 Knowledge and understanding.

On graduating with an honours degree in social work, students should be able to demonstrate:

- A sound understanding of the five core areas of knowledge and understanding relevant to social work, as detailed in paragraph 5.1, including their application to practice and service delivery.
- An ability to use this knowledge and understanding in an integrated way, in specific practice contexts.
- An ability to use this knowledge and understanding to engage in effective relationships with service users and carers.
- Appraisal of previous learning and experience and ability to incorporate this into their future learning and practice.
- Acknowledgement and understanding of the potential and limitations of social work as a practice-based discipline to effect individual and social change.
- An ability to use research and enquiry techniques with reflective awareness, to collect, analyse and interpret relevant information.
- A developed capacity for the critical evaluation of knowledge and evidence from a range of sources.

7.4 Subject-specific and other skills.

On graduating with an honours degree in social work, students should be able to demonstrate a developed capacity to:

- Apply creatively a repertoire of core skills as detailed in section 5.
- Communicate effectively with service users and carers, and with other professionals.
- Integrate clear understanding of ethical issues and codes of values, and practice with their interventions in specific situations.
- Consistently exercise an appropriate level of autonomy and initiative in individual decision-making within the context of supervisory, collaborative, ethical and organisational requirements.
- Demonstrate habits of critical reflection on their performance and take responsibility for modifying action in light of this.

Glossary

Accommodation The process of modifying existing schema to fit new experiences or to create new schemas (Piaget).

Adolescent development The physical changes associated with puberty; the process of development of 'self' and the changing nature of relationships with others.

Ageism Where negative generalisations, assumptions or stereotypes result in people being treated unfairly, or discriminated against because of their age.

Assimilation The process of taking in new elements of experiences and information in terms of the schemas that a child already possesses (Piaget).

Attachment A positive emotional link of affection between two people or more.

Attachment theory Theory that explains the significance of attachment and relationships, in particular the bonds between children and care givers.

Behaviourism Theories that focus on our behaviours and how these behaviours and the consequences of our actions influence our learning (e.g. Skinner, Bandura).

Bonding A bond between the mother and child (or child and significant other).

Cabinet Office: Social exclusion task force The role of the Task Force is to co-ordinate the Government's drive against social exclusion, ensuring that the cross-departmental approach delivers for those most in need. Their stated aim is to ... *champion(s) the needs of the most disadvantaged members of society within Government, ensuring that as with the rest of the public service reform genda, we put people first*. www.cabinetoffice.gov.uk/strategy aspx

Cabinet Office: Strategy unit The role of the Unit is to provide a cross-departmental perspective on the major challenges facing the UK, to work with departments in developing their key policies, and to provide strategic advice and support to the Prime Minister/No 10 www.cabinetoffice.gov.uk/social_ exclusion_task_force.aspx

Cognitive development The mental processes by which we acquire and process knowledge (e.g. Piaget).

Department for Children, Schools and Families (DfCSF) Government department whose stated purpose is to ... *make this the best place in the world for children and young people to grow up.* www.dcsf.gov.uk

Department of Health (DoH) Government department that provides health and social care policy, guidance and publications and whose defined purpose for social care is to ... *(work) to define policy and guidance for delivering a social care system that provides care equally for all, whilst enabling people to retain their independence, control and dignity.* www.dh.gov.uk

Development A complex, continuous, progressive series of changes that occur as a result of maturation and experience.

Developmental Relating to growth, progression and advancement.

Developmental pathways/Developmental trajectories Both of these terms relate to the different courses or routes, through a range of experiences and transitions that individuals may take as they grow and progress through the life course.

Developmental psychology How people develop across the life course exploring their thoughts, ideas, feelings and behaviours.

Disengagement theory A theory built on the premise that withdrawal from social participation and interaction is an expected and natural process in later adulthood. Disengagement and detachment is perceived as positive and normal for older people.

Ecological Relating to the environment in which people live their lives.

General Social Care Council (GSCC) The workforce regulator and guardian of standards for the social care workforce in England. They were established in October 2001 under the Care Standards Act 2000. They are responsible for the codes of practice, Social Care Register and social work education and training.

Generativity A concept that relates to *generating* or being productive and contributing in some way to future society. This is discussed in detail in Chapter 5 of this text.

Holistic An approach that focuses on the whole of something, in the case of social work, this would usually be the whole of the person's life and current circumstances, and not just one element. Holistic approaches view the different aspects of a person as being closely interconnected and understandable only by reference to the whole.

Identity development A process of forming an awareness of 'who we are'. Understanding ourselves as a person, developing personality and a concept of self in relation to others in the social world. Becoming conscious and confident about one's personal life history, sexuality, race, gender and ethnicity.

Life course The progression and path an individual takes from conception to death.

Life course perspective A viewpoint that considers the whole of a life (from conception to death) as offering opportunities for growth, development and change.

Life cycle An alternative term used to describe the life course.

Life-span An alternative term used to describe the life course, often used in developmental psychology.

Lifestage development How people develop their identity as they move through stages or 'crisis' points in their lives (e.g. Erikson).

Milestones Expected stages of sequential development of skills and abilities, usually in children and commonly related to age. These stages are based upon that which is deemed *normal* and are used to gauge children's development and identify potential developmental problems.

Multidimensional (human development) Human development across the life course that is recognised as complex and influenced by the interaction of biological, social, psychological and environmental factors.

National Service Framework (NSF) The national service frameworks are national strategies which set out goals and programmes for change within specific areas of health and social care. The National Service Frameworks for Children (2004) and the one for Older People (2001) are particularly pertinent to this book.

Narrative or **biographical approach** The narrative approach is a way of working with individuals that focuses on the importance of their own first hand account of their life, their experiences and the meaning they attach to them.

Personalisation This is intended to mean starting with the person as an individual with strengths, preferences and aspirations and putting them at the centre of the process of identifying their needs and making choices about how and when they are supported to live their lives.

Post registration training and learning (PRTL) This is the term used by the GSCC and is taken here to mean the activities that individuals may undertake in order to achieve Continuing Professional Development (CPD).

Psychosocial theories Theories that arise from aspects of both sociological and psychological perspectives.

Puberty A stage of human development which is defined by biological, physical change – the reproductive organs, in males and females, become functional.

Reflective practice A form of mental processing – a form of thinking that we may use to fulfil a purpose or to achieve some anticipated outcome or we may simply 'be reflective' and then an outcome may be unexpected (See Crawford, 2006).

Transition Phases, stages or life events that people move through during their life course.

Social Care Institute for Excellence (SCIE) The Institute's mission is to identify and spread knowledge about good practice to the large and diverse social care workforce and support the delivery of transformed, personalised social care services.

Schemas The basic building blocks and the internal representation of a physical or mental action (Piaget).

Social construction Where a common understanding or meaning of a concept is taken for granted, so that the notion appears to be obvious to those who accept it. However, the meaning actually emerges from ideologies, images, values and beliefs in a particular culture or society.

A systems perspective A theoretical stance that views individuals as part of social systems that are dynamic and interconnected. This perspective focuses on the interaction and relationships between people and their environment.

References

Age Concern (2005) *Death and dying*. Policy Position Papers. London: Age Concern England. **www.ageconcern.org.uk**

Ainsworth, MDS, Blehar, MC, Waters, E and Wall, S (1978) *Patterns of attachment: a psychological study of the strange situation*. Hillsdale NJ: Erlbaum.

Aldgate, J, Jones, D, Rose, W and Jeffry, C (2006) *The developing world of the child*. London: Jessica Kingsley.

Ariès, P (1962) *Centuries of childhood*. New York: Vintage.

Baltes, P (1987) Theoretical propositions of life-span developmental psychology: on the dynamics between growth and decline. *Developmental Psychology*, 23, 611–626.

Bandura, A (1977) Self-efficacy: Toward a unifying theory of behavioural change. *Psychology Review*, 84, 191–215.

Bandura, A (1986) *Social foundations of thought and action*. Englewood Cliffs, NJ: Prentice Hall.

Banks, S (2004) *Ethics, accountability and the social professions*. Basingstoke: Palgrave Macmillan.

Baumrind, D (1971) Current patterns of parental authority. *Developmental Psychology Monograph 4*. 1, part 2.

BBC News Online 17 November 1999 **http://news.bbc.co.uk/1/hi/education**

Bee, H (1994) *Lifespan development*. New York: HarperCollins College.

Bee, H (1995) *The growing child*. New York: HarperCollins.

Beinart, S, Anderson, B, Lee, S and Utting, D (2002) *Youth at risk? A national survey of risk factors, protective factors and problem behaviours among young people in England, Scotland and Wales*. London: Communities that Care.

Bellamy, C (2005) *The state of the world's children 2005: childhood under threat*. New York: UNICEF. **www.unicef.org**

Berger, KS (2003) *The developing person* (6th edition). New York: Worth.

Berryman, J, Smyth, P, Taylor, A, Lamont, A, Joiner R (2002) *Developmental psychology and you*. Oxford: BPD Blackwell.

Birch, A (1997) *Developmental psychology: from infancy to adulthood* (2nd edition). Basingstoke: Palgrave.

Bowlby, J (1953) *Child care and the growth of love*. Harmondsworth: Penguin Books.

Bowlby, J (1969) *Attachment and loss: Vol. 1 Attachment*. New York: Basic Books.

Bowlby, J (1973) *Attachment and loss: Vol. 2 Separation anxiety and anger*. New York: Basic Books.

Bowlby, J (1988) *A secure base: clinical application of attachment theory*. London: Routledge.

Bronfenbrenner, U (1979) Contexts of child rearing: problems and prospects. *American Psychologist*, 34, 844–850.

Bronfenbrenner, U (1979) *The ecology of human development*. Cambridge MA: Harvard University Press.

Buss, AH and Plomin, R (1989) The EAS approach to temperament, in R Plomin and J Dunn (eds) *The study of temperament: changes, continuities and challenges* (pp.67–80). Hillsdale, NJ: Erlbaum.

Butrym, Z (1976) *The nature of social work*. London: Macmillan.

Chamberlayne, P, Bornat, J and Weingraf, T (eds) (2000) *The turn to biographical methods in social science: comparative issues and examples*. London: Routledge.

Children's Workforce Development Council/Department of Children, Schools and Families (2010) *Common core of skills and knowledge for the children's workforce*. Available from: **www.dcsf.gov.uk/everychildmatters/**

Cobb, N (1995) *Adolescence: continuity, change and diversity* (2nd edition). Mountain View, CA: Mayfield.

Cochran, W and Tessor, A (1996) The 'What the hell' effect: Some effects of goal proximity and goal framing on performance, in LL Martin, and A. Tessor (eds), *Striving and feeling: Interactions among goals, affect and self regulation*. New York: Lawrence Erlbaum Associates.

Codd, J (1997) Knowledge, qualifications and higher education: a critical view, in M Olssen and K Morris Matthews (eds) *Education policy in New Zealand: The 1990's and beyond*. Palmerston North: Dunmore Press.

Cole, M and Cole, SR (2001) *The development of children*. New York: Worth.

Coleman, J and Hendry, L (1999) *The nature of adolescence* (3rd edition). London: Routledge.

Coopersmith, S (1967) *The antecedents of self-esteem*. New York: WH Freeman.

Crawford, K (2006) *Reflective reader: Social work and human development*. Exeter: Learning Matters.

Crawford, K and Walker, J (2004) *Social work and older people*. Exeter: Learning Matters.

Cree, V and Davis, A (2007) *Social work: voices from the inside*. London: Routledge.

Crittenden, P (1996) Research on maltreating families: implications for intervention, in J Briere et al. (eds) *The APSAC handbook on child maltreatment* (pp. 158–74). Thousand Oaks, CA: Sage.

Cumming, E and Henry, W (1961) *Growing old: the process of disengagement*. New York: Basic Books.

Daiute, C, Beyont, Z, Higson-Smith, C and Nucci, L (2006) *International perspectives on youth conflict and development*. New York: Oxford University Press.

Daniel, B, Wassell, S and Gilligan, R (1999) *Child development for child care and protection workers*. London: Jessica Kingsley.

Dawson, CR, Cragg, A, Taylor, C and Toombs, C (2007) *Video games*. British Board of Film Classification. **www.bbfc.co.uk**

Department for Children, Schools and Families (DCSF) (2007a) *The children's plan: building brighter futures*. Norwich: The Stationery Office.

Department for Children, Schools and Families (DCSF) (2009) *The children's plan: Two years on.* Norwich: The Stationery Office.

Department for Children, Schools and Families (DCSF) (2010) *Working together to safeguard children*. Norwich: The Stationery Office.

Department for Children, Schools and Families and Department of Health (DCSF) (DoH) (2007a) *Aiming high for disabled children (AHDC): Better support for families*. Norwich: Stationery Office.

Department for Children, Schools and Families and Department of Health (DCSF) (DoH) (2007b) *(AHDC) Best practice to common practice*. Norwich: Stationery Office.

Department for Education and Skills (DfES) (2002) *Birth to three matters: A framework to support children in their earliest years*. Nottingham: DfES Publications Centre. **www.standards.DfES.gov.uk**

Department for Education and Skills (DfES) (2003) *Every child matters*. Norwich: The Stationery Office.

Department for Education and Skills (DfES) (2004) *Every child matters: Change for children*. Norwich: The Stationery Office.

Department for Education and Skills (DfES) (2004) *Children Act 2004*. London: The Stationery Office.

Department for Education and Skills (DfES) (2005a) *Youth matters*. Cm 6629. London: The Stationery Office. **www.dfes.gov.uk**

Department for Education and Skills (DfES) (2005b) *Every child matters change for children: Young people and drugs*. London: The Stationery Office.

Department for Education and Skills (DfES) (2006a) *The Common Assessment Framework for children and young people: Practitioner's guide*. Nottingham: DfES Publications Centre.

Department for Education and Skills (DfES) (2006b) *Care matters: transforming the lives of children and young people in care*. Nottingham: DfES Publications Centre.

Department for Education and Skills (DfES) (2007a) *Practice guidance for the Eary Years Foundation Stage*. **www.standards.dfes.gov.uk**

Department for Education and Skills (DfES) (2007b) *Every parent matters.* Norwich: The Stationery Office.

Department for Education and Skills (DfES) (2010) *Support for all: The families and relationships green paper.* Norwich: The Stationery Office.

Department for Education, Schools and Families, Department of Health, Department for Business, Innovation and Skills with Social Work Reform Board (2009) *Building a safe and confident future: implementing the recommendations of the social work task force.* Available from: **www.desf.gov.uk**

Department of Health (DoH) (2000) *Framework for the assessment of children in need and their families*. London: The Stationery Office.

Department of Health (DoH) (2001a) *The National Service Framework for older people.* **www.doh.gov.uk/nsf/olderpeople.htm**

Department of Health (DoH) (2001b) *Valuing people: a new strategy for learning disability for the 21st century*. London: The Stationery Office.

Department of Health (DoH) (2002c) *The requirements for social work training.* Norwich: The Stationery Office.

Department of Health (DoH) (2004) *National Service Framework for children, young people and maternity services*. London: The Stationery Office.

Department of Health (DoH) (2005) *Independence, well-being and choice: our vision for the future of social care for adults in England*. Cm 6499. London: The Stationery Office.

Department of Health (DoH) (2006a) *Our health, our care, our say: a new direction for community services: a brief guide*. London: DoH Publications.

Department of Heath (DoH) (2006b) *A new ambition for old age: next steps in implementing the National Service Framework for Older People*. London: DoH Publications.

Department of Health (DoH) (2007) *Advance care planning: a guide for health and social care staff*. Leicester: End of Life Care Programme.

Department of Health (DoH) (2010) *The future of social work in adult social services in England*. Available from: **www.dh.gov.uk/**

Dillon, L, Chivite-Matthews, N, Grewal, I, Brown, R, Webster, S, Weddell, E, Brown, G and Smith, N (2007) *Risk, protective factors and resilience to drug use: Identifying resilient young people and learning from their experiences.* Home Office Online Report 04/07.

Erikson, E (1982) *The life cycle completed. A review*. London: WW Norton.

Erikson, E (1987) *A way of looking at things: selected papers from 1930–1986*. London: WW Norton.

Erikson, E (1995) *Childhood and society*. London: Vintage.

Eyer, DE (1992) *Mother–infant bonding: a scientific fiction*. New Haven, CT: Yale University Press.

Fahlberg, V (1991) *A child's journey through placement*. London: BAAF.

Farington, D (1996) *Understanding and preventing youth crime*. York: Joseph Rowntree Foundation.

Fook, J (2002) *Social work: critical theory and practice*. Sage: London.

Freud, S (1949) *An outline of psychoanalysis*. London: WW Norton.

General Social Care Council (GSCC) (2002a) *National Occupational Standards for social work*. London: GSCC. **www.gscc.org.uk**

General Social Care Council/Topss (GSCC) (2002b) *The National Occupational Standards for social work*. Leeds: Training Organisation for the Personal Social Services.

General Social Care Council (GSCC) (2002c) *Codes of practice for social care workers and employers*. London: GSCC.

General Social Care Council (GSCC) (2005) *Post Qualifying Framework for social work education and training*. London: GSCC.

Gessell, AL (1928) *Infancy and human growth*. New York: Macmillan.

Giddens, A (1991) *Modernity and self-identity*. Cambridge: Polity Press.

Gilligan, C (1982) *In a different voice: psychological theory and women's development*. Cambridge, MA: Harvard University Press.

Gilligan, P and Furness, S (2006) The role of religion and spirituality in social work practice: views and experiences of social workers and students. *British Journal of Social Work*, 36, 617–37.

Goldson, B, Lavelette, M and McKechnie, J (eds) (2002) *Children, welfare and the state*. London: Sage.

Gordon, D et al. (2000) *Poverty and social exclusion in Britain*. York: Joseph Rowntree Foundation.

Gubrium, J and Holstein, J (eds) (2003) *Ways of aging*. Oxford: Blackwell.

Harter, S (1999) *The construction of self: a developmental perspective*. New York: Guilford Press.

Havighurst, R (1972) *Developmental tasks and education* (3rd edition). New York: David McKay.

Hayflick, L (1977) The cellular basis for biological ageing, in CE Finch and L Hayfick (eds) *Handbook of the biology of ageing*. New York: Van Nostrand Reinhold.

Hester, M and Pearson, C (1998) *Preventing child abuse: monitoring domestic violence*. Bristol: The Policy Press.

Hockey, J and James, A (2003) *Social identities across the life course*. Basingstoke: Macmillan.

Hollis, F (1970) The psychosocial approach to the practice of casework, in RW Roberts and RH Nee (eds) *Theories of social casework*. Chicago: University of Chicago Press.

Holmes, TH and Rahe, RH (1967) The Social Readjustment Rating Scale. *Journal of Psychosomatic Research*, Vol II, 213–318.

Howe, D (1987) *An introduction to social work theory*. Aldershot: Arena.

Howe, D (1998) Psychosocial work, in R Adams, L Dominelli and M Payne (eds) *Social work: themes, issues and critical debates*. Basingstoke: Macmillan

Howe, D (1995) *Attachment theory for social work practice*. Basingstoke: Macmillan.

Ingel, E (2010) *Applied psychology for social work* (2nd edition). Exeter: Learning Matters.

Institute for Health Research (2005) *The impact of person centred planning*. University of Lancaster. **http://valuingpeople.gov.uk**

Johns, R (2007) *Using the law in social work* (3rd edition). Exeter: Learning Matters.

Jowitt, M and O'Laughlin, S (2005) *Social work with children and families*. Exeter: Learning Matters.

Karmiloff, K and Karmiloff-Smith, A (2001) *Pathways to language: from fetus to adolescent*. Cambridge, MA: Harvard University Press.

Katz, P (1979) The development of female identity. *Sex Roles*, 5, 155–178.

Kitwood, T (1993) Frames of reference for an understanding of dementia, in J Johnson and R Slater (eds) *Ageing and later life*. London: Sage.

Kohlberg, L (1976) Moral stages and moralisation, in T Linkons (ed.) *Moral development and behaviour.* New York: Holt, Rinehart and Winston.

Kroger, J (2007) *Identity development: adolescence through adulthood* (2nd edition). London: Sage.

Laming, H (2003) *The Victoria Climbié inquiry report*. Cm 5730. London: The Stationery Office. **www.victoria-climbie-inquiry.org.uk**

The Lord Laming (2009) *The protection of children in England: A progress report*. London: The Stationery Office.

Levinson, D (1978) *The seasons of a man's life*. New York: Knopf.

Lorenz, K (1970) *Studies in animal and human behaviour*. Vol 1. Translated from the German by Robert Martin. London: Methuen.

Maccoby, E (2002) Parenting effects: issues and controversies, in J Borkowski, S Landesman Ramey, and M Bristol-Power (eds) *Parenting and the child's world: Influences on academic, intellectual and social-emotional development*. Hillsdale, NJ: Erlbaum.

Maccoby, E and Martin, J (1983) Socialization in the context of the family: parent–child interaction, in E Hetherington (ed.) *Handbook of child psychology: socialization, personality and social development* (Vol. 4). New York: Wiley.

Marshall, M and Tibbs, MA (2006) *Social work and people with dementia: partnerships, practice and persistence.* Bristol: The Policy Press.

Meggitt, C (2006) *Child development: an illustrated guide* (2nd edition). Oxford: Heinemann Educational.

Mezirow, J (1991) *Transformation dimensions of adult learning.* San Francisco: Jossey Bass.

Milburn, A (2001) *The national service framework for older people.* Department of Health. **www.doh.gov.uk/nsf/olderpeople.htm**

Moon, JA (2004) *A handbook of reflective and experiential learning: theory and practice.* London: RoutledgeFalmer.

Mullender, A and Morley, R (eds) (1994) *Children living with domestic violence: putting men's abuse of women on the child care agenda.* London: Whiting and Birch.

Newman, T and Blackburn, S (2002) *Transitions in the lives of children and young: resilience factors.* Barnardo's Policy Research and Influencing Unit.

Novak, T (2002) Rich children, poor children, in B Goldson, M Lavelette and J McKechnie (eds) *Children, welfare and the state.* London: Sage.

Office for National Statistics (2006) *Social Trends 36.* London: The Stationery Office.

Ogbu, JU (1993) Differences in cultural frames of reference. *International Journal of Behavioural Development,* 16, 483–506.

Oliner, SP and Oliner, PM (1988) *The altruistic personality: rescuers of Jews in Nazi Germany.* New York: Free Press.

Paludi, MA (ed.) (2002) *Human development in multi-cultural contexts. A book of readings.* New Jersey: Prentice Hall.

Parker, J and Bradley, G (2010) *Social work practice: assessment, planning, intervention and review* (3rd edtion). Exeter: Learning Matters.

Payne, M (2005) *Modern social work theory* (3rd edition). Basingstoke: Palgrave Macmillan.

Phinney, JS (1993) A three stage model of ethnic identity development in adolescence, in ME Bernal and GP Knight (eds) *Ethnic identity: formation and transmission among Hispanics and other minorities.* New York: State University of New York Press.

Piaget, J (1936) *Origins of intelligence in the child.* London: Routledge & Kegan Paul.

Piaget, J (1970) *The science of education and the psychology of the child.* NY: Grossman.

Prior, V and Glaser, D (2006) *Understanding attachment and attachment disorders: theory, evidence and practice.* London: Jessica Kingsley.

Quality Assurance Agency for Higher Education (QAA) (2008) *Subject Benchmark Statements.* Gloucester: QAA. **www.qaa.org.uk**

Race, D (2002) *Learning disability – a social approach.* London: Routledge.

Rathus, (2008) *Childhood and adolescence: voyages in development* (3rd edition). Belmont, CA: Thompson Learning Inc.

Redmond, B (2004) *Reflection in action: developing reflective practice in health and social services.* Aldershot: Ashgate.

Ritchie, JH, Dick, D and Lingham, R (1994) *The report of the inquiry into the care and treatment of Christopher Clunis.* London: HMSO.

Ronen, T (2002) Cognitive-behavioural therapy, in M Davies (ed.) *The Blackwell companion to social work*. Oxford: Blackwell.

Rowe, J W and Kahn, R L (1987) Human ageing: usual and successful. *Science*, 237.

Rutter, M (1981) *Maternal deprivation reassessed* (2nd edition). Harmondsworth: Penguin.

Schön, DA (1983) *The reflective practitioner*. London: Temple Smith.

Schön, DA (1991) *The reflective practitioner: how professionals think in action*. Aldershot: Ashgate.

Shropshire, J and Middleton, S (1999) *Small expectations: learning to be poor?* York: Joseph Rowntree Foundation.

Sidell, M (1993) Death, dying and bereavement, in J Bond, P Coleman and S Peace, *Ageing in society: an introduction to social gerontology* (2nd edition). London: Sage.

Siegler, R, DeLoache, J and Esienberg, N (2003) *How children develop*. New York: Worth.

Smith, PK and Cowie, H (1991) *Understanding child development*. Oxford: Blackwell.

Social Exclusion Taskforce (2007) *Reaching out: Think family*. Norwich: The Stationery Office.

Steinberg, L (1993) *Adolescence*. New York: McGraw-Hill.

Stevenson, O (2004) The future of social work, in M Lymbery and S Butler, *Social work ideals and practical realities*. Basingstoke: Macmillan.

Sugarman, L (1986) *Life-span development concepts, theories and interventions*. London: Routledge.

Sullivan, HS (1953) *The interpersonal theory of psychiatry*. New York: WW Norton.

Svejda, MJ, Campos, JJ and Emde, RN (1980) Mother–infant 'bonding': a failure to generalise. *Child development*, 51, 775–9.

Thom, B, Sales, R and Pearce, J (2007) *Growing up with risk*. Bristol: The Policy Press.

Thomas, A and Chess, S (1977) *Temperament and development*. New York: Brunner.

Thomas, A and Chess, S (1986) The New York longitudinal study: from infancy to early adult life, in R Plomin and J Dunn (eds) *Changes, continuities and challenges*. Hillsdale, NJ: Erlbaum.

Thompson, N (2000) *Theory and practice in the human services*. Buckingham: Open University Press.

UMIST News (11 January 2002) Manchester.

UNICEF Innocenti Research Centre (2007) *Child poverty in perspective: An overview of child well-being*. Available from: **www.unicef-irc.org/publications/**

Walker, L, Pitts, C, Hennig, K, and Matsuba, M (1995) Reasoning about morality and real life moral problems, in M Killen and D Hart (eds) *Morality in everyday life: developmental perspectives*. Cambridge: Cambridge University Press.

Wood, J, Ashman, M, Davies, C, Lloyd, H and Lockett, K (1996) *Report of the independent inquiry into the care of Anthony Smith*. Derbyshire: Southern Derbyshire Health Authority and Derbyshire County Council.

Index